Media and Morality

This book is dedicated to my grandchildren both present and future.

Media and Morality

On the Rise of the Mediapolis

ROGER SILVERSTONE

polity

Copyright © Roger Silverstone 2007

The right of Roger Silverstone to be identified as Author of this Work has been asserted in accordance with the UK Copyright, Designs and Patents Act 1988.

First published in 2007 by Polity Press
Reprinted in 2008 (twice)

Polity Press
65 Bridge Street
Cambridge CB2 1UR, UK

Polity Press
350 Main Street
Malden, MA 02148, USA

ISBN-10: 0-7456-3503-2
ISBN-13: 978-07456-3503-3
ISBN 10: 0-7456-3504-0 (pb)
ISBN 13: 978-07456-3504-0 (pb)

A catalogue record for this book is available from the British Library.

Typeset in 11.25 on 13pt Dante
by SNP Best-set Typesetter Ltd, Hong Kong
Printed and bound in the United States by Odyssey Press Inc., Gonic, New Hampshire

The publisher has used its best endeavours to ensure that the URLs for external websites referred to in this book are correct and active at the time of going to press. However, the publisher has no responsibility for the websites and can make no guarantee that a site will remain live or that the content is or will remain appropriate.

Every effort has been made to trace all copyright holders, but if any have been inadvertently overlooked the publishers will be pleased to include any necessary credits in any subsequent reprint or edition.

For further information on Polity, visit our website: www.polity.co.uk

Contents

Preface and Acknowledgements

This book picks up where my previous one, *Why Study the Media?*, left off. It deals with what I am beginning to see as the second of the great environmental crises with which global societies are increasingly having to deal: the crisis in the world of communication. This is a moral and an ethical as well as a political crisis, and I argue in this book not only that the pollution of this mediated environment is threatening our capacity to sustain a reasonable level of humanity, but that it is only by attending to the realities of global communication, but also and even more so to its possibilities, that we will be able to reverse what otherwise will be a downward spiral towards increasing global incomprehension and inhumanity.

Many individuals have helped me along the way both directly and indirectly. Some indeed have had the dubious privilege of reading portions of the manuscript way before they should have been released for any kind of consumption other than my own; and I thank Lilie Chouliaraki, Richard Sennett, Steven Lukes, Nick Couldry, Maggie Scammell, Tom Hollihan and Helena Bejar for undertaking what none of them reasonably should have been asked to do. Terhi Rantanen was the first to read the whole of the manuscript in near final draft and made a huge number of helpful suggestions for its improvement. Otherwise, and it is not at all an otherwise, thanks are due to my many students, colleagues and friends in the Department of Media and Communications at the LSE, whose intellectual presence has been, and indeed remains, constantly invigorating.

Thanks are also due to my colleagues, especially Dean Geoffey Cowan, at the Annenberg School of Communication, University of Southern California, who generously hosted a period of sabbatical time in the spring of 2004, which was sufficiently calm and stimulating to enable me to undertake the research which led to the writing of chapter 3.

The last year of the manuscript's writing was by no means straightforward. Many doctors, both in London and Mexico City, are owed immeasurable gratitude for keeping me alive. But beyond anything, I want to record the extraordinary care and devotion of my wife Jennifer, my children, Daniel, Elizabeth and William, and their partners, and my brother Anthony for supporting me (and each other) at moments and indeed periods of great stress. Let this book, in part, be a token of my love and thanks to them.

Parts of the book have involved significant rewriting of previously published material, as follows:

- Chapter 5 substantially develops arguments in my 'Complicity and Collusion in the Mediation of Everyday Life', *New Literary History*, 33 (4), 2002, 761–80.
- Chapter 7 does likewise with respect to 'Regulation, Media Literacy and Media Civics', *Media, Culture and Society*, 26 (3) 2004, 440–9.

1

Morality and Media

O wad some Pow'r the giftie gie us
To see oursels as others see us!
It wad frae mony a blunder free us,
And foolish notion.

Robert Burns, To a Louse

I have a memory of an interview broadcast on BBC Radio 4 on *The World at One* during the height of the war in Afghanistan which followed hard on the heels of the attack on the World Trade Center. It was with an Afghani blacksmith who, having apparently failed to hear or understand the US airplane based, supposedly blanket, propaganda coverage of his country, offered his own account of why so many bombs were falling around his village. It was because, his translated voice explained, Al Qaeda had killed many Americans and their donkeys and had destroyed some of their castles. He was not, of course, entirely wrong.

There is much that is striking in this otherwise insignificant piece of reportage. And much of what is striking goes to the heart of what I want to explore and argue during the course of this book.

The first point of note has to do with the blacksmith's mere presence in the British media. The second has to do with what he says. In one sense presence is all – a certain kind of presence that has transcended geographical, social and linguistic distance; a certain kind of presence which brought this voice into the living rooms of suburban England, not just from a war zone, a soon to be replicated war zone, our war zone which is almost by definition, now, somewhere else, but from another age, distant in time as well as space. This was a real voice, but an unfamiliar voice. And its unfamiliarity had everything to do with, was overdetermined by, the blacksmith's capacity to offer an account *of* us as well as *to* us: we, in the West, with our donkeys and our castles, we with our losses, we in our equivalence. His understanding, his misunderstanding, was touching, naive, easily patronized. Yet it was true: a translated truth, a cultured truth, and

1

a truth meaningful for him. Just as we had and have our views of what life might be like for a blacksmith in Afghanistan, he has his views of what life, and death, might have been like in downtown Manhattan on the morning of 11 September 2001. In both cases those views are, at best, filtered through the prejudice of ages and the immediacy of images. At worst they enter into judgements and through judgements into actions which, for those who have the power, are likely to be consequentially misinformed and fatal in their consequences.

His appearance in our mediated space, albeit in this case his audible appearance only, represents the appearance of the other, the strange and the stranger, in the familiarity and comfort of home. He appears to us as a representative, a rare representative, of the doubly distant: the proverbial man in the street, or in this case the man in the smithy, and as someone as far away from us, perhaps in time as well as space, as it is possible to conceive. Ordinary and usually unheard. But now speaking about our misfortune as well as his. And his appearance represents a life, too, when we might otherwise only see – indeed we normally do only see – a body. A silent body, a body perplexed, a body in pain, a dead body. A victim.

So here is the blacksmith speaking, and he is speaking, albeit briefly, about us. Here he is talking about us in his terms, through his view of the world. Are we going to listen? What are we going to hear?

His appearance is only an appearance. And it is his only appearance. For one lunchtime only. His forty seconds of fame. It is, of course, a mediated appearance. The voice, because it is radio, is disembodied. It is translated. It is heard somewhere else, somewhere where he is a stranger. We can try and imagine what he looks like, where he is sitting. We can try and imagine, and will indeed imagine, because we have a stock of images and sounds on which to draw, the setting. The bombing, the dust, the children, the distant women. But can we imagine him imagining us? What will he have seen or heard about the attack? And can we imagine ourselves to be his strangers?

This unnamed blacksmith is a double, and his appearance, his representation, involves a doubling. Actually it involves many doublings. The sound bite is a tiny shard mirroring the conventions of western media discourse, representing, misrepresenting, naturalizing us. Indeed his appearance involves representation in many dimensions. He is represented, characterized as an Afghan, as a blacksmith, as someone who can speak and, thanks to the BBC, can claim an audience. But he is also a representative. Chosen to speak on behalf of others: a minor synecdoche within the western media's reporting of the war. And then he is re-presented. Taken out of context and put into another. Or put into many: the context of his framing in the narrative of the newscast; the context of the reception of that newscast in the homes and heads of British listeners at 1.20 p.m. on a weekday lunchtime. And then the fading context of individual memory and forgetfulness, as well as that defined by, and the property of, the juggernaut of relentless news.

It is these contexts and their complexity, the contexts most broadly of discourse and reception, which are of course the concern. And I should point out that the pronouns 'we' and 'us', and the possessive 'our' here and elsewhere in my text, are both singular and plural, expressing a shared or shareable, as well as a distinct and individual, entity and locus of understanding and participation in the world, both mediated and immediate. No presumptions should be made about an unreflecting, universal, generalizable, uncomplicated, *we*. The 'we' is not substantive, though it does inevitably reflect an orientation from the Anglophone western world. It is rather more an invitation, to invite the reader to join me in my space, but not to feel subsumed by it, nor to feel excluded from it. The 'we' here and in the rest of the book is, but crucially is also not, the plural of the 'I'.

The blacksmith's doubling is, of course, also unusual insofar as we do not often see, nor indeed do we often allow, others to comment on us on our screens. The continuing dismay with which Al Jazeera is received in western societies, most especially in the United States, is not only because of the graphic horror of some of its images (we provide those on a daily basis) or the ferocity of the political rhetoric (likewise). It is much more fundamental. It is based on the breaking of a media taboo and the reversal of the customary taken-for-granted nature of media representation, in which we in the West do the defining, and in which you are, and I am not, the other.

So in the massive inequalities of global media power, the blacksmith's appearance, and his version of the world, is relatively rare. But it mirrors, however faintly and briefly, the much wider representational culture of western media, whose gaze, alternately crystalline and cloudy, but always culturally specific, dominates the screens and speakers of the world. And for those in the West, or indeed for those in the UK, he is who he is only on those screens and speakers. He has no existence otherwise. He, in his unfamiliarity and distance as speaker, on the one hand, but in his famil-iarity and closeness as visible or audible presence, on the other, is a pres-ence that those who hear him can neither touch nor interrogate. They have no other link with him, with his experience, or with his world, not at least through the broadcast media. And he will disappear at the end of the programme. For ever.

Meanwhile his life connects with ours because our forces have been bombing him, and in the global uncivil society in which we live, he is believed to be connected in some way to those who momentarily made us the victims. Briefly the BBC chose to reverse the usual framings and offer a western audience, otherwise far removed in reality and imagination from the conflict, an opportunity to connect with someone else's lived and sentient difference, with someone who mirrors, and therefore reverses, albeit only in a single sentence, the customary polarities of interpretation.

There are possibilities to identify with this man, and to engage with him on his terms, though in the inevitable absence of any shared interactive space, this would, perforce, be confined to the imagination. There are, however, many more possibilities to reject that identification. And the opportunities for rejection and denial are, as is the way of things, cultural, ideological and technological things, likely to be much easier to accept. Yet he represents the other, and in his speech, and in the journalists' decision to give him space to speak, there is an invitation to make a connection to someone who, in his humanity, and despite everything else, might have something in common with the rest of us.

Notwithstanding the blacksmith's distinctiveness, the mediated world is full of such strangers and such images. Indeed I can reverse the sentence and say, with increasing confidence, that the mediated images of strangers increasingly define what actually constitutes the world. The relationships that are made, or which are refused, with the other extend across social, geographical and indeed historical space in ways which would be unimaginable in the everyday lives of ordinary people (as opposed to elites) as little as fifty years ago. And since it is the relationship we have with others which defines the nature of our own being, then such links as we might have with these mediated individuals are increasingly becoming the crucial ones for us too.

Such images are not often so benign. Nor do they always or only represent otherness at a distance, from somewhere else. From time to time the consistency with which otherness, especially dark otherness, is kept at one mediated remove breaks down, and the horror of our own otherness appears. This is how the images from Abu Ghraib came home: not so much as faithful representations of real transgressions and real crimes, but more as a transgression of the norms of media representation. These were people like us (at least if you lived in the United States), our sons and daughters, our defenders and our heroes, who seemed to see no problem in their behaviour or in its digital display. They were only following orders, or following the crowd, or following the increasing trend of personal publication, the publicity of the private.

Introducing morality and ethics

My argument in this book builds from this rather modest and unexceptional beginning. It concerns the role of the media in the formation of social, civic and moral space. And when I say media I mean media: the mass, the globalized, the regional, the national, the local, the personal media; the broadcast and interactive media; the audio and audio-visual and the printed media; the electronic and the mechanical, the digital and the analogue media; the big screen and the small screen media; the dominant and alternative media; the fixed and the mobile, the convergent and the stand-alone media. And this lack of discrimination, this inclusivity, is deliberate. Of course different media allow us to do different things; they provide different social and political affordances. But together, in the array of possible technologies, delivery systems, platforms, discourses, texts, modes of address, as well as in the patterns of our use of them, they define a space that is increasingly mutually referential and reinforcive, and increasingly integrated into the fabric of everyday life. As Marshall McLuhan might have said, we put the media on, like clothing, to hide our nakedness, to protect us from the elements and to enable us to leave home and explore the world.

The media are becoming environmental. Not in the Baudrillardian sense of the media as generating a distinct sphere, a separation of the symbolic from the realities of everyday life, a kind of more or less escapist excursion into the realm of fantasy and simulation. More a sense of the media as tightly and dialectically intertwined with the everyday. We have become dependent on the media for the conduct of everyday life. They have become the *sine qua non* of the quotidian. But they are also inexplicable and insignificant without the everyday, without in turn their being resources for thought, judgement and action, both personal and political.

I am aware that such a starting point, and such a position, opens me to the challenge of media-centrism, that I am presupposing what needs to be demonstrated, and that if I assume and insist on the media's importance *a priori* then I will be in no position to challenge or to test it. Indeed, in simple and commonsensical empirical terms, it is quite clear that the media are not, cannot be, everything. Life is lived outside the media and for many, if not statistically most, around the world, the media, at least many of them, are absent, unavailable, irrelevant. And even in advanced industrial societies personal and political decisions are often made away from microphones and cameras. Life is lived, in families, organizations and states without reference to the media. We live. We die.

My argument presumes all this. But it also insists on the significance of the media for our orientation in the world, in a world that is available to us, within reach, albeit only symbolically, in ways unimaginable before the electronic age. Indeed my argument does not need an exclusivity clause. I can insist, as I already explicitly have begun to do, on the salience of the presence in our world of such figures as the Afghan blacksmith, and others like and unlike him, simply because without that appearance, the world which includes them would not exist at all, at least not for us. And I can ask, as I will now and for the remainder of the book, what the significance of that appearance might be, without insisting that it is the only thing of significance. The media are both context and themselves contextualized. They both construct a world, and are constructed within and by that world. And of course the world is plural not singular. The world as it appears on Al Arabya is different from that on CNN. My world is different from yours. Experience, both mediated and non-mediated, is culturally specific.

At the core of my questioning is the nature of our mediated relationship to the other person. And my question, consequently, concerns ethics. Isaiah Berlin defines the term:

> Ethical thought consists of the systematic examination of the relations of human beings to each other, the conceptions, interests and ideals from which human ways of treating one another spring, and the systems of value on which such ends of life are based. These beliefs about how human life should be lived, what men and women should be and do, are objects of moral enquiry: and when applied to groups and nations, and, indeed mankind as a whole, are called political philosophy, which is but ethics applied to society. (Berlin 1990: 1–2)

Berlin here deliberately elides ethical thought, moral enquiry and political philosophy. In doing so he begs a number of questions as to their distinctiveness and prioritization. While I am aware of the significance of these questions, I do not intend to dwell on them, though the relationship between the ethical and the political will continue to be troublesome. For the most part I will use the terms the *ethical* and the *moral* as synonymous, but I will tend to distinguish, and hope to do so in a consistent fashion, ethics from morality in the following, no doubt oversimplified, way. I am taking the moral to apply to first principles; to the judgement and elucidation of thought and action that is oriented towards the other, that defines our relationship to her or him in sameness and in otherness, and through which relationship our own claims to be a moral, human, being are defined. Implicitly and explicitly such morality assumes an idea of the good, a set of values to which one will aspire, and in their unlikely achievement, would define those who do so achieve them as themselves good. The moral refers to the generality of principles, and to the possibility of their justification. Ethics, I intend, is the application of those principles in particular social or historical, personal or professional contexts.[1]

In the context of the present discussion, then, the morality of the media refers to the generality of orientation and procedure within which the world is constructed by the media and within which the other appears. Or to put it the other way round, it is because the media provide, with greater or lesser degrees of consistency, the frameworks (or frameworlds) for the appearance of the other that they, de facto, define the moral space within which the other appears to us, and at the same time invite (claim, constrain) an equivalent moral response from us, the audience, as a potential or actual citizen.

Media ethics, on the other hand, relates to practice and procedure: to the ways in which the journalists go, don't go, or should go, about their business; and to the ways in which the relationships between reporters, film makers, storytellers and image producers and their subjects and their viewers and listeners are constructed or assumed. Whereas ethics can be, and maybe should be, codified, morality can only be argued. And which of the two takes precedence: whether morality has to be seen as the product of ethics, as a distillation of practice, or whether judgements of morality take precedence as a precondition for ethical behaviour, the ethical life, is a question that I cannot, philosophically, begin to judge. The answer will be presumed, as I have already suggested, in the latter's favour, without too much, I hope, hanging on that presumption, at least in the current text.

Notwithstanding the importance of these both subtle and significant distinctions, the baseline of my argument is that the world's media are an increasingly significant site for the construction of a moral order, one which would be, and arguably needs to be, commensurate with the scope and scale of global interdependence. Insofar as they provide the symbolic

connection and disconnection that we have to the other, the other who
is the distant other, distant geographically, historically, sociologically,
then the media are becoming the crucial environments in which a morality appropriate to the increasingly interrelated but still horrendously
divided and conflictful world might be found, and indeed expected. In
short, any ambitions for a genuine, meaningful and ethical civil society
that might extend beyond states (but not only beyond states) and to
include an idea of the global citizen, must take how that world is represented in the world's media seriously.

There is one further philosophical issue to be addressed. It is the
problem intrinsic to any proposal which involves judgements that extend
beyond the self to include the other. This is the universalist–relativist
problem. There do not appear to be any conclusive arguments for defending either relativism or universalism. Relativist arguments fail, logically,
on the basis of their own relativism ('I am not able to persuade you to
accept the argument that all thought is relative to a given society, because
you live in a different society from me, and the relevance of my thought
is by definition confined to my own'). Universalist arguments fail, politically, because they fail to recognize that socially distinct and incommen-
surate values and positions can be genuinely and validly held. Any attempt
to specify a generality or universality of position therefore involves an
imposition, a violence, which undermines even (or especially) any claims,
for example, for tolerance or mutual understanding.

It follows that the proposal both to investigate, and to establish the
possibility for, a morality for media, at any and every level of its manifestation, can be seen to be, in its otherwise faded liberalism, at best ethno-
centric and at worst an expression of precisely the kind of cultural
imperialism that it seeks to redress. I don't think there is any simple way
out of this. But as I shall now argue, social, political and cultural terms
and conditions are changing in such a way as to suggest that there may
be life beyond the incommensurable. And those changing terms and
conditions can be characterized quite simply: as globalization.

Globalization

Globalization has become an essentially contested term. Palpably useful
in identifying many of the distinctive characteristics of late modernity,
distinctive perhaps more in their convergence than in their singularity,
globalization, from one particular and somewhat dominating perspective,
characterizes a view of the world which privileges the interconnection

and integration of networks and capital flows, of corporate control and commercial exploitation. Here globalization is constructed as a phenomenon of rampant capitalism, arguably benefiting all those who, however weakly, are drawn into the global market economy, but clearly also benefiting the few at the expense of the many. In political economy the globe has become a single, competitive, productive, consuming, self-consuming, marketplace. Globalization is seen therefore as both a precondition for the production and distribution of increasing global wealth (and therefore a good thing) and the *deus ex machina* of increasing inequality, the economic repression of global populations and the destruction of the environment.

Globalization is also seen as a social phenomenon. Here the dominant metaphors are also of networks and of flows. The globe is seen as being constituted through the intense and endless movement of capital (as above), people, technology, ideas and media, a rhizomatic structure of multiple connections where individual quantities on the move become liquid, fluid, sticky, solid, in their convergent and divergent passages across political, natural and cultural boundaries. Indeed such is the scale of these movements that they appear to congeal into a new whole: postmodern rather than modern; palpable but ineffable; a whole which is abstracted from the tangible materialities of territory, nationality, identity and power; a whole which exists only in the substantial insubstantiality of post-modernity.

And globalization is, necessarily, a political phenomenon. The almost infinite range of neo-imperial power on the one hand, and of terror on the other; the emergence of covenantal institutions with global remits and global reach (Held 2004); the interdependence of states with each other and with transnational organizations; the dreams of a global civil society and the nightmare of a global civil war; the emergence of environmental and human rights, and anti-globalization, movements; the struggles of states to maintain control of populations, markets, national culture. Each of these dimensions of the politics of globalization registers one aspect of what many see as the tectonic shifts in the exercise of, and struggle over, power in a post-Cold War globe.

Finally, globalization is a cultural phenomenon. And this too involves struggle. From one perspective culture, as meaning, value, experience, has become disconnected from the chains of the immediate and the local. Time and space are compressed. New media, new technologies, have extended the range and reach of communication, and access to information is infinite. The result is a quantum shift in the homogenization of cultures, in the undermining of the traditional, and in the disembedding of culture from locality and particularity. But the globalization of culture also involves reaction: fundamentalism, localism, the emergent cultures of diasporas, lifestyles, genders and sexualities: the tensions between roots and routes; proximity and distance.

I want to extract the media, and the process of mediation, from these disparate arguments and positions. My argument will be that it is impossible to conceive – and I mean conceive in both senses of the word, that is to imagine and to bring into being – globalization without the media. This is not as wild a notion as it might appear, though it is one either overlooked, underplayed or taken for granted in many accounts. It is principally and predominantly through our mediated culture that it is possible, I am inclined to say as never before and as I have already illustrated, to be in touch with, to see or hear, to be informed about, events and circumstances, people and settings, far removed from those that are otherwise only experienced in the local neighbourhood. Whatever our views, whatever our responses, the globe *appears* on the world's screens, on a continuous if uneven basis: from the reporting of a motor racing grand prix, to the satellite broadcast of a world cup football match, to the live commentaries of crisis or catastrophe, risk or ritual; to the daily dubbing, drubbing and subtitling of soap operas, telenovelas and Hollywood movies. Otherness and sameness (of which more shortly) appear side by side, intertwined but constantly available as resources to construct both individual and collective global imaginaries: a sense of there being an elsewhere; a sense of that elsewhere being in some way relevant to me; a sense of my being there. But the global media do not just make the global appear symbolically; they are of course a material component of the infrastructure that makes the globe possible as a lived-in place, managed, travelled across, and crucially, relatable to the contingencies and uncertainties of everyday life.

The media have this unique role in global culture. They provide a technological and cultural framework for the connectivity, positive or negative, without which the globe would be merely a shadow. They provide the resources, productive as well as of course counter-productive, to lock the possibility and potentiality of connectivity into the fabric of the quotidian. It is within the media's framing, in image and narrative, home page and chat room, that increasingly the world is becoming global and liveable. It is at this interface, the interface of media and the life-world, where the media as a moral force becomes most relevant, where the world in its otherness is at its most visible. And it is here, in this role and with this responsibility, where the world's media become, indeed must become, ethically constitutional.

There are a number of threads running through this argument, and it would make sense to identify them now, even though they will be developed more fully at various points in the chapters that follow.

The first is a matter of phenomenology. It concerns the relationship between proximity and distance. This is a relationship crucial to our very being as responsible and moral selves. There is a simple point to be made, and that is that the media, as indeed other technologies, enable the stretching of action beyond the face-to-face, and consequently undermine the expectation of responsibility and reciprocity that action and communication in face-to-face settings conventionally require. Technologies disconnect as well as connect. The distance they create between interlocutors, between subject and subject, is a precondition, as many have argued, for the erosion of any sense of responsibility that individuals would be expected to have for the other. The media function as technologies in this respect, but they do so paradoxically. For in establishing and maintaining a material disconnection they simultaneously create a symbolic connection. Distance and presence coincide in ways that fundamentally challenge the necessary proximal relations that are assumed to be a precondition for an ethical life. How the media choose to represent, or conventionally find themselves representing, the other, the other who is otherwise out of reach, becomes a fundamental issue for any kind of project seeking a more virtuous, more ethical, public space.

The second is more sociological. It concerns the status of the cosmopolitan. The cosmopolitan has emerged in recent sociological theory as the figure who represents the phase of late modernity that some call postmodern, and who emerges from the dynamics of the intensification of globalization processes. There have always been cosmopolitans, those who are as comfortable abroad as at home, those whose identities consist in their willingness to be both here and there, inside and outside, and those whose spheres of action and loyalty shift with setting and situation. The cosmopolitans have mostly been confined historically to elites; and where they were not (and sometimes when they were) the word cosmopolitan became derogatory, describing an individual not with two or more homes, but with none; and not with more than one loyalty to place or nation, but with no loyalty to any nation, and therefore a threat.

Now, it is argued, globalization has brought with it an intensification of the condition of the cosmopolitan and an increasing legitimation of the cosmopolitan's status. The new cosmopolitan is assumed to be free from the tying and oppressive loyalties of the singular community. In the ideal world such a figure is mobile, flexible, open to difference and differences. And such a figure is no longer seen as marginal but rather as central to the civic project (Beck 2003), and the construction of a global public sphere. The question this raises, of course, is the possibility of envisaging the media as enhancing a global cosmopolitan culture, one that might not require, indeed will not require, physical mobility, but mobility through the symbolic.[2]

The notion of the cosmopolitan is of course still problematic in a number of ways. It is romantic (in the sense of its wishfulness), anti-romantic (in the sense that it is precisely the cosmopolitan which was anathema in the Romantic reaction to the Enlightenment); unsociological (insofar as it appropriately describes only a very small slice of the world's population)[3]; too singular (there are many cosmopolitanisms, and the cosmopolitan might be thought of rather more productively as being a condition rather than a status, and as such something one moves in and out of); and finally it is a particularly western, and therefore a somewhat exclusive, idea. It survives, like so much in this book, as an analytic and normative category, notwithstanding these weaknesses and as long as it is used with care, for it will stand as an actuality (for some), a possibility (for many) and as the basis for a plausible moral foundation of a global civil society (for all).

The third is political. The public space which reflects, expresses, as well as distorts the appearance of the global on the screens of both broadcast and on-line media, is a contested space. The presumption of uniformity or homogeneity within global mediated culture is palpably absurd. It is a cacophonic space. It is indeed barely a space at all. It is dominated by a few multinational companies who have managed to extend control based on their existing dominance within broadcast media into the otherwise open territories of the internet, one key dimension of the global commons.[4] Yet it is also full of alternative voices, minority presences and individual performances. It is expressive of public service agendas, state-sponsored and controlled agendas as well as commercial agendas. It is fractured by contradiction, as the footprints of national broadcasters are overlaid and compromised by the networks of communication which emerge from diasporic cultures and other transnational movements whose lines of connection transcend state boundaries. Fractious, disputed, imperial, repressive, unjust, the global media space is nevertheless the place where any viable framework for the culture of globalization will need to be forged and where, if at all, an ethical and moral infrastructure for the future of civil society will emerge.[5]

The final point to be made here is technological. Much of what I have been arguing over the last few pages presumes a particular model for media. And it does this, once again, with a descriptive as well as a normative intention. It refuses a model of the media which depends on influence and effects, and it proposes a model of media as environmental. One needs to be careful here, of course, for in unsophisticated hands such a presumption will lead directly to a kind of technological determinism unyielding to the social and to its construction. Yet, as I have already suggested, the media, the global media, albeit guided by the hand of global capital, increasingly have become a key component of the cultural infrastructure of contemporary society, one in which the conduct of personal and private life as well as public and political life increasingly depends. In this sense, and without expecting specific effects to follow from specific media or their intervention, I want to endorse the idea of the media as an environment, an environment which provides at the most fundamental level the resources we all need for the conduct of everyday life. It follows that such an environment may be or may become, or may not be or may not become, polluted.

Cosmopolitanism and pluralism

I need now to return to the philosophical: to the question of the way in which this discussion of globalization might enable a move towards approaching, if not actually resolving, the problem of relativism and universalism in media ethics.

Global interdependence is the setting. It is both the problem and the context in which the steps towards ameliorating the problem might be taken. For global interdependence, both conflictful and conciliatory, involves increasing awareness of, and interaction with, the stranger. In this late modern world of ours the stranger's otherness is constantly in our face: in the lived realities of urban spaces, in the imagined and communicated realities of mediated places. There is a huge debate emerging as to how this new world can be, and should be, lived in. By what, if any, general principles? Does difference condemn humanity either to indifference or to a fundamental refusal of its value? Can that difference be dignified (Sacks 2002) in a project of global or cosmopolitan virtue?

These are questions that go way beyond what it is possible satisfactorily to deal with here. So what I intend to do is to draw on, and try and summarize, a range of overlapping arguments, broadly speaking within the same liberal tradition, which provide a necessary, though certainly an insufficient, basis for the position I want to develop in my discussion of the morality of media. Together they provide a framework which I would like to think bridges the sociological and the philosophical in such a way as to ground morality and ethics in the specific conditions of contemporary society and its mediation.

To begin with Ulrich Beck's notion of the cosmopolitan:

> Today there is a new cosmopolitanism in the air. The term 'cosmopolitan' can easily be misunderstood. It does not mean ruthlessness – the perspective of the global player, global capitalist; not recolonisation, nor universalism either; because there are *many* cosmopolitanisms – not one language of cosmopolitanism but many languages, grammars, tongues. It is *not* multiculturalism either because multiculturalism presumes some essentialistic understandings of cultural differences . . . We all are living by birth in two worlds, two communities – in the cosmos (that is *nature*) and in the *polis* (that is, the city/state). To be more precise: individuals are rooted in *one* cosmos but in *different* cities, territories, ethnicities, hierarchies, nations, religions – all at the same time. This creates not exclusivity but rather an inclusive plural membership. It means that all humans are equal in nature, yet belong to different states, organised in territorial units (polis). (Beck 2003: 6)

The key to this, for the moment, is the claim for an empirically grounded plurality as the condition of humanity in late modernity. It is a limited empirical claim of course, given what we know about the world and its population, but it is one that has meaning within an analysis of the contemporary character of at least European society, and in terms of its generic moral and political implications. This will become significantly more relevant as my own argument develops, not least in my intention to take seriously the duality of the polis and the media, as environment and as cosmos, in chapter 2.

The cosmopolitan individual embodies, in his or her person, a doubling of identity and identification; the cosmopolitan, as an ethic, embodies a commitment, indeed an obligation, to recognize not just the stranger as other, but the other in oneself. Cosmopolitanism implies and requires, therefore, both reflexivity and toleration. In political terms it demands justice and liberty. In social terms, hospitality. And in media terms it requires, as I will argue in chapter 6, an obligation to listen, an obligation which I will suggest is a version of hospitality.

Cosmopolitanism, finally, requires a philosophical and an ethical response. This response goes by the name of pluralism. In Isaiah Berlin's hands, pluralism is the product of the thinking of, perhaps ironically, three anti-Enlightenment figures of the eighteenth century, Giambattista

Vico, J. G. Herder and J. G. Hamman. The irony lies in each of these men's contribution to the emergence of Romanticism and, in the last's case, to the origins of nationalism. It was an irony not lost on Berlin. The principal focus of their critique, however, was the universalist tendencies in the Enlightenment, the misplaced omnipotence of reason and the Enlightenment's *de jure* refusal to acknowledge the distinctiveness, indeed the irreducible distinctiveness, of human cultures. For Hamman individual experience, and its empirical observation, was what counted against all the otherwise presumed certainties of rational argument. For both Vico and above all Herder, it was their pluralism that was both distinctive and revolutionary: 'the belief not merely in the multiplicity, but in the incommensurability of the values of different cultures and societies, and . . . the incompatibility of equally valid ideals' (Berlin 2000: 176).

Berlin subsequently attempted to rescue his interpretation of those men (and indeed himself) from the charge that he had failed to establish their thinking as anything other than relativist, and it is in this defence where he most clearly articulated what he meant by pluralism. It needs to be quoted fully:

> There are many objective ends, ultimate values, some incompatible with others, pursued by different societies at various times, or by different groups within the same society . . . any one of which may find itself subject to conflicting claims of uncombinable, yet equally ultimate and objective, ends. Incompatible these ends may be; but their variety can not be unlimited, for the nature of men, however various and subject to change, must possess some generic character if it is to be called human at all . . . There is a limit beyond which we can no longer understand what a given creature is at: what kinds of rules it follows in its behaviour; what its gestures mean. In such situations, when the possibility for communication breaks down, we speak . . . of incomplete humanity. But within the limits of humanity the variety of ends, finite though it is, can be extensive. (Berlin 1990: 80)

There are a number of elements of this specification which require brief elucidation for they need to be disentangled, as Berlin in fact seeks to do, from the pre- and non-liberal context in which they were originally formulated. The baseline is the insistence on both the objectivity of certain aspects of the human condition, which for Berlin would include the universal value of liberty, the existence of a common human nature, rational criticism and the tractability of many but not all conflicts of value in public and private life (Lukes 2003). Pluralism insists on difference, but not irreducible difference. It insists that the shared fundament of the human condition imposes limits on the range of meaningful difference and likewise enables the possibility of communication, some kind of communication, across the widest and deepest channels. Pluralism in this sense is compatible with Berlin's negative version of liberty, a moral minimalism which acknowledges the basic shared experience of humanity, in its vulnerability to suffering, in its desire for personal or collective freedom, which is defensible and at the same time compatible with cultural variation and profound differences of value. Pluralism also insists, in Berlin's hands, on the absence of conclusivity in human thought. There is no Archimedean point from which to make any final judgements or impose what he (apparently without any hint of irony) calls a final solution (Berlin 1997).

Berlin's moral minimalism is constitutive. In Michael Walzer's (Walzer 1994) account, a similar moral minimalism appears, only this time as epiphenomenal. For Walzer our capacity, or incapacity, to engage with the other is not based on the irreducibility of the human condition, but on the fact that each culture provides in its thick uniqueness a set of values which enable us to recognize something similar in the cultures of others. It is because every society has a notion of truth or justice, that truth or justice as an abstraction can surface as a component of a shareable, albeit, in Walzer's terms a thin, morality.

Moral minimalism, that which is, then, shareable across cultures, is the product of this mutuality of recognition. It is not sufficient to sustain identity but it is a necessary component of any kind of community. Moral maximalism is grounded in the particularity of experience and history, which together define the distinctiveness of any individual culture, and it is this particularity, a particularity which we all share, each in our distinctive ways, which Walzer sees, perhaps counter-intuitively, as the basis for a wider commonality and for a community of discourse. Moral minimalism is a version of relativism that both recognizes that there are limits to what can be accepted, as well as one which sees sameness emerging from the otherwise incommensurability of difference.[6] And perhaps this is the crucial point, however simple: it is in the experienced dialectic of sameness and difference that the possibility of a personal or communal ethics emerges, and it is in the mediated *representation* of that dialectic that the equivalent possibility of a media ethics emerges.

Such experience, an experience which only knows the stranger because it already knows the friend, and vice versa, is the precondition for toleration. Contemporary society still has its boundaries, however porous, however conflictful; and fences and walls are still being built and dismantled both in the material world and in the symbolic. And in such a world, one increasingly accustomed to living with ambivalence, both internal and external, but one also resisting that ambivalence in the creation of ever new and intransigent polarities, these discriminations are the vital raw material for a global media ethics. They are what constitute its possibility. As Walzer himself suggests in insisting that modernity has not been erased by the post-modern, but merely overlaid by it: 'We still know ourselves to be this or that, but the knowledge is uncertain, for we are also this *and* that' (Walzer 1997: 90; italics in original). We also increasingly know ourselves to be vulnerable, again in both material (body, environment) and symbolic (culture, identity) domains.

There is, I hope, a convergence of argument and position emerging in the discussion so far. It lies in the grounding of both a general and a media ethics in the varieties, but also the consistencies, of human experience. And it is in the claims, albeit differently inflected, and notwithstanding the manifest and often punishing differences of such experience across cultures, that there is at the same time the possibility of sameness: the possibility of recognition, the possibility of identification, the possibility of communication. And in another modality, not just its possibility but its necessity.

Ulrich Beck calls this possibility/necessity 'cosmopolitan realism' (Beck 2004).[7] Cosmopolitan realism, like Berlin's pluralism, presupposes a universalist minimum with a range of self-evident principles and prohibitions, and also like Berlin's pluralism, it is, or should be, aware of its limits and the contradictions that even such a basic morality sets for itself – not least the possibility of having to break those principles in order to defend them. It also includes the troubling and dangerous elision between the taking of global responsibility, humanitarian intervention, and what might otherwise be considered (and used to be so considered) as colonialism. Cosmopolitan realism, in the acknowledgement that there are no separate worlds, represents a kind of contextual universalism, one which suggests that non-intervention in the crisis of the other is no longer possible because we are, in this new global era, intimately connected to each other as never before. In today's world there is no out there there. Cosmopolitan realism involves an affirmation of the other as at once both different and the same. And cosmopolitan realism, as Walzer's moral minimalism, leads to a cosmopolitanism of humility. It requires an acknowledgement of our own vulnerability.

There is inevitably an intimate connection between any promotion of an ethics for the newly emerging global society and one, mine, which addresses the possibility of a global media ethics. This intimacy is, increasingly, a natural one. It is also a necessary one. Otherness, difference, sameness are the differentiating and connecting categories that appear on our screens on a daily basis. Media are technologies which both connect and disconnect, but above all they act as bridges or doors, both open and closed, to the world. If there is to be fair and just action in that world, as there must be, then what those who act see and hear as electronically contrived, as well as what they learn from the direct immediacy of social experience, are its preconditions.

Media work

It is generally believed that late modernity, or post-modernity, is a fuzzy world, a world of flux, a world of ever shifting identities, of fractures and faults, flaws and freedoms. We live in societies that, supposedly, no longer are societies. Borders are transgressed; indeed the notion of transgression itself is no longer available as an evaluative term. And borders are there only to be crossed. How much of this is a conceit, a prerogative of the thought of the western, dislocated intellectual, is an open question. As a relative judgement it is hard to dispute: traditional societies, those inscribed and constrained by inflexible boundaries, are, and have been now for generations, on the wane. As an absolute judgement of social and cultural change, and its irrevocability, it stands less secure. Cultures and societies are always in tension, always having to manage the clash of creativity and conservatism. And human beings cannot live without the play of sameness and difference, individually or collectively. In this, and despite radical social change, we are no different; we are the same.

The generalized state of ambivalence, the fear of chaos, the need for both friends and enemies, these are constants of the human condition. Fortunately or unfortunately. The present world is struggling – though it seems quite banal to say so – with these problems of differentiation and judgement no less than its predecessors. The Cold War has merely been replaced by a liquid one. Terror is the ultimate destroyer and defender of boundaries.

So, it might be said, are the world's media. This is not meant as just a provocation. Nor is it a reference to the presence of violence, both real and symbolic, on our screens. It is intended as a way of registering the kind of work which the media undertake as they go about their representational business. And this work is not confined to that undertaken in the news or current affairs, where claims for truth and trust and literalness are most obviously articulated in the directness of the engagement with the world as it appears in all its vivid immediacy. This representational work extends to the play of narrative and performance across all the genres and platforms of media: to the construction of heroes and villains, friends and strangers, in drama and soap opera as well as on the sports and gossip pages. And it also extends, of course, to the work that audiences do, or fail to do, in their engagement with what they see and hear. For media are part and parcel of the everyday, just as the everyday is part and parcel of the media.

I want to identify media's work as boundary work. And in a number of dimensions. The media, in their centripetal phase, articulated the boundaries of national and linguistic cultures. Beginning in the first age of print, they enabled the fixing and spreading of vernacular languages and, through that emergence, the boundaries and identities of the embryonic modern nation-state (Eisenstein 1979). The newspaper, and perhaps above all, radio and television broadcasting, continued with this project, throughout the twentieth century (Anderson 1983; Scannell and Cardiff 1991). Written language, and public service broadcasting together, had, and to a degree still have, that consequence and that significance: the work of boundary and community construction at national but also at subnational, regional and local, levels.

And now in an age where the media are more centrifugal, and where the internet, above all, is helping to spread the loci of cultural and political activity to the social margins, and in so doing is upsetting the integrative role of broadcasting and the national press, this boundary work is becoming even more significant, if not more complex and challenging. Everyone is doing it, in the reporting of global media events and global crises: in the centripetal rush to the established media when we are, collectively, at our most anxious; and in the centrifugal assertion of identities and connectivities in accordance with shared interests, lifestyles or political persuasions on websites and in alternative and minority media.

This is the media's macro-boundary work. But there is, constantly, micro-boundary work too. Work which involves the continuous inscriptions of difference in any and every media text or discourse: from the crude stereotypes of otherness to the subtle and not-so-subtle discriminations of dramatic characterization, narrative construction, political punditry, internet chat rooms and talk radio. It would not be too far-fetched to suggest that this is what the media do – their primary cultural role: the endless, endless, endless, playing with difference and sameness. Such is the source of both the pleasure and the irritation which they provide.

Such is the source of their significance in the articulation of a public space, in its most ridiculous as well as its most sublime manifestations. If this seems unnecessarily reductive, then so be it. It need not be an exclusivist claim. It is however the necessary basis for any judgement of the media as a moral force, either positive or negative. As such it is the connection between the media's discriminative practices in terms of self and other, the dominance and consistency of some of these practices, the weakness and inconsistency of others, with our capacity and willingness to make judgements and to pursue distinct courses of action in our everyday lives, that becomes salient. And this is the case not just in propagandist regimes but in the consistencies of representation and rhetoric in the most democratic of global societies.

It follows that the third dimension of the media's boundary work is to be found here, at the double interface between the symbolic and the real, and between the public and the private. And it is here where it becomes most clear that media work itself is actually boundless. It spills over. It involves audiences and readers, as well as producers and participants. It involves the continuities of talk, of response and rejection, as what is seen and heard, understood or misunderstood, loved or hated, is incorporated, both consciously and unconsciously, into the cultures of the everyday. In these continuities and complexities of practice, the media become a multiply reflexive project, one in which we can take what appears on screen and page not merely as read, but as providing many of the secondary, if not the primary, resources for being and living. The media, then, are not the only locus of reflexivity in this, the late modern world, but they are one of its key stimuli, and they themselves are, or indeed should be, the objects of reflection and criticism, just as they themselves, at best, provide the materials for that reflection and criticism. The media are both contained by, and are the container of, the everyday.

Consider the screen. A boundary *par excellence*. The screen is an interface, a frame, a window, a mask and a barrier. It is an interface and as such a space for inscription, the literal inscriptions of image and text, and the projected inscriptions of readers and audiences. As frame it acts as a container, limiting what is seen and heard and marking the boundary between the experienced world and its representation. And as a frame the screen separates transmitted sacredness from experienced secularity, the heightened manifestation of appearance from the mundane ordinariness of the everyday. As window it reveals. It reveals a world otherwise beyond reach, a world of otherness in its supposed transparency, and with the invitation, reinforced by immediacy and liveness, or the supposed liveness, of reality television or synchronous on-line communication, to see and to believe. As window it delivers the mimetic. As mask, it disguises that same reality, distorting, disturbing, truth or authenticity as it simultaneously reclaims them both. As mask too the screen offers its fictional accounts of the world, another kind of disguise, but one rarely completely removed from a world which can be recognized and read by its viewers as relevant and real. Masks too are mimetic. As barrier it separates the worlds which otherwise it might connect: the celebrity from the fan; the terrorist from the victim; the bomber from the bombed; the self from the other. As barrier the screen fails us.

And what of these failures? The world's media is replete with its own self-criticism. Though this is, for the most part, an impotent self-critique, and one without irony, as for example when NBC once condemned the 'media circus' gathered to welcome Michael Jackson at his arraignment on child molestation charges in Santa Maria County California, a circus it needs hardly to be said in which they themselves were participating. More fundamentally, but just as ubiquitously, dumbing down, 'Hollywoodization', commercialization, the loss of trust, the failures of distance, the disregard of privacy, the trivialization of the serious, the exploitation of the weak and vulnerable, the celebritization and the inevitable cannibalization of the not-so-famous, the erosion of the boundaries between the real and the imagined, between fact and fiction, and between news and entertainment, all are versions of a constant media critique, one which does not only emerge from the literati of the world but also from many ordinary people who are as profoundly disenchanted, and whom, for reasons that need not concern us now, the dominant media persistently ignore (while, for the most part, insisting they are doing the opposite).[8]

To parcel these together, as many have done, is basically to suggest that the media have lost their role as guardians of the public good, that they are no longer an effective fourth estate, and that their current practices are being pursued without regard to basic ethics or to their responsibilities and duties to citizens or states. The defence is usually one which insists, among other things, that we get the media we deserve, or are willing to pay for. I am not going to engage in this argument, for while I am quite willing to acknowledge the media's manifest weaknesses, it is the juxtaposition – though pursued in different ways – of the attack and the defence that grounds what follows.

The media, in all their differentiation, do have responsibilities and indeed these responsibilities are not confined only to the nuts and bolts of reporting and representation. They include these of course, but the net has to be cast much wider: to the principles which underlie those responsibilities, and which in turn need to be based on an interrogation of the context, the increasingly global context, in which they have to be exercised and which significantly increases them. But the reverse is also true. It is that we (readers, audiences, citizens) need to take responsibility for our media. Our dependence on them is no longer at issue. That dependence therefore can no longer be innocent. What follows is therefore an attempt to secure, or at least begin to secure, a doubly ethical project for the media, one which interrogates the media's role in, and ultimate responsibility for, a global civic space, what I call in chapter 2, the 'mediapolis', the space of appearance. And one which also requires something, indeed quite a lot, from us.

The sequence

The next and framing chapter builds an argument through an examination of the writing of Hannah Arendt, a political theorist whose thinking was in turn framed by her experience of her life and the life of others in Germany before, during and after the holocaust, and whose writing on the human condition, on the nature of thought, judgement and action, as well as on the nature of responsibility in public life, have, in my view, massive relevance to my own problematic and to the current state of mediated affairs. Her work on totalitarianism and evil is well known. Her concern with modernity's undermining of the quality of public, democratic life equally so. Her approach to communication is implicit but vital. And it is in particular her characterization of communication in public space, the space of appearance, on which I focus. It leads me to develop the idea of the mediapolis, as the condition of media, and as both an empirical and a normative term, in which relations between self and other are to be conducted in a global public sphere. The mediapolis becomes, then, a core concept in the book as a whole as I explore both the reality and the possibility of global communication, and its significance for the future of what I will have to say is the human condition.

Chapter 3 involves a slight stepping back from the previous abstractions and is, effectively, a reflection on evil, and on the presence of a discourse of evil in American public culture. It draws once again on the work of Hannah Arendt, but takes a much wider historical, sociological, and even philosophical view of what I argue is the continuity, and the continuous availability, of a rhetoric of evil in the United States. Such a presence is guaranteed, as it were, by a convergence of belief, exposition and narrative to be found in US religious, popular and political culture, and one which, in particular, has been drawn upon, principally but not exclusively, by Republican presidents in the years since the beginning of the Cold War. The media are key to such a rhetoric's formation and its acceptance. In the context of my argument overall in this book, this case study provides, in a sense, a cautionary tale, one that addresses issues of polarization and demonization, and as such the dangers of refusing the legitimate presence of the other in public space. This chapter looks at the dark side of a singularizing media.

The next, in reversing that polarity, introduces the second of the intellectual stimuli, perhaps, it could be said, in the minor key. This is provided by Edward Said, particularly in his work reflecting his own exilic status and analysing the place and significance of imperialism in English and French nineteenth- and early twentieth-century literature. Drawing on my own empirical work on minority media in Europe, I offer an account, again both empirical and normative, of his use of the notion of counterpoint (strictly, the contrapuntal, in his terms) as a starting point for a model and metaphor for the analysis of the dynamics of what would otherwise be called the multicultural. The significance of this is twofold. In the first instance it draws attention to (and is based on my own empirical research in) Europe as a society of complex media, and differentiated public spaces, in which media can, and increasingly will, articulate both distinctive and distinctively shared cultures. And secondly it provides a case study for the exploration of mediation as engaged with pluralities of judgement, action and belief, and of the multiplicity and complexity of otherness, in a case study which contrasts quite radically with the one that precedes it, based, as it was, in the United States of America.

So far the focus has, principally, been on the producers of media. Chapter 5 reverses the polarities and considers the role of the media in everyday life from the perspective of audiences, and in relation to their responsibility. It is quite clear that mediation extends beyond what appears on screen and speaker, and it is equally clear that in a world of global mediation and representation, we need to consider audiences and readers as necessarily responsible for their own participation in that culture. The everyday is a site of media work; and mediation, in turn, needs to be understood as the product, in significant part, of the actions and inactions of audiences. This chapter discusses these issues through an analysis of complicity, collusion and compassion, and explores the value of a notion of *proper distance* as a measure for ethical positioning in media work.

Media justice, hospitality and responsibility are the topics of the penultimate chapter. It takes me fully into the realms of moral philosophy, in an attempt to offer a set of principles upon which to ground a media ethics. The argument rests on a discussion of an obligation as opposed to a rights-based model for what I call representational ethics: and principal among the obligations proposed is that to ensure that the mediated other will be listened to and heard. It also rests on the implications of the tension between responsibility and justice, between the individual and the procedural as sites for the grounding of a media ethics. Both, I argue, are necessary. So too is a commitment to media hospitality, a version of which I develop from a reading of Jacques Derrida, and one which, or so it seems to me, is a precondition for the effective emergence of the mediapolis as a space for connection and compassion in the late modern world.

And lastly to issues of application. The final chapter addresses how these questions of responsibility can be operationalized in media practice. It does so through a consideration of the relation between regulation and literacy, and generates what I hope is a productive discourse on the range of responses that seem to be required if we are to enable a more moral media culture and a more viable global civic space. The argument challenges the presumption that regulation is the be-all-and-end-all of that possibility, and it defends a wider and more critical approach, one which crucially depends on education as an instigator of an engaged and informed media literate citizenry.

2

Mediapolis or the Space of Appearance

The sight of hostages, British, US, French, Italian, on the television screens of the world, pleading for their lives and pleading with governments to change their policies or free their own prisoners, became a commonplace, notwithstanding its horror, in the months after the invasion of Iraq. And indeed perhaps as such a commonplace, it quite quickly became absorbed into the slew of reality television, just another version of the world's perversity appearing on the global screen, just another manifestation of its inhumanity, presented for our momentary delight. These images were intended, at least by those who produced them, as a weapon in their own political battle, a weapon that would extend the reach of their struggle to the four corners of the earth. Their expectation of such global reach was dependent on the world's media's collusion with them. And for good reasons and bad, disinterested news on the one hand, and the draw of the terrible on the other, they would not be disappointed. But how quickly such images fade, and how easily they meld into the dailiness of the media's momentary attention and their capacity to roll the exceptional into the numbing flow of daily reporting and representation.

The contemporary rhetoric of terror is dramatic in its immediacy and blunted in its contextualization. It fights for attention in the political spaces that the media uniquely provide. It fights for response, from global audiences, from those who might see, who might respond, who might judge and who might wish to act on what they have seen and understood. Terror, of course depends on what has been called the oxygen of publicity. But not just terror. All public life depends on it. And politics is inconceivable and unsustainable without its appearance and its performance on the screens and through the speakers of the world's media.

The pathological often offers a window on the normal: a focus on the perverse often provides a view of the ordinary. Here the images and the sounds of unbearable cruelty and inhumanity provide, or so I shall argue, a starting point for believing that the media can be a place for civility and humanity. This is more than merely trying to make a virtue out of necessity. Perhaps it is, on the contrary, arguing for making necessity out of incipient virtue. For this, the space the media create, its omni-ever-present, indestructible, ephemeral, relentless, fractured, encompassing, intrusive, mediated space, is *the* public space, perhaps the only viable public space now available to us in a world of global politics and global interconnection. It is a public space grounded in appearance, in what John Thompson (Thompson 1995) has called the new visibility. It is my intention in this chapter to explore and interrogate this space of appearance, and to argue for the need to grasp its significance, its possibilities and its implications for the future of global civil society.

Things appear. They are pushed to the front, like children at a family photograph. Sometimes those things are unwelcome, sometimes they are forced onto the screen. Western mainstream media collude with those images. They will say they have no choice. Even the murders and the decapitations. If they do not show them, others will, and indeed are doing so, on the internet at least, and on global satellite channels. They are available, somewhere in media space; they are available everywhere.

Once the media have opened the door to the visibility of the world, we cannot pretend that it is not there. But the claims and expectations of the rights to access, of the rights to see, need to be accompanied, and indeed conditioned, by the responsibility to listen and to respond. Seeing is neither believing nor knowing. The image without its context and its interrogation is no royal route to the truth, nor even, more properly, to understanding. Appearance must become more than mere appearance. Seeing is not enough. And visibility is only just the beginning.

Appearance, mediated appearance, however, constitutes our worldliness, our capacity to be in the world. Such worldliness is not quite we what we are used to. It is both more and less than the worldliness of the face-to-face. Less, obviously, because it does not press on us with its interrogatory demands, with its smell and touch. More, equally obviously, because it offers a range of connections that both enhance and supplement experience, and which replace the material by the symbolic, the as-if of touch.

This offer of worldliness, this offer of a shareable world, extends across the whole range of media and communications technologies and services. The world is shareable in novel and increasingly intensive ways in its constant availability and its accessibility. Mediated connection and interconnection define the dominant infrastructure for the conduct of social, political and economic life across the globe. The possibility of seeing and talking to globally dispersed family and friends on the internet; the possibility of sharing information in real time with business partners or colleagues; the possibility of knowing what is happening on the other side of the planet as well as what is going on down the street, these are the components of a world in which many, if not most, interactions take place through the media of various kinds, and one where our dependence on these media knows no bounds.

The world is shareable but not necessarily shared. Not only does communication palpably break down, but it is structurally flawed. Distances are maintained even in the immediacy of the live broadcast or the long-distance telephone call or web-cast. There is noise and dissemblance; there are falsehoods and absences; there are biases and exaggerations; there are exclusions. Against the albeit still flawed gold standard of the face-to-face, all mediated communication is lacking (though it has many advantages). In the world of mediated communication, as in all others, we have to learn to live with imperfection. But we also have to challenge those imperfections and our tendency, perhaps unwittingly, but also structurally, to magnify them.

Yet the world of globally mediated communication offers and to a degree defines the terms of our participation with the other. When things appear, when images of suffering or crisis or joy, or indeed the banality of everyday life's stuff, surface on page and screen, they are brought to our attention. And without our attention they can have little meaning and little effect. The mediation of the world requires its audience; but to be an audience it is not enough to sit back, pumping the key pad, clicking the mouse. It requires our participation, our engagement. It requires us to take responsibility for our part in the process, one way or another.

Media culture could be, and indeed will be here, defined as late modernity's space of appearance, both in the sense of where *the world appears*, and in the sense of *appearance as such* constituting that world. This doubling, this overdetermination, defines the media's absolute distinctiveness, and indeed its claims for power. The attack on the World Trade Center appeared on the screens of the global media and, apart from those living within a small radius of the catastrophe, and even for many of those who did, its appearance on those screens constituted its reality. A defining moment, perhaps, in world history, was however not a defining moment in media culture, merely an intense manifestation of what otherwise is entirely taken for granted: the *sine qua non* of media as underpinning and overarching the experiences of everyday life. The media bring immediacy.

As I have already begun to argue, we live in a world with others who are not like us, but also in a world in which, precisely, it is the commonality of difference that is shared. This is what constitutes the world as plural. For generations, perhaps, we could avoid, disguise or deny such plurality. Our everyday lives were not necessarily lived in ways that forced the issue, at least on a scale beyond the face-to-face of village or community. But now they are. The mediated globe involves lifting the veil on difference. It cannot be avoided. It is seen and heard daily. The problem is that while globalized media have lifted the veil, they have provided few or no resources to understand and respond to that difference, nor do they necessarily represent it adequately. And the consequences of that representation have tended to produce either worldly indifference or hostility, both strategies for denial. If the media are – and they are in a sense by definition – the bridge between private and public worlds, as well as between the social and the personal, then we ought not to be satisfied with their limitations, their narrowness and intransigence. There is too much at stake.

In this chapter I explore the implications of these preliminary observations for an understanding of the global media as a moral space, and as a necessary, if not sufficient, site for the emergence of a civic culture that encompasses and engages with the very realities that claim our attention on an hourly and daily basis. In doing so I draw directly, and intensely, on the work of the political theorist and philosopher, Hannah Arendt.

Arendt's work, informed by the experience of totalitarianism and her status as an exile and a Jew, rarely deals directly with the media, except in critically dismissive ways that insist on their homogeneity as well as their insidiousness. Her intellectual position is distinct and of its time and her experience. But her commitment to analysing the roots of, and threats to, the body politic, and her approach to the problems of communication, of speech and action in the post-holocaust world, have huge contemporary relevance, especially in the polarized and polarizing global culture currently emerging. Indeed much of her writing is an exercise, a critical and albeit an often deeply pessimistic exercise, in the analysis of human communication, its responsibilities and its vulnerabilities, and the implications of communication's successes and failures in enabling or disabling public life and public morality (Cmiel 1996).

This is the thread that links her concerns with mine. Perhaps the most significant and salient difference is that generated by the presence of the global media, not simply as an addendum to the social or the political, as Arendt might have seen it, but as one of its major constituents. The media's pervasive presence has sucked up what was left of the public and the political, after its battering by fascism and communism, into its own framework of representation. Arendt's own critique juxtaposed her apparent, but by no means uncritical, endorsement of the politics of Athens with the vulnerability of political space and action in her own time, when it might be said that the dominant political institutions had recently revealed the consequences of their capacity to commandeer the communication infrastructure – its very mass-ness was both novel and crippling. Yet in the present world it is possible to suggest that the positions have been reversed, and that if we are to search for, and interrogate, the presence and character of the public and the political we need to start, and possibly finish, with the media themselves.

Doing so involves more than asking the familiar question of the presence or absence of a mediated public sphere, a question that media scholars (for a review see Dahlgren 1995) have been debating for some time. It involves cutting a swathe through the arguments that insist that the national and transnational media have led to a fragmentation of any vestige of a public sphere and a consequent disenfranchising and disempowering of its putative citizens. But it also involves a refusal of the opposite argument, that the media in their current form are virtuously extending the range of communication meaningfully in ways that are fundamentally enhancing the democratic process. Neither of these presumptions are right, neither are wrong. Both are right. Both are wrong.

What I want to suggest is that in significant respects, for better and for worse, the media do in fact constitute the world's publicness – there is, arguably, no other – and therefore it behoves us to interrogate what kind of publicness this is, what its strengths and weaknesses are, what its consequences might be, what its responsibilities, and what might be changed. This is the task of the present chapter, and to a significant degree, of the book as a whole.

The mediapolis

It is a commonplace to presume that the Greek *polis*, a public space of face-to-face communication among an elite whose capacity to debate and judge was in part dependent on the exclusion and exploitation of large sectors of the Athenian population, is in no respect a relevant model for current political life. However this may not necessarily be the case.

Contemporary media enable a face-to-faceness which, both in broadcast and interactive modes (and of course the differences are not insignificant), involves the coming together of speech and action and, albeit in the symbolic realm of mediated representation, they reproduce, though of course in an intensely technologically mediated form, the discursive and judgemental space of the *polis*. Like the *polis* this mediated space is often, indeed mostly, elitist and exclusive. Like the *polis* it depends on visibility and appearance, performance and rhetoric. The world and its players appear in the media, and for most of us that is the only place they do appear. Appearance itself becomes, in both senses of the word, the world.

And although it is not formally constituted as a space of judgement and decision making, the mediated space of appearance nevertheless provides the setting where such judgements and decisions are presented and represented, debated, and sometimes, to all intents and purposes, made. Increasingly what passes for public life in contemporary societies takes place, more or less exclusively, on the screen. And what takes place on the screen is fought over by those political interests, including the media themselves, whose continuing power and influence depends precisely on that appearance. Such appearance is a measure of political, and other, status. Political status is measured according to such appearance. Status leads to influence, and influence to power (and of course vice versa). Both mainstream politics (national and global) as well as the politics of those who aspire to influence – the politics of the disadvantaged, the marginalized, the minorities – depends on that visibility. And through such visibility judgements are formed, decisions made and actions set in train, both among the participants and amongst those who constitute the audience, players too, albeit invisible, whose response to what they see and hear will always be, even in its absence, material.

Of course, like the classic *polis*, this mediated space of appearance offers one thing and delivers another, contradictions and paradoxes not lost on Hannah Arendt with respect to its prototype any more than they are lost on a range of current critics of the way in which the media currently represent or constitute public life. However, if such a space exists and is becoming increasingly salient for the conduct of public life, then its inclusions and exclusions, systematic or otherwise, and its capacity to enable or disable public debate, are the key issues. And it becomes imperative, if we are to realize its potential, to understand both critically and constructively how it might be otherwise, as well as how it might be wise to the other.

I propose to investigate in this chapter and in one way or another throughout the book, consequently, something which, albeit with some hesitation, I will call the mediapolis, the mediated public space where contemporary political life increasingly finds its place, both at national and global levels, and where the materiality of the world is constructed through (principally) electronically communicated public speech and action. There is of course no integrity within the contemporary mediapolis. The public space which it constitutes is fractured by cultural difference and the absence of communication, as much as it is by the homogenization of global television and genuine, if only momentary, collective attention to global events, crises and catastrophes. Viewers watching Al Jazeera will obviously be seeing a different world from those watching Fox. And those differences are palpable and crippling. Yet they will be seeing that world through the media, and to a significant degree so do we all.

I therefore propose mediapolis, in the singular, notwithstanding the manifest fragmentation of the delivery platforms, channels and the cultures of global media. And I propose mediapolis as both a descriptive and a normative category, for the invitation is to visualize the wholeness of media culture and then to interrogate it both for its weaknesses and its possibilities. The mediapolis is, I intend, the mediated space of appearance in which the world appears and in which the world is constituted in its worldliness, and through which we learn about those who are and who are not like us. It is through communications conducted through the mediapolis that we are constructed as human (or not), and it is through the mediapolis that public and political life increasingly comes to emerge at all levels of the body politic (or not).

The mediapolis is not dependent on a specific location. It is no longer even the equivalent of the city square in which presumptions of sameness outweigh those of difference. It does not need nor depend on the nation-state, or arguably the regulation of specific national institutions. It emerges in the interaction of human beings within the space of mediated appearance, and in this deterritorialized, but intensely social, environment, it reproduces something of the *polis*, at least as Hannah Arendt herself understands it. As she writes:

> The *polis*, properly speaking, is not the city-state in its physical location; it is the organisation of the people as it arises out of acting and speaking together, and its true space lies between people living together for this purpose, no matter where they happen to be . . . It is the space of appearance in the widest sense of the word, namely, the space where I appear to others as others appear to me, where men exist not merely like other living or inanimate things but make their appearance explicitly . . .

> To men the reality of the world is guaranteed by the presence of others, by its appearing to all; 'for what appears to all, this we call "Being" and whatever lacks this appearance comes and passes away like a dream, intimately and exclusively, our own but without reality'. (Arendt 1998: 198–9, citing Aristotle, *Nicomachaean Ethics*: 1172b36ff)

The reality of the world, a world that is by definition shared, is guaranteed by the presence of others in a space of appearance. This space of the mediapolis is a mediated space, and the space of appearance is provided by the screen and the speaker. This is not an exclusive space. It may be that being in the world increasingly becomes dependent on such appearance, but there are other tangible and material spaces, the spaces of institutional and everyday life, in which life is also lived, and reality maintained. So the mediapolis does not replace the world of experience, nor does it deny the validity and the materiality of the face-to-face, as Jean Baudrillard might see it as doing. However, it frames it and, in framing it, it also liberates the possibility of collective action. This possibility is exactly what is envisaged, of course, by those who see in the internet, as well as in the potential of new forms of mediated deliberative democracy, the opportunity for new forms of networking and new forms of alternative political discourse and action.

The media provide in their full range of narratives and images, of suffering as well as hope, of conflict as well as cooperation, as well as in the direct representation of parliaments, senates or select committees, a tangible manifestation of the space in which men and women make their appearance to each other. Mediated appearance, the visibility of the other, of the stranger as well as the neighbour, the capacity for dialogue and the manifestation of discord, the presence of alternative views and the struggle for an audience, are what constitute the publicness of the mediapolis, and what grounds its claims for the kinds of freedom that being in public, in principle and ideally, should enable.

The question which arises, and it is one central to Arendt's own analysis of the Greek *polis* and subsequent imperfect realizations of the space of appearance in different historical circumstances, is the nature of power which is enabled by such appearance. Arendt has quite a distinct notion of power. It is different from violence. It emerges in the convergence of word and deed. It emerges in the coming together of men and women in public space. It is worth quoting her again:

> Power is what keeps the public realm, the potential space of appearance between acting and speaking men, in existence . . . Power is always . . . a power potential and not an unchangeable, measurable and reliable entity

like force or strength. While strength is the natural quality of an individual seen in isolation, power springs up between men when they act together and vanishes the moment they disperse. (Arendt 1998: 200)

The space of appearance is, therefore, where, in an ideal world, speech and action converge, and when they do converge the world appears in its materiality. But Arendt is clear that such presence does not, of itself, guarantee that materiality, only its possibility. The mediated space of appearance is, likewise and at best, a space of potential and of possibility. At worst, of course, when freedoms of expression are restricted or denied, or when voices are muted and transformed in their representation, it becomes tyranny, and power becomes force. We know about this. Just as we know about the impotence guaranteed by the fragmentation of voices and the blank incomprehension of distrust and hostility, an impotence which marks so much of contemporary global communication.

Media power is a hugely contentious issue, and power exercised through the media, likewise. The mediated space of appearance is vulnerable to loss of trust, misuse of power, deception and violence, just as its face-to-face precursor was. It is also asymmetric, since neither I appear to others, nor others appear to me, in equivalence, as equals. The mediapolis does not, cannot, involve everyone. Power is only shareable in principle, never in practice. But the power which is available in the mediapolis, the power that emerges in the coming together of 'word and deed', in the integrity of speech and the facilitation of action, is tangible and sought after. We need to find ways of realizing its potential, to find institutional and individual resources, in education and regulation, in literacy and professional practice, to ensure that the public space that the media create is one which works for the human condition and not against it. I return to these tangible questions in my final chapter.

The mediapolis is manifestly, now, embryonic and imperfect; and even in its potential can never be imagined as fully realizable. But it has to be seen as a necessary starting point for the creation of a more effective global civil space. In a sense I am arguing that there is no choice, for there is no alternative site for this to be created, but I am also arguing that there is sufficient, intellectually as well as politically, in what we see and what we know about the nature of global communication at least to make the case for it.

The mediapolis differs from the classic formulation of what might otherwise be seen as Jürgen Habermas's similar notion of the public sphere. There are, of course, close resemblances between the two models of public participation and civic life, resemblances which to a degree

Habermas would be bound to acknowledge, since he too draws on Arendt in his own formulations. But there are differences too, and these are significant, above all in the way in which the media can be theorized. For Habermas, as indeed for Arendt, modern media have become, in the pincer age of grasping capitalism and clawing state power, mere pawns in a bigger game, a game which he calls refeudalization. Such a view has generated increasing despair (albeit with substantial empirical justification) when the media's democratic role is under the microscope.

Habermas's public sphere depends on full equity and equality of participation. It also depends on a commitment, which is pure and essential, to rational debate and argument. If anything is utopian, then this is. But it is also misleading, since a space where only reason, and a singular and narrow kind of reason at that, determines the viability of discourse and the possibility of action, seriously misrepresents both the possibilities and the limits of human communication in the world. It also leads to premature condemnation, a misrepresentation of the failures of this publicly mediated space, this public sphere, to survive the depredations of state and market.

The mediapolis, on the other hand, as I intend it, is both more and less than the Habermasian public sphere. It is more, because within it communication is multiple and multiply inflected: there is no rationality in an image, and no singular reason in a narrative. Both rhetoric and performance subvert the simple order of logic. The political, civic space of mediated representation, globally, nationally, locally, depends on both the capacity to encode and to decipher more complex sets of communications than mere reason enables. Since the world in its living and being cannot be so contained, neither can the public discourses that might express and account for it.

It is also more than the public sphere because of its ambition and its hope.

The mediapolis is less than the public sphere, in its modesty. There is no expectation that all the requirements for fully effective communication can be met by those responsible for its initiation, and those, in good faith, who contribute to it. On the contrary, what is required is both a mutuality of responsibility between producer and receiver, notwithstanding differences of power in the structure of things, and a degree of reflexivity by all participants in the communication, notwithstanding the inevitable imperfections of the process. What is also required is the recognition of cultural difference. The mediapolis is both an encompassing global possibility and an expression of the world's empirical diversity.

What kind of reality is created in the mediapolis, in the mediated space of appearance? What kind of publicness? How do we appear, or do not appear, to each other within it?

I would like to begin with the notion of plurality.

Plurality

For Hannah Arendt, as indeed for John Dewey, it is communication which defines the possibility of social and political life, and communication can only emerge meaningfully among those who acknowledge both what they share and what distinguishes them. This has to be the case for the global as well as for the face-to-face.

Indeed Arendt begins her interrogation of the human condition with the following simple but telling observation:

> There may be truths beyond speech, and they may be of great relevance to man in the singular, that is, to man in so far as he is not a political being, whatever else he may be. Men in the plural, that is, men in so far as they live and move and act in this world, can experience meaningful- ness only because they can talk with and make sense to each other and themselves. (Arendt 1998: 4)

Political life depends on plurality, on both the presence of the stranger in the world, and on the acknowledgement of that presence in the commu- nication that seeks comprehension, intelligibility and ultimately the jus- tification for action in the world. Political life depends on what Arendt calls natality, the continuous and continuously challenging novelty that both birth and arrival produce, and the continuous and continuously unpredictable nature of action, always new and always irreversible. The plurality of the human condition guarantees its humanness. Isaiah Berlin, notwithstanding his poor opinion of Arendt, makes a similar argument. Totalitarianism, and this is what distinguishes it from any other political force including tyranny, is its refusal of difference, its destruction of dif- ference in the name of the same.

Plurality, either as fact or as possibility, both separates and connects; and the space between the familiar and the strange, myself and the other, is the space of appearance, the space that guarantees the possibility (though only the possibility, as we have already learned) of public life and political action. As Arendt insists at the end of *The Origins of Totalitarian- ism*, '. . . not one man, but men in the plural inhabit the earth' (Arendt 1994a: 476), a judgement which both insists at one and the same time on the principle of commonness, a prioritization of common sense and on the plurality of man as the precondition for the establishment of human rights, and of their principal, the right to have rights.

In what does this plurality consist? It is not simply a matter of difference, though this is its beginning. Difference without acknowledging a shareable identity leads to isolation and reification, as can be seen in many versions of multiculturalism. The individual in his or her isolation is vulnerable to terror, condemned to the private world of self-interest and political impotence (Arendt 1994a: 474). Plurality constitutes the public, and it is only in public that action can take place, in the recognition of a shared space in which the appearance of actors, and their presence in each other's company as visible and audible acting beings, forms the precondition for an effective engagement with the world. It is that engagement which gives the world its materiality, its reality. Arendt's metaphor is of a table around which we sit, and which both connects and separates us. The table is the metaphor for the common world, the material world which we share, and which is a precondition of our commonness, a commonness which is not necessarily community, but which underpins our sixth sense, common sense. Once again it is in the destruction of common sense, its radical undermining in the isolation of the individual that totalitarianism was so effective. And once again it is the presence of the media, and their materiality, which is a precondition for our commonness, our common sense, in the twenty-first century.

The dialectic of sameness and otherness, for all its abstraction, is crucial. In the late modern world it is increasingly the acknowledgement of otherness, that *in* ourselves as well as that *of* others, that constitutes that commonness. This is perhaps the essential paradox that the media must express, for it is their worldliness which is a precondition for ours. For Arendt the fundamental defining characteristic of our humanity is our presence among other human beings (Arendt 1998: 21), a presence that the media both enable and disable. As she says, '. . . without a space of appearance and without trusting in action and speech as a mode of being together, neither the reality of one's self, of one's own identity, nor the reality of the surrounding world can be established beyond doubt' (Arendt 1998: 208). Mediated communication is only possible through a shared commonness of sense. We have the opportunity to see ourselves in the reflection of the other. But we have to know how to look.

Arendt bewailed the loss of common sense in the post-totalitarian world, a loss manifested in its internalization, its withdrawal into the individual and the private. She suggests that what is now common is no longer the world but the structure of our minds, and this we cannot have in common 'strictly speaking' (Arendt 1998: 283). Her critique is premised on a singular and much criticized distinction between the public and the private: the public where political action and speech are the means for effective judgement and just behaviour; the private, the realm of the domestic and of self-interest, in which there is no separation of self and other, no plurality. It is the bane of modernity to have suffered both the colonization of the public by the private (self-interest, private property) – this is what she calls *society* – and at the same time the undermining of the security of the private home, '. . . the warmth of the hearth and the limited reality of family life' (Arendt 1998: 59). And mass society is the villain of the piece.

In her argument plurality, the public realm and permanence combine. The latter is what is desired and sometimes achieved by entry into public life and in the construction of objects and institutions that would outlive the individual and sustain, by their longevity, the common rather than an individual world. The public realm is enabled and guaranteed in 'the simultaneous presence of innumerable perspectives':

> For though the common world is the common meeting ground of all, those who are present have different locations in it . . . being seen and being heard by others derive their significance from the fact that every- body sees and hears from a different position. . . . Only where things can be seen by many in a variety of aspects without changing their identity, so that those who are gathered around them know they see sameness in utter diversity, can worldly reality truly and reliably appear. (Arendt 1998: 57)

This is the prize. But it is also the challenge, the fundamental challenge to any notion of a viably mediated public realm. This is not just a chal- lenge to the otherwise invisibility of diversity, but also a challenge to the ephemerality of representation. And of course it is a challenge to the media's manifest erosion of the distinctiveness of public and private space and of the boundary between them. And it is, finally, a challenge, arguably the most difficult one of all, to the inequities of representation and the persistence of exclusion that mark the mediapolis as a site for the exercise of media power, both by capital and by the state, and within the ideological and prejudicial frames of unreflexive reporting and storytelling.

We are dealing with great imperfection. The presumption of the mass media's role in the creation of a mass society in which sameness, transi- ence and the loss of trust and security are its defining characteristics is a well-trodden one. Yet I want to suggest that the dismissal is both premature and self-defeating, not because the mediapolis is virtuous and effective. On the contrary. But because it exists and because the emergence of a global civil society, in whatever form we imagine it or indeed desire it, will depend on it. And as such it must be understood and interrogated if it is to be a constructive rather than a destructive force in global as well as national public culture.

Thinking, speaking, listening and acting

Appearance, therefore, is a necessary but not a sufficient condition for the emergence of the mediapolis. Appearance cannot be mere appearance, any more than mediation is merely mediation. For both require the active participation of human beings as thinkers, listeners, speakers and actors. Appearance has to be created. Mediation is a practice in which producers, subjects and audiences take part, and take part together.

Thinking, speaking, listening and acting[1] – the basic components of life in the world, and the precondition for the constitution of publicness. In Arendt's view of it, the space of appearance only has meaning, only has effectiveness, when human beings think, speak and act in relation to each other, for each other. Such requirements do not change in a mediated environment. On the contrary, but they are often overlooked and indeed often absent. Neither appearance nor mediation is possible without recognition of the other, in his or her identity and difference. Both involve a commitment to communication, and an acceptance of the responsibility, and reciprocity, which follows such a commitment. And thinking, speaking and acting are also the links between the mediated and the real world, links between the public and the private, for the work of mediation goes on before and after its appearance on the screen. It follows, as I have already indicated, that the publicness of the mediapolis is not an exclusive publicness, a publicness confined only to its presence in media space, but depends on, just as it sustains, the world of political action in the widest realm.

Not that this is happening much at the moment. It would be foolhardy to deny the depth and intransigence of discord and division within the contemporary mediated space of appearance. The battles between good and evil, between radical fundamentalisms of one kind or another as they appear unchallenged or reinforced on page and screen, the polarization of reporting on the one hand, and the rampant individualism, celebritization and marginalization of the weak and the minor, on the other, express much that Arendt herself recognized as both components of a totalitarian society (if not a totalitarian world) and those of the more long-term, post-Athenian, erosion of the possibility of a genuine public, political, space.

Here lies the challenge. What makes the human condition human is the possibility, and ultimately the necessity, of the conjunction of both thought and action, and of speech and of judgement. The capacity for thought, action, speech and judgement, in turn, depends on the presence of the public in us. And the presence of the public in us depends on our willingness to recognize and to take responsibility for the other, that other person who appears to us, in our space, in our world, and whose presence cannot be ignored. It also depends on honesty and integrity, however pious this sounds, of the communications we construct for each other.

The space of appearance is a space of speech and action, but its precondition is thought, since without thought, without radical doubt and without challenge to the taken-for-granted, the received wisdoms, our capacity for speech and action does not get to first base. It was the absence of thought which was at the heart of Arendt's analysis of the banality of evil with which she charged Adolf Eichmann. It was banal, not because it was deliberate or motivated, but because, on the contrary, it involved perfect complicity and collusion with a regime that both encouraged and depended on, absolutely, an absence of thought. Thinking, she argues, is what we do to avoid such complicity and collusion; thinking is what we do to free ourselves from the constraints of an otherwise totalitarian force. Without thinking, free and critical thinking, nothing, no humanity at all.

And without thinking no speech, no action and no effective acknowledgement of the capacity to be creative in the world nor any acknowledgement of the signal and material presence of the other, of the world's plurality. There is an intimate and potent relationship between action and speech:

> Power is actualised only where word and deed have not parted company, where words are not empty and deeds not brutal, where words are not used to veil intentions but to disclose realities, and deeds are not used to violate and destroy but to establish relations and create new realities (Arendt 1998: 200)

Arendt's notion of power, benevolent power, is dependent on this necessary convergence between thought, speech and action, and it is to be distinguished, as we have already seen, from violence and from force. Power is a generalized capacity to act that depends on the coming together of men and women, in the plural and in their diversity. And this generalized capacity for action, this willingness to accept the views and interests of the other and to transform self-interests into a common goal is a precondition of political life, as she understands it. Indeed Arendt defines interest as *inter-est*, that which lies between, that is something, by definition, shared (Arendt 1998: 182). Power and communication are intimately related.

Action and speech invite, indeed demand, disclosure, the disclosure of the individual, the individual as actor, the individual persona in the classical sense of the presence of authentic speech through the public mask (*per-sona*), and as such the individual as human being. The viability of the political realm is therefore dependent on this visibility and on the appearance of the person, warts and all (Arendt 1998: 179–80). The meaningful, just and responsible, exercise of power results from common action coordinated through speech. The ideal, and arguably idealized, public space which results, is both agonistic and discursive: both are necessary. So, central to the constitution of an effective public space is the presence of living speech and the possibility of effective action. It is the coming together of speech and action in public which is, as Seyla Benhabib notes in her elegant discussion of the work of Hannah Arendt, a precondition for viable, deliberative, democracy (Benhabib 2003: 209).

Speech and action are, then, both expressions, and in turn, the preconditions, of freedom and of its manifestation in political life. 'A life without speech and without action . . . is literally dead to the world' (Arendt 1998: 176). And freedom is not the freedom of speech as such, the freedom of expression so beloved of the liberal imagination, but the freedom to grasp reality in one's capacity to move between positions and different perspectives: the freedom to recognize both difference and commonness in a plural world (cf. Canovan 1992: 112–13). And it is the freedom, it might be added, to be heard. This is the kind of freedom which creates and sustains worldliness, and without worldliness, that being in the world among others, we lose all humanity. It is a freedom which can never be free of responsibility. The human predicament, is not, as Martin Heidegger would argue, solitariness, the loneliness before death, but what is shared and what is common. And it is birth, natality, which is its precondition. Plurality, once again, is the measure of all things political.

The Greek *polis* fractured and has never re-emerged. There are very few points in subsequent political history where Arendt is willing to grant endorsement to the flowering of the authentically political. And she is not just intensely mindful of the vulnerability of political life, as she both defines it and requires it, both to human weakness and the march of modernity, but she is absolutely clear about the capacity of violence and terror, usurpers of power, to destroy it and destroy humanity. Yet her despair is never total and her critique, though melancholic, seems both accepting of modernity and also involved with its possibilities. Why bother to engage so radically if you don't care about the well-being of the object of your concern?

Likewise with the mediapolis, and what I want to argue is the promise of the appearance of living speech and effective action that must emerge if it is to fulfil its role in enabling the creation of a global public space. Perhaps the omens are not good. The early years of optimism in which public service broadcasting was expected to lay a foundation for inclusive national culture have long gone. In this context Habermas is correct. The capacity of the world's media to construct the world in any image other than that of the interest of capital or the state has been mortally weakened. The globalization of media has not yet materialized in any meaningful way, notwithstanding the press of the occasional media event, the traumatic as well as the sporting. The world's television viewers and internet users gain even in the globally live transmission, the instant report, the streaming video, the blog and the chat room, a version of that world which is tarred by self-interest and, in Arendt's terms, by the private. These spaces are conflicted, intransigent and often inflaming.

In the present manifestation of the mediated space of appearance, the public has little meaningful status. Thought, speech and action are disconnected, and compromised by the absence of context, memory and analytic rigour, and increasingly, the absence of trust. It is possible to suggest too that the claims for publicness that appearance on the global screen de facto are making are actually those of intimacy and claims for a spurious identity, since it is the connection between individuals who believe only in their sameness that emerges instead. A connection of assimilation, incorporation, a denial of difference. I discuss the implications of this representational move in the next section of this chapter.

Underlying these generic failures, failures which mark above all the global press and broadcasting, is the progressive withdrawal of a genuine commitment to communication, a withdrawal into the bowels of private worlds which masquerade as the public, a withdrawal into commercial worlds which pretend disinterest and objectivity, and a withdrawal into the realms of information as if mere information was sufficient to order the world.

Yet insofar as technologies are changing, and the digital revolution is gathering pace, it is possible to recognize significant possibilities for change in the mediapolis too. Optimism once again abounds, particularly around interactive radio and television, but especially on the internet.

Optimism, however, is not enough. The potential in networking and in interactivity (two distinct but increasingly inseparable qualities of the new media environment) has to be mobilized socially and politically. This requires a recognition of the importance both of understanding the dynamics of global mediation and of developing institutional and other responses to it. These are themes that I address, in various ways, in the remaining chapters of this book.

The emergence of interactive and network media, therefore, notwithstanding the ease of their misuse and the limitations of connectivity, as well as the dissemblance of person and the vulnerability of trust which seem to be endemic within them, can be seen to be providing an important step in the direction of what Arendt calls, approvingly, *publicity* (Arendt 1998: 55).[2] Interactivity, from this perspective, is seen as a form of power, a muscle-flexing by those who are otherwise denied access to, or marginalized by, the mainstream, and which, in its intensity as well as its persistence, some kind of permanence (an ersatz eternity) is realized to set against the ephemerality of discourse created by the established and dominant media platforms and institutions.

But perhaps we can recover some ground even from the latter. Mediation is not just a matter of what appears on the screen, but is actually constituted in the practices of those who produce the sounds and images, the narratives and the spectacles, as well as, crucially, those who receive them. In these practices, in this work, all participants in the process become actors, and as actors they have to take responsibility for what they say and do. For audiences respond to what they see and hear, and in that response engage simultaneously with the mediapolis and the world which constitutes their everyday life. Indeed Luc Boltanski (1999) argues, at the conclusion of an analysis of the contemporary mediation of suffering, opinion formation, effective speech in his terms, is a form of action: '. . . speech, which . . . was the spectator's main resort for coping with the moral demands raised by the representation of distant suffering, can be understood as effective speech and *so be an adequate response to the demand for action*' (Boltanski 1999: 184–5; my italics). I will develop these arguments more fully in chapter 5.

Thought without communication, that is without the other, is self-defeating and solipsistic. Thought with communication is a precondition for action. Arendt's notion of communication is, first of all, not that of a shared understanding, a precondition for community, as many media scholars would like to believe, but a process of collective reasoning. Communication, she argues, and as we now know, is a bulwark against tyranny, and as such a precondition for citizenship (Cmiel 1996: 98). But such communication is not to be too narrowly defined. It includes the performative. It includes the narrative. It includes the personal. It includes the rhetorical.

So for Arendt in the *polis*, and for me in the mediapolis, the issue is not just the rationality of human communication, but a recognition that communication is grounded in a feeling for the world, and in the condition of being in the world among others. Publicity becomes, as I have already suggested, a positive rather than a negative term, as it is for Jürgen Habermas. And what emerges, notwithstanding its vulnerability, is the possibility of a public culture which has a wider range of reference and context. And what emerges too, and above all, is the case for publicness, and for a commitment to the creation of a mediated civic space for a global society which depends on that publicness, that publicity, but which does so reflexively, taking nothing for granted.

The mediapolis is just this manifestation of publicness: one which we should not dismiss too quickly with arguments of massification or refeudalization. The question is perhaps not so much the extent to which contemporary media are abstractions from the world and the reality of worldliness, but the extent to which they provide various versions of worldliness and refuse or ignore others. The question is also the extent to which such manifestations of publicness may be amenable to change in the light of critique and of political intervention consequent upon that critique.

We have also to decide how far such versions of public worldliness constitute expressions of media power in the Arendtian sense of the convergence of speech and action in a common space of appearance, and how far, on the contrary, they are expressions of symbolic violence, denying by virtue precisely of their representation or misrepresentation of speech and action the possibility of an effective, public, space of appearance.

At issue too are the faculties of judgement and imagination, and the capacity of the mediapolis to provide, and enable, the resources for the exercise of both in pursuit of more effective understanding and participation in the world. This is an issue to which I now turn.

Conditions for the mediapolis

There are a number of issues raised in this discussion that have, I believe, a direct bearing on the quality of the mediapolis, the mediated space of appearance.

The first involves the provision of resources for judgement, for cognitive, aesthetic and moral judgement, in our confrontation with the world, both that of face-to-face and that of mediated experience. This is the media's primary responsibility in its functioning as *polis*. This is an enlargement of its traditional role as a fourth estate. The second is that of the significance of perspective, what Kant called 'enlarged mentality', and which I will be discussing in terms of the phrase 'proper distance'. The third, which I address in the last two chapters of the book, is the issue of responsibility, equally, though differentially, shared by the subjects, producers and audiences within the processes of mediation.

There is a difference between thinking and judgement, and that difference is material, intensely material, for any consideration of the role of the media in creating and sustaining a global civic space. I shall argue in this section that the key to the capacity of the media to do this, the key effectively to the existence of the mediapolis, is in the provision of what I will refer to as resources for judgement. Once again Hannah Arendt provides the stimulus.

Thinking, in Arendt's terms, is something that takes place in private. It is a solitary activity. Its aim is truth. Judgement, on the other hand, is concerned with the formation of opinion by an actor in the world who needs to, and does, confront human plurality. Judgement is, or should be, liberatory. Thinking, in the Socratic sense, is a midwife, a process of reflection, discrimination and critique, a slowing down. Judgement is a talking through, a bringing forth, a constant engagement with one's own thought and that of others.

Judgement is linked to, and underpins, opinion. This is opinion not so much of the collective, nor of public opinion in the sense in which it is commonly understood. Indeed Arendt has a rather poor view of public opinion as it appears in the aggregates of contemporary measurement, a view which I think is eminently still defensible. Opinion, real opinion, she argues, is an achievement, one which nevertheless has been neglected in accounts of the rationality of public life. Public opinion cannot be then a technical summary of a range of private thoughts, but the product of an individual's participation in, and work upon, the world, the world which is shared with others. Arendt insists on the distinctive characteristics and importance of judgements made in public, on the vital importance of political thinking that is engaged in the world of appearance, and which is not determined by the solitary abstraction of philosophy or the imperial rigour of disinterested logic.

Judgement, then, is in many ways an awesome responsibility which, ultimately, rests on the individual, but on the individual in the world, in public.[3] While it is a precondition for effective action, it is also a precondition for freedom. Without the capacity for judgement the public realm atrophies, for without judgement there is no independence of mind or action. Judgement involves risk, and mostly risks are not taken. Judgement involves stepping out of line, brushing 'history against the grain' (Benjamin 1970: 259). The absence of judgement signals the absence of thought and the absence of one's responsibility in the world of appearances, in the public realm. It was Adolf Eichmann's inability to think, as I have already mentioned, which Arendt saw as his extraordinary shallowness, which disabled judgement and cemented his capacity for evil. The absence of thought results in an absence of conscience, an absence of conscience results in the defeat of judgement and the defeat of judgement results in the collapse of the political. This of course has a crucial bearing on the media and our, the audience's, participation in its global reach. As the American scholar Dana Villa suggests: 'In a world in which the opportunities to be a "participator in government," to share words and deeds on a public stage, have been dramatically curtailed, we still have the choice between being passive consumers of media-packaged spectacle, or independent judges of the events which constitute the "spectacle" of the public world and history' (Villa 1999: 103). If judgements are effectively decisions made in, and on behalf of, the public – in, and on behalf of, what is shared or common – then public media must provide the resources to make such judgements effectively. There is no option. It is their *sine qua non*. And their failure to do so, the ever threatened and often realized bias against understanding, the absence of context, or of history or debate, in the presentation of the world which is otherwise, materially or symbolically, beyond reach, is arguably culpable. Early twenty-first century cases of such misadventures, in the BBC (the dossier justifying the Iraq War), NHK (comfort women in the Second World War), CBS (the Bush military service record), the *New York Times* (invented stories), are probably only the tip of an iceberg of such significant failures. These are the ones that have made it as stories in the global media.

The media are, precisely, mediators between the present and immediate realities of everyday life and the world which is spatially and temporally beyond immediate reach. What do I need to understand now, here, and for tomorrow, if I am to make sense of my life and of the lives of others intimately and remotely connected to me? How do I balance the relative claims of those who are near and familiar and whose claims are always immediate and pressing with those who are far but may be suffering and in despair? How, given its visibility, and the ever-present noise within personal as well as global communication, do I make the decision to connect or refuse to connect to the world beyond my front door? The variations and ironies in the global (both institutional and personal) response to the big environmental tragedies of 2004, the tsunami, Hurricane Katrina and the earthquake in Pakistan Kashmir, are illustrative of the effects of material and symbolic distance on the capacity of the West to respond (strongly in the case of the tsunami, weakly in the case of the earthquake) and of course in the rest's response to the West (the offer of aid for New Orleans to the US from Afghanistan was politically telling).

Such mediation does not of course only involve the supply of naked facts, a disingenuous transparency which is in many, if not in most, respects self-defeating. The factual may be necessary but it will never be sufficient as a resource for judgement. Mediation also involves the production of narrative – a crucial component of the present and future of the mediapolis's discourse and one which I discuss more fully shortly – and personal performance; it involves the multiple rhetorics of voice and image; it involves (though not yet sufficiently) the deployment of media literacies. And mediation also involves both the reflection and expression of the diversity of the world. But the resources for such judgements cannot only come from the media. Both subjects and audiences bring their own resources, and must do so, if they are to be participants in the mediapolis.

All such judgements require imagination. Let me quote Hannah Arendt once more:

> Imagination alone enables us to see things in their proper perspective, to be strong enough to put that which is too close at a certain distance so that we can see and understand it without bias and prejudice, to be generous enough to bridge abysses of remoteness until we can see and understand everything that is too far away from us as though it were our own affair. This distancing of some things and bridging the abysses to others is part of the dialogue of understanding, for whose purposes direct experience establishes too close a contact and mere knowledge erects artificial barriers. Without this kind of imagination, which actually is understanding, we would never be able to take our bearings in the world. It is the only inner compass we have. We are contemporaries only so far as our understanding reaches. (Arendt 1994: 323)

Imagination here is that human quality which opens the doors to understanding and in turn to the capacity to make judgements in and through the public world. Imagination, the Kantian enlargement of mentality beyond the individual and the solitary self, requires taking the position of the other, the creation of the appropriate distance to enable effective communication, the formation of opinion and the materialization of a political life. The enlargement of mentality involves bringing as many others into one's imagination as it is possible to do: 'The more people's standpoints I have present in my mind while I am pondering a given issue, and the better I can imagine how I would feel and think if I were in their place, the stronger will be my capacity for representative thinking and the more valid my final conclusions, my opinion' (Arendt 1977: 241).

The media have extended reach, but have they also extended understanding? The media have provided the resources for an enlarged mentality, but have they facilitated representative thinking and judgement?

This is a problem that I want to address through the concept of *proper distance*. Proper distance refers to the importance of understanding the more or less precise degree of proximity required in our mediated interrelationships if we are to create and sustain a sense of the other sufficient not just for reciprocity but for a duty of care, obligation and responsibility, as well as understanding. Proper distance preserves the other through difference as well as through shared identity. In other words proper distance is a component, and a precondition of plurality. The idea of proper distance draws on the momentary, but intensely significant, convergence in the thinking of both Arendt and Emmanuel Levinas, both of whom see the issue of proximity as a crucial determinant of politics (Arendt) and morality (Levinas). Proper distance involves both imagination, understanding and a duty of care: an epistemological (Arendt) and an ontological (Levinas) commitment to finding the space to express what is both experienced (Arendt) and essential (Levinas) in our relationships to the other.[4]

And the construction of such relationships in contemporary culture is intensely dependent on the media who, for the most part, and perhaps increasingly, fail in this respect, as in so many others. The media trade in otherness, in the spectacular and the visible, and in so doing inevitably refuse the possibility of connection and identification. The media, just as often, trade in identity: in the elision of the different to the same and in the refusal to recognize the irreducibility in otherness. Both of these familiar representational moves are symptomatic of the failures of current media, but they also echo – though not only echo, for they also sustain – the palpable failures of modernity *tout court* to acknowledge plurality and the rights of the stranger. Arendt explores these failures in her own critique of the nature, origins and consequences of imperialism and totalitarianism, as does Levinas in his discussion of responsibility for the other as a precondition of any kind of social life.

The embedding of journalists within the armies of occupying forces, the intrusion into the private life of public figures and the drafting of images of the exotic into global advertising are all, in their different ways, examples of incorporation, of the denial or reduction of difference. *Too close.*

The representation of the other, a Moslem, an Iraqi, a Palestinian (or in its mirroring, a Jew or an American) as beyond the pale of humanity, is even in its convention, and perhaps especially in its convention, an example of the irresponsibility of distance. *Too far.*

The contemporary cult of celebrity, more complex perhaps than we often realize, destroys difference by exaggerating it (the ordinary made exceptional) as well as naturalizing it (the exceptional made ordinary), and denying, in its seductive dialectic, the legitimacy of difference. *Neither close nor far.*

Proper distance – *both close and far* – requires imagination, both from those who construct the narratives and images of the media, and those, the audiences and readers, who, more dependently, construct their own images and narratives based upon them. The mediated enlargement of mentality which is necessary for independent judgements to be made and for opinions to be formed in the late modern age is necessary but not sufficient for imaginative thought and the formation of what Arendt means by opinion. The consequences of failure, likewise any modest achievements, are political and, in the broadest sense of the term, moral. Without the understanding which follows the experience of contemporaneity, but which is not possible without it, there is little possibility of humanity. This has powerful resonance, as I have just suggested, in our current struggle to represent and understand, for example, the Islamic world, and indeed its equivalent failure, arguably, to understand us.

There is a doubling of responsibility involved. Both actors and spectators are present in public space, and both actors and spectators must carry the burden of judgement. Both have choices. Media representation, indeed the process of mediation as such, involves not just those who produce and their resulting texts. The mediated world of appearance includes those who view and read and take away what they have appreciated or understood of what they view or read. In this sense the mediapolis extends to, and includes, both those who are represented on screen and page, as well as those whose judgements in life increasingly depend on that representation.

Judgement, then, is a generalizable faculty. It involves, as Arendt notes, the capacity to distance oneself from the abstractions of thinking, as well as the immediate exigencies of action, to engage with the particular and with the things close at hand. And as she also points out, writing about the presence of evil in the world, the thinking which is a precondition for judgement is 'not a prerogative of the few but an ever present faculty of everybody' (Arendt 1984: 36).

The context of what otherwise might well be seen as entirely pious remarks is the now familiar one of the presence and aftermath of totalitarianism, though they are far, in Arendt's mind, from being limited to that context. If it is the case that the political and moral significance of thinking, as Arendt defines it, is limited to the rare moments when society is in crisis, then it might modestly be suggested that modernity has brought with it a state of constant crisis and that thinking, and judgement, now just as ever, are likely to be very much in demand as a consequence. It might also be said that the current so-called soft-war world of terror and increasing polarization between the West and Islam is rapidly producing the symptoms of an all too familiar version of the totalitarian, as democracies, both old and young, retrench and feed the culture of paranoia and hatred. And it should not be forgotten that the media in many states in the world are still subject to the kind of political and cultural controls which inevitably, and by design, restrict, sometimes to the point of nullity, the possibilities of judgement and the freedom of speech which are a primary condition for the viability of the mediapolis.

Nevertheless the mediapolis is the site where the resources for understanding and judgement, the benevolent as well as the malevolent, are to be found. In this space of mediated appearance, the worldliness of the world emerges, an environment of perceptions and constructions of otherness and sameness. The civic space which is underpinned by these representations, is not one of perfect rationality, nor indeed of imperfect, or distorted or depleted rationality, if by the rational we require adherence to the disinterested logic of abstract reasoning. On the contrary it is a space of conflicting and competing discourses, of stories and images and performances; one that requires a different logic in its construction and in its reception. One that requires, too, different kinds of responsibility. And one that we can only begin to understand and influence if we recognize its integrity as well as its diversity.

The burden of representation

The mediapolis is a space of appearance. And such a space is a constant, even if the things that appear on it come and go. The global media have raised the art of the ephemeral to radical new heights. Nothing escapes what Milan Kundera called, in another context, the unbearable lightness of being. The representations of the world which the media second by second provide are as light and as fragile as a feather. Nothing lasts. The occasional image, maybe, becomes iconic, though in the process its meaning shifts and the memorial line either fades or distorts. News and celebrity, two sides of the same coin of impermanence, are nevertheless constant smudges on the screens of the world. The grounding paradox of media representation, although not uniquely for it is a paradox of all that is communicated, is that between transience and permanence. We know it elsewhere as the paradox of speech and language: the former on the lips and the latter in the grammars, the texts, the technologies and the institutions.

However, Hannah Arendt's notion of the public requires its permanence, and it is hard to gainsay her. There has to be something to transcend mere mortality. There has to be continuity in the symbols and the meanings that sustain the plurality of public space. The question, of course, is whether the mediapolis is up to the job. On the face of it, it manifestly is not.

In the last chapter of *The Human Condition*, Arendt reflects on the key moments in the birth of modernity. The one she sees as most significant is the invention of the telescope. Galileo's telescope, she argues, had a profound ontological significance for it allowed the separation of Being and Appearance. For the first time things seen were not as they appeared, and the explanation for them was no longer to be found exclusively within them.

The telescope changed the way the world was seen, and it did so in quite fundamental ways. What the telescope revealed was a world that had been changed not by the force of reason but by the force of technology. And the path from technology to science was direct, as was the effect on epistemology. As Arendt argues, 'If Being and Appearance part company forever . . . [which is] the basic assumption of all modern science, then there is little left to be taken on faith; everything must be doubted' (Arendt 1998: 275).

Descartes, she argued, picked up Galileo's baton. It was this loss of certainty that marked the distinctiveness of the modern age, and truth or reality became a matter of practical test, one which resulted in the *measure* of appearance as the only, yet as always the inadequate, measure of truth. But it was also a loss of certainty which was, paradoxically, accompanied by a certain hubris, for man now believed that *he* could be the measure of all things: *dubito ergo sum*. And reason became the ground for the permanence of what might become the public, the political.

The word television has the same verbal structure as the telescope. And both refer to seeing from (and to) a distance. Yet I would argue that their epistemological consequences are quite opposite to each other. The *television* is not merely a different kind of tele*scope*, one which extends reach and enhances appearance, albeit principally towards the social rather than the cosmic. It is quite otherwise. For television (and other media too, of course), in its focus directly on the world, the world of lived experience, offers and represents a move towards what could be called a post-modern reconciliation of Being and Appearance. In television's world Appearance *is* Being: the two, as in the pre-Galilean, mediaeval world, are no longer distinct.

In the contemporary mediated space of appearance, what we see is what we get. What we get we tend to accept uncritically. With such a reconciliation, visible on a daily basis in the narratives and images of everything from news to soap opera, the need for doubt falls away, for the invitation is to accept the world as it appears on the screen, an appearance which is, for all its superficial variety, ubiquitous, eternal and to all intents and purposes, real (though of course it is nothing of the sort). In the mediated space of appearance we no longer need to, nor wish to, nor are for the most part capable of, doubt. The mediated world is what is mediated, and there is no difference between being and appearance, just as there is no longer significant difference between the world as it appears on the screen and the world that is lived.[5] At one level we no longer doubt, and the disappearance of doubt is concomitant with the world's re-enchantment. Yet truth and the search for truthfulness remains, as I argue in chapter 6. The mediapolis is the site of the tension between the two. How they are resolved is its crucial challenge.

As doubt disappears, so too does common sense, literally speaking the sense of the world we have in common, without which the public as a space for deliberation and decision, cannot survive. Arendt's melancholia finds its justification in these losses. Are they irrevocable? My argument in this chapter and indeed in the remainder of the book, in different ways, is that they are not, or more accurately, perhaps, that they must not be.

Such a position, it should be clear by now, rests both on the status of the mediapolis as a structural component of global communications and on the theory of mediation which informs my understanding of the process of global communication. Crucial to both at this point and in the foreseeable future is the recognition that the mediapolis is not self-sufficient and that it must be understood as being a component of a wider social and political reality, one that is centrally and intimately connected to the sphere of lived social relations. And crucial too is the recognition that mediation is, effectively, a practice, one which involves individuals in social and cultural (not to say also political and economic) activities for which they bear a responsibility. These individual actors are obviously the editors, journalists, producers, directors and subject-participants, but they are also, notwithstanding the asymmetry in power and control, the media's audiences. Indeed it is the participation of the audience as actor in the process of mediation that ensures, in principle, that the mediapolis can fulfil its role in the creation of a global civic society. Their mutual responsibility is to provide and then respond to the resources for judgement which alone enable a degree of reflexivity sufficient, one would hope, for an effective engagement with the world.

Such a position also rests on an expectation of the continued significance in global communication of the broadcast, disseminative mode (Peters 1999). It presumes that the dialogical structure of the internet will be unable substantially to leave the private domain of personal interaction, even in its most political manifestations. Perhaps this is overly radical (it is certainly contentious), but it is increasingly clear that on its own, that is without the link to other more inclusive media like television, or radio or the press, the internet is a private, exclusive and fragmenting medium: centrifugal rather than centripetal. And it follows that to count on it being the harbinger of a new kind of global political culture, by itself, is a mistake. The internet is not yet, and may never be, strictly a plural medium. It is singular: it significantly relies on, and reinforces, identity not plurality. And it has real problems with narrative.

Indeed narrative, as I have already briefly indicated, is central for an understanding of the media's role in the creation of a public space for deliberation and judgement. It is through narrative that the world appears in its vividness and in its capacity to create and sustain significance. It is in the stories we tell ourselves, the historical and the contemporary as well as the fantastic, that we seek and sometimes find the shareable meanings that create the possibility for a shared understanding of the world. Narratives are inclusive even though they exclude. Notwithstanding the obvious vulnerability to distortion and deception, the telling of stories about ourselves and others, about the actions that have been completed or are envisaged 'teach[es] acceptance of things as they are' (Arendt 1977: 262).

Narrative, like so much in Arendt's work, bears a substantial burden, for it is in the telling of public tales that we gain both access to the truth and to the reality of the actor (what Martin Heidegger and Emmanuel Levinas might call his or her *ipseity*) whose actions and life are recounted. It is in the telling of tales that memory is recovered and the future is touched. It is the telling, but above all the completion, of a narrative, its ending, that guarantees remembrance and creates significance. Arendt suggests that actions which are lived are meaningful, but only actions which are narrated have value. And it is, in her view, on the fecundity of plural narrative rather than the aridity of singular reason on which the *polis* most obviously depends.

Narration lies, then and now, at the heart of the political, offering a shareable culture and a framework for common understanding, for making sense. Disclosure, drama, performance, the telling itself, are, and have always been, the stuff of the political realm, though often emanating, and properly so, from outside it. Arendt requires of the *polis* that it enables a plurality of stories and histories, not the singular and the totalitarian. Narratives are agonistic. They compete with each other and in their competition and in their performance they define both the reality and the possibility of public life. Paradoxically, perhaps, their presence in public space is one dimension of its permanence. As long as we tell each other stories, stories about ourselves and about others, and as long as those stories are heard and understood, the telling itself is enabling, and there is continuity in theme and character.

But it is not the actor, but the spectator and the narrator who, in Julia Kristeva's summary of Arendt's position, '. . . accomplish history . . . This accomplishment takes place through recollection, without which there is simply nothing to recount. It is not the actors but the spectators (provided they are capable of thinking and recollecting) who make the *polis* a productive place to organise memory and/or history and stories' (Kristeva 2001: 72). If the spectator, the listener, the audience (as well as the narrator) is to 'accomplish history', the stories that make that history have to be engaged with, and such engagement requires both responsibility ('these are my stories: what are they saying to me?') and literacy ('these are my stories: how do I understand them?'). These issues of responsibility and literacy will be pursued again in later chapters.

The telling of stories lies at the heart of media representation, and at the heart of the mediapolis's capacity to create and sustain a public space, or what Seyla Benhabib in her recent study of Arendt's political thinking calls the civic imagination, and what I have called the construction of proper distance. To quote her:

> [The] process of self-representation and articulation in public is still the only means through which the civic imagination can be cultivated. The process of articulating good reasons in public forces one to think from the standpoint of all others. . . . The ability of individuals and groups to take the standpoint of others into account . . . is a crucial virtue in a civic polity . . . The public sphere is like the pupil in the eye of the body politic; when its vision is murky, clouded, or hindered, the sense of direction of the polity is also impaired. (Benhabib 2003: 211)

The media, it now appears, carry a huge, one might even say an impossible, burden of representation. For it is, as I have been arguing, within the mediated space of appearance, the mediapolis, that this project of the civic imagination stands or falls. And from this perspective, Benhabib's metaphor of the pupil has more meaning than perhaps she intended, for not only can it stand for what sees, but also for the person who studies and learns and criticizes.

To summarize and conclude.

At the core of my argument in this chapter has been a view of the media as occupying a space of appearance, providing on and through the screen a version of the world which increasingly constitutes the world. That space is political insofar as it is a space within which judgements are made, judgements of inclusion and exclusion; a space in which speech and actions are represented; and a space which provides, however, inadequately, and of course it is inadequate, a glimpse of the plurality of that world. As I suggested in my introduction, the media have enabled a lifting of the veil on difference, and that this lifting is a necessary but not a sufficient condition for the creation of a viable global public realm. I hope that some of the aspects of this insufficiency, but also some of its potential, have become evident in the intervening discussion.

Mediated worldliness is not a substitute for the worldliness of the face-to-face, but must be understood as related to it contrapuntally. These two aspects of the human condition are both present and necessary, and both gain (and lose) in their constant interaction with each other. And mediated worldliness itself, notwithstanding the singularity of the mediapolis, is nothing if not fragmented and contrapuntal. I will be discussing contrapuntality in chapter 4.

From this perspective, the mediapolis stands as both a descriptive and a normative term. In its first guise it seeks to acknowledge the reality of the political space which the media occupy and, for better and for worse, enable. In its second, it offers the beginning of an account of what that politics could, and should, be. Its singularity should not be misunderstood. I am not insisting on its current coherence or on its immediate viability. Neither would be easily sustainable. However, I do not want to point both to a socio-technical reality and a desired outcome. For without an effective mediated space of appearance, without in other words an adequate expression of the plurality of the world which the mediapolis must provide, both on the screen and in the interaction of screen and spectator, then there is little to look forward to. Arendt's critique of the post-totalitarian world is both a lament and a lash. I have tried to suggest that engaging with her work provides a basis for the investigation of current media presence and practice, but that it can also be a starting point for both asking substantive questions and making the substantive judgements that only grounded thinking of the kind that she herself undertakes can provide.

3

The Rhetoric of Evil

In this chapter I take a modest step back from a more or less direct discussion of the mediapolis, in order to address both a wider and a more focused issue. The wider issue is the relationship between media and the broader political and popular culture. The more focused one is the presence of evil in global society and in the global imaginary.

Through an interrogation, principally, of the mediated culture of the United States, I want to explore the problem of evil as a singularly important one for an understanding of the contemporary moral order and the media's place within, and indeed responsibility for, that order. I want to suggest that the identification of evil is a problem for practical morality, in the capacity to make the singular judgements of absolute right and wrong that humanity must make if it is to survive. It is a problem for ethics and politics, in the rhetoricization of those judgements, judgements which in their convenient direction towards the status of the other, say a great deal about ourselves. And it is a problem for the media who, in their willingness to collude with such appellations, in that collusion both legitimate and amplify them.

Susan Neiman distinguishes an evil from a crime against humanity: '. . . a crime is something for which we have procedures – at least for punishing, if not for preventing. To say this is to say that a crime can be ordered, can be fitted in some manner into the rest of our experience. To call an action evil is to suggest that it cannot – and that it thereby threatens the trust in the world that we need to orient ourselves within it' (Neiman 2002: 8–9). Evil, in this account, is a sober, but telling, reserve. It is a kind of standing reserve against the failures of reason in humanity's Enlightenment and post-Enlightenment project. Evil is what we call upon to explain an otherwise inexplicable world. Yet evil might be both real and imagined. And this complicates things rather. It denies the passing comfort of a singular discourse. And it defines the parameters of an ultimately insoluble contradiction in which evil both appears and disappears, real, eternal, but at the same time essentially constructed and contested.

Since Kant we know that evil comes with freedom, not as a deficit but as a fundamental component of what the human condition both requires and rejects.[1] Nothing about evil is without contradiction. Nothing about evil is certain. Yet no aspect of the human condition needs to be more certain. And no thing, consequentially, is more pressing.

The media have a central role to play in this discussion, and doubly so, for my concern is with the radical moral judgements that are made both on, for and through the media, and with the radical consequences of the presence of those judgements of evil within the media, both in image and word, for our everyday lives. Both presence and consequence are radical insofar as those who wish to articulate judgements of good and evil for public consumption will do so through the media, and within frameworks well established for that purpose. And insofar as the media are effective as platforms for, and conduits of, those communications, their significance as defining the discourses and agendas of public culture, and through that framing the way we think about the world which is otherwise beyond reach, is equally real and radical. It is because without the media we would not know the world in its global extent, that the judgements about that world which pass across the pages, speakers and screens of press, radio, television and the internet are so important.

The mediated judgements of good and evil are therefore radical – in the sense of radical as root and branch – because through them we are being invited to establish a relationship of connection or disconnection to the other, to other human beings distant from us in time or space. The mediated judgements of good and evil are the most trenchant and uncompromising articulations of difference in global civil society. They speak to, and to a degree determine, practices of inclusion and exclusion, and as such define the boundary of what it is to be human. And yet, at the same time, the salience of such judgements in public discourse, and their increasing presence in the post-9/11 world, provides, just as radically, a smokescreen for authentic or at least sustainable moral judgement. It is on the social and political significance of the anagrammatic difference between veil and evil that the discussion in this chapter will, effectively, turn.

There is another side to this of course. One that is dramatically revealed, shamefully revealed, in the puncturing of everyday mediated space, even during the long-running misery generated by the war in Iraq, by the publication of pictures of the torture of Iraqi prisoners in the prison of Abu Ghraib. And that is the presence of evil within. I refer to the otherness of ourselves. Such images break the illusion of virtue which US and western culture (as indeed all cultures, to some extent) need to preserve themselves. It is an illusion that is sustained through the projection of evil onto the stranger and its denial to the neighbour or to the self. Such images as these, circulated with such horror and shame, are there to constrain, at the very least, the hubris of the imperial powers in Iraq. Such images are anamorphic. They fracture the singularity of dominant media representation, provide an arguably necessary caution, and in so doing they express a certain constancy in western art and culture.

Anamorphosis relies on the deliberate distortion and subversion of the normal visual angle of sight and representation in order to remind the canny viewer of his or her vulnerability. This is most famously visible in Holbein's painting of *The French Ambassadors* (1533) in which two grand figures who embody power, wealth, glory and not a little smugness, stand on either side of a series of objects symbolic of early Enlightenment knowledge, learning and art. At their feet, as if projected from another place, is a distorted image that can only be deciphered by looking at the picture from an angle, from the side. Doing so reveals the image of a skull, an indication, for those who know how to read the Christian symbolism, of a hidden reality, a message of the instability of the world, the necessity of abandoning vainglory and of human mortality (Melchior-Bonnet 2001: 237). For those who know how to read the images of naked prisoners, taunted and tortured, and perhaps that is most of us, the message will be similarly familiar. Suddenly we (at least in the West, at least those in the US) are being asked to see ourselves both as other and as vulnerable.

The problem of evil

Susan Neiman (Neiman 2002) has recently argued that the problem of evil has been a defining characteristic of western philosophy, certainly since the Lisbon earthquake of 1755 and arguably until, and beyond, Auschwitz. Evil is both the answer to a question and itself a question. It is an answer to the question about the possibility of suffering and its otherwise incomprehensibility. Evil is a category of thought which has emerged to try and account for the horrors of the world, horrors beyond understanding. And evil is a question insofar as its own meaning is constantly in doubt, and in its continuing presence in public discourse it is the source of a considerable, and an inevitably punishing, confrontation.

Evil has been, or can be, understood as absence. It is perceived as the manifestation of the absence of God. Theodicies are, correlatively, what have emerged to recover God in the presence of evil.[2] Evil refers to actions and thoughts beyond reach, beyond imagination, beyond justification, beyond defence. Evil goes beyond crime, for crime has been imagined and framed in law. To say something or someone is evil is to say that they are beyond appeal, beyond redemption. To call on evil is to call on the other as human. To see the other as inhuman is itself the progenitor of evil. This circularity is, of course, at the heart of evil's viciousness.

Suggestions that Satan is dead (Delbanco 1995) and that we have in the West lost the power to define evil, to the contrary (Baudrillard 1993), there appears to be a sustained naturalness to the contemporary discourses of evil, especially in the United States. Richard Bernstein (Bernstein 2002) calls such discourses 'vulgar Manichaeism'. Yet, as he also point outs, we are bound to ask (even in a modern and post-modern world) for an explanation of the wrongs that are done to us, or the sufferings that we observe which we otherwise cannot explain and for which the explanations of reason (or social science) are unavailable or are rejected.

Evil is becoming, once again, a taken-for-granted category of analysis and judgement, particularly in the post-9/11 world, in both West and East. The problem comes when the notion of evil is seen as sufficient explanation for those wrongs, and worse, as a justification for action. The paradox is, of course – under such circumstances – that in a world in which evil is believed to be only a property of the other, it is almost inevitable that such an imposition will rebound. Those who call it become it. Evil has the potential to be perniciously double-edged.

This is an argument which, in some of its aspects, I want to take to the work of Hannah Arendt. The theme of evil runs like a dark and burning thread through much, if not all, of her writing. Her arguments emerge from her own experience of the rise of fascism and the destruction of the holocaust, and they are sustained in her reporting of the trial of Adolf Eichmann. She describes evil as both radical and banal and both characterizations have elicited huge controversy.

Radical evil is the evil of totalitarianisms, an evil manifested in the refusal of individuality, the denial of plurality, the creation of superfluousness, and the destruction of humanity. It is real in its consequences. The evil of totalitarianism has undermined all the securities to be found in tradition, in the morality of an ordered society. It has created and exploited personal isolation. It is in all these dimensions radically incomprehensible. A significant portion of Arendt's life-work is to try and redeem some of that incomprehensibility. It has, she believes, to be confronted, not sidestepped.

But evil is also banal:

> It is indeed my opinion now that evil is never 'radical', that it is only extreme, and that it possesses neither depth nor any demonic dimension. It can overgrow and lay waste the whole world precisely because it spreads like a fungus on the surface. It is 'thought-defying' . . . because thought tries to reach some depth, to go to the roots, and the moment it concerns itself with evil, it is frustrated because there is nothing. That is its 'banality'. Only the good has depth and can be radical. (Arendt 1978: 251)

The banality of evil is the evil that comes with the absence of thought (Arendt 1984). At the end of her controversial account of Eichmann's trial in Jerusalem, she speculates that the kind of evil manifest in his participation in the annihilation of the Jews resulted not so much from a radical commitment of an aware and intelligent being, but from the blank unthinkingness of a unreflective and self-serving bureaucrat. In her postscript to the account of the trial, she makes this clear. Eichmann *'never realised what he was doing* . . . He was not stupid. It was sheer thoughtlessness . . . that predisposed him to become one of the greatest criminals of that period . . . . That such remoteness from reality and such thoughtlessness can wreak more havoc than all the evil instincts taken together . . . that was, in fact the lesson one could learn from Jerusalem' (Arendt 1994b: 287–8; italics in the original).[3]

In one sense Arendt's agenda remains valid and vital. Yet there is something quite radically different in the various expressions of contemporary mediated discourse. For Arendt evil was an objective dimension of the human condition, a presence in the world which results from an absence of thought. For us, arguably, in the rhetorics of both the West and the Middle East, the supposed presence of evil has become a reason for not thinking. It has become a claim against thought. Consequence has become cause. And in the re-enchantment of the world which such mediated rhetoric signals, evil becomes once again a force for the denial and destruction of difference, both in the symbolic and the material worlds. The claims for, but crucially against, the evil embodied in the beliefs, thoughts and actions of the other are used as a weapon against thought in ourselves, and in so doing they reflect and reproduce the terrifyingly familiar, and ultimately totalitarian, speech which legitimates the perpetration of evil in the same breath as it condemns it.

The relationship between evil and the absence of thought and indeed judgement so clearly articulated in current discourse is a significant component of the mediapolis, its dark side, as it were. To point to its possible consequences is at the same time to condemn it. Yet, it is also to require its interrogation. As Arendt points out in the context of her own discussions, thinking is something that releases man, and crucially men in the plural, all men (and women), from the otherwise pernicious dreams of omnipotence. Insofar as totalitarianism is the manifestation of evil, then its presence results in the denial of the political in its ideal sense as a space for thought and action. The irony to which I have just referred is that it is the challenge to the evil seen in the words and deeds of others which represents an expression of the potential of our own. The media's unthinking reproduction of this dialectic is, when it occurs, therefore culpable.

The mediation of evil

There are a number of general points to be made about the mediation of evil and its consequences. The first is to say, and this will be argued in some detail in the discussion of the US case shortly, that its presence in public culture needs to be understood as deeply embedded in the values and ideas of the wider culture which the media reproduce as well as produce. The second is to say the representation of evil is merely the tip of an iceberg of a moral discourse which is omnipresent in the various representational practices of the modern media. What follows from both these observations is the following.

Media discourse consists essentially in a dialectic of narrative and event; of continuity and its interruption. The reporting of the attack on the World Trade Center on 11 September 2001 and its aftermath was, in its awesome extremity, paradigmatic.

Forms of narration, conventions of storytelling, metaphors of representation in text and image are deeply inscribed in the eternities of news and reporting, as well as in the various manifestations of serial drama on the established national and global broadcast media. It is a commonplace to observe that such consistencies provide a more or less secure framework of the familiar within which the new, the outrageous or the threatening can be absorbed and contained. Such consistencies are highly ritualized but also ideological. They provide comfort and entertainment, but they also become a screen. They are the taken-for-granted, deeply embedded components of contemporary culture, as mythic and as enchanting as they are superficial and persuasive.

Such discourses, indeed all of them in their various ways, are fundamentally moral. They orient the reader and viewer to a world that embodies the primary values of the society that produces them, notwithstanding the inevitable differences and contradictions within and between societies in such matters. They inscribe judgements of good and evil, of benevolence and malevolence, both in the narratives of global and national reporting, as well as in the dramatization of fiction. There is in all of these frameworks a narrative of us and them, of origins and futures, of boundaries and the articulation of difference, without which our culture, indeed any culture, could not survive. Such forms of narration are, or have been in a world of broadcasting, key to the formation and sustaining of nations, and on occasion, to a sharing of global comfort or grief. Such are the continuities of mediation.

From time to time such reassuring continuities are fractured by media events, that is events in the world which are of such intensity that the media must stop, interrupt the schedule and take notice. These have been seen, for the most part, as moments for community, for the discarding of difference and for a more or less benevolent engagement of the population of a state or global society. They have also been seen as moments of change, in which the media register, but at the same time reinforce, the trauma of reality by inscribing it into the symbolic. The ensuing contests, conquests and coronations are the expressions of that media work and of its social implications (Dayan and Katz 1992).

The paradox of media events, of course, lies in the consistencies with which they are, despite their uniqueness, dealt with by the media. The media have developed a range of more or less established and ritualized responses which ensure their reduction from the heights of uniqueness. Events become 'de-evented', a process which the analysis itself somehow reproduces. Such an analysis tends to underestimate both the political and moral power latent in many of these globally reported events, albeit still for the most part through the frame of a national agenda. It does not, in particular, register their vulnerability to incorporation into a wider politics in which media and state will collude in particular exercises in the construction of the heroes and villains of history, and where they will be written and rewritten as the defining moments in an ongoing narrative of national or ethnic identity.

So, for example, as Emily Rosenberg has argued (Rosenberg 2003), the history of Pearl Harbor is a history justifying righteous revenge and divine retribution, as well as providing a key component of both the media's, and the wider political, rhetoric framing the attacks on the World Trade Center and the Pentagon.

The event to mark the sixtieth anniversary of the attack on Pearl Harbor took place on 7 December 2001. In attendance at Oahu, Hawaii, were some 600 New York City police officers, some 350 family members of those who had died in New York and Washington on September 11, and President Bush, who neither for the first nor last time claimed Pearl Harbor as a component of national memory and as 'a symbol of American military valor and American resolve, but also a reminder of the presence of evil in the world and the need to remain vigilant against it'. The President then flew to the deck of the *USS Enterprise*, accompanied by a number of witnesses to Pearl Harbor, and of course the national and the global media, where he spoke again, this time reflecting on the continuities of fascist aggression and the need for US resolution in the face of terror. As Emily Rosenberg comments, Frank Capra, the director of World War II's *Why We Fight* series of films, could have written the lines (Rosenberg 2003). I will come back to the convergence of media representation and political rhetoric shortly.

For the moment let me merely say this. Pearl Harbor and September 11, each distinct in place and time, have been, and continue to be, endlessly folded and refolded into media narratives that, notwithstanding their contestation and their variation, lie ready for use and re-use in wider projects of representation and mobilization. Each separately, but even more significantly, at least in this case, each in their juxtaposition, assume the status of moral events, not so much in the terms in which Luc Boltanski (Boltanski 1999) refers to them in the context of the representation of suffering, but as tools for the determination of good and evil.

Such events, decontextualized and recontextualized as they will continue to be, are liberated in the shock of their initial framing from the determinations of history, and the *longues durées* which would otherwise give them the complex significance of the past. They stand ready to fall into frames that they provide for each other as well as those that, in the media's own imaginary, lie close at hand in the present and popular reservoir of dramatic images and stories of evil, destruction and Armageddon.

There are other dimensions, of course, in the emergence or re-emergence of evil as a category in the framing of media events and global relationships and conflicts. Two of these dimensions will be addressed and developed in what follows. For the moment the first is simply stated. The capacity to construct the world in terms of these basic polarities signals the failure of the Enlightenment to banish the irrational from public and popular culture. No surprises here, perhaps, more a recognition of the continuing power of myth and magic as supports for the conduct of everyday life. The continuing presence or resurgence of evil in the rhetoric of the elite is equally an expression of a certain kind of populism as well as an operational failure to distance political discourse from the demonization which has been a component of religious and neo-religious discourse since the birth of Judeo-Christianity.

The second aspect of the presence of evil in contemporary mainstream culture is its tendency for discounting. If evil is everywhere it is nowhere. If everything is evil then nothing much is. Such discounting and devaluation has a number of consequences. Above all, in denying the distinctive particularity of wickedness in the world, the loud-hailing of evil undercuts the possibility of confronting it when it is really threatening. Like so much in contemporary culture, a devaluation of this kind leads to failures of critical judgement. And the good, as a consequence, also disappears. The polarization, too, which ensues is both pernicious insofar as nothing can resist its incorporation, and pathetic, insofar as the moral judgements which are embodied become increasingly ineffective. Evil becomes a slogan.

Evil emerged as a, possibly the, major dimension of the narrative constructed around and after September 11 in the US media and in presidential rhetoric. And it has remained so. What factors have enabled this distinct framing? How come it has found so ready an audience? What consequences does such mediation have?

The presence of evil in American popular and political culture

> The last time I spoke here, I expressed the hope that life would return to normal. In some ways, it has. In others it never will. Those of us who have lived through these challenging times have been changed by them. We've come to know truths that we will never question: evil is real, and it must be opposed [Applause]. Beyond differences of race or creed, we are one country, mourning together and facing danger together. Deep in the American character, there is honor, and it is stronger than cynicism. And many have discovered again that even in tragedy – especially in tragedy – God is near [Applause] . . .
>
> President George W. Bush, State of the Union Address, 2002[4]

President George W. Bush is good at it. President Reagan was even better. In a speech to the National Association of Evangelicals, in Orlando, Florida, on 8 March 1983, he referred to C. S. Lewis' description of the ordinariness of evil in *The Screwtape Letters*, the (Eichmannesque) evil hatched in the minds and the back offices of the quiet men of bureaucracy, and linked such evil-mongering with the voices and actions, if not exactly the forked tongues, of the Soviets.

> So, I urge you to speak out against those who would place the United States in a position of military and moral inferiority. . . . So, in your discussions of the nuclear freeze proposals, I urge you to beware the temptation of pride – the temptation of blithely declaring yourselves above it all and label both sides equally at fault, to ignore the facts of history and the aggressive impulses of an evil empire, to simply call the arms race a giant misunderstanding and thereby remove yourself from the struggle between right and wrong and good and evil.[5]

This is a speech full of unintended irony, in which the charge of hubris is directed not at those who believe in their divine rightness, but to those (the same ones) who might believe that their divinity commands them to be above the material struggle. Its significance, apart from the coining of what became the infamy, but also the legitimation, of the epithet 'evil empire', was that it signalled, though by no means for the first time nor indeed the last, the presence of divinely ordained judgement at the heart of the United States' contribution to global politics. In doing so it condensed, and provided a framework for, a manifestation of a hugely powerful public culture which took God for granted, and which drew on, as I shall now argue, a convergence of religious and popular imagery preparing the way for the Bush administration's mobilization of the rhetoric of evil in and for the media, and the post-9/11 media's complicit appeal to the American public.[6]

My argument will be as follows. Starting with Reagan's own distillation and synthesis of his religious beliefs and his experiences in Hollywood in the post-Cold War era, I want to suggest that the presence of a rhetoric of evil in the US is one that has a long and deep history, so much so that the construction of the pernicious polarities in the US's global imaginary expressed in post-9/11 politics and rhetoric was an inevitable and indeed natural consequence of what was already deeply embedded in the collective psyche. The resources for it were already there. The attack was anticipated in the sense that it fitted into a well-established messianic and apocalyptic narrative, and the response was prepared insofar as media narratives and popular demonology in the US had already articulated familiar threats and appropriate responses. It was not just Hollywood's imagery (the images of urban destruction, for example, in the film *Independence Day*) which informed the reporting of the attack on the World Trade Center, but Hollywood's and other expressions of popular culture's storytelling, both ascribing blame and indicating the appropriate rhetorical and military reaction to the threats of otherness, that prove telling.

I also want to suggest that the significance of such an analysis lies in what it tells us about the media's role in creating and sustaining such a version of the world, what that role tells us about the relationship between media and the politics of US society, and what consequences it has for a wider understanding of the media's responsibility for global morality. Such an analysis also speaks, of course, to the continuing significance of the pre-Enlightenment in late modernity, of the sustained power of the religious and the mythic, long after it was supposed to be dead and buried.

Michael Rogin (Rogin 1987) has shown the extent to which Ronald Reagan's political persona was forged by his experiences in Hollywood, both in his roles and in his immediately subsequent career in the local politics of McCarthyite Los Angeles. It is a component of a wider thesis on the persistence of demonology in American politics, a politics of conspiracy, dehumanization and paranoia.[7] Rogin points out, of course, that such a politics is not exclusive to the US, but likewise makes the point, as I do, that nowhere is it so significant nor so uncompromising. As he spells out in the preface to his book:

> American demonology has both a form and a content. The demonologist splits the world in two, attributing magical, pervasive power to a conspiratorial centre of evil. Fearing chaos and secret penetration, the countersubversive interprets local initiatives as signs of alien power . . . the countersubversive needs monsters to give shape to his anxieties and to permit him to indulge his forbidden desires. Demonisation allows the countersubversive, in the name of battling the subversive, to imitate his enemy. (Rogin 1987: viii)

Rogin's argument stresses the convergence of the personal and the political in Reagan's career. Communism was the evil and its presence was both internal, buried within the otherwise homely fabric of American society, as well as abroad, where it manifested itself as a singular demonic threat. What Reagan succeeded in doing was to make himself, both physically and spiritually, the benign centre of America, placing all malignancies outside its borders.

Reagan's key roles in *Love is on the Air* (1937), *Brother Rat* (1938), *An Angel from Texas* (1940), *Murder in the Air* (1940), *Desperate Journey* (1942), *The Hasty Heart* (1949), but most especially in *Knute Rockne* (1940) and *Kings Row* (1942) collectively provided the resources for the formation of a powerful persona and a world view. In *Knute Rockne* Reagan plays George Gipp, the legendary Notre Dame half-back who died very young after an attack of pleurisy (a disease which actually nearly killed Reagan), a character who appears for no more than fifteen minutes in the film. Gipp was immortalized in Reagan's own subsequent identification with the character and in lines such as 'Win this one for Gipper' which he included in his first speech after his shooting in 1981, and 'Wherever I am, I'll know about it and it'll make me happy' during his exhortation of Republicans in the 1984 presidential campaign. In *Kings Row* (1942), a gothic film involving many doubles and an ideology of good and evil, and indeed the film which made him a star, Reagan plays a crippled hero whose line on discovering the loss of his legs after being run over by a train, 'Where's the rest of me?', was used as the title of his autobiography and his own summary description of his search for, and discovery of, his political identity (Rogin 1987).

This identity was also formed through a range of films that cast him very firmly at the heart of battles between good and evil: as General Custer in *The Santa Fe Trail* (1940), and an RAF pilot in *International Squadron* (1941). Often in these roles, as well as others, he is cast as a character who is physically and emotionally vulnerable, weak in his relationships with women, or as a character who dies. It was not until 1950 and his departure from Warner Brothers in order to choose his own roles, those that did not involve such vulnerability and personal victimhood, that he was able to command a filmic status as the defending champion of the West – against the Indians in *The Last Outpost* (1951), *Cattle Queen of Montana* (1954) and *Law and Order* (1953), as well as against the Communists (*Hong Kong* (1952)) and the Klu Klux Klan (the 'Communists within') in *Storm Warning* (1951).[8]

The films portrayed recognizable conflicts with familiar adversaries and in accordance with well-established narratives of threat both from within and beyond US society, threats that remained structurally in place despite their shifting from right to left, from west to east, and from fascism to communism. And these evils were indeed perceived, in the immediate post-war period and as the Cold War began to take shape, as coming very close to home. As Reagan's time in the movies was drawing to a close he entered studio politics, leading Hollywood's campaign against communist infiltration of the industry. It is quite clear that this political identity and commitment emerged from both the unconscious and conscious blurring of life and movies: an individual embodiment of the fictional and the factual.

I want to suggest, however, that there is another deeply engrained component of American culture which needs to be taken into account in both placing and understanding Reagan's politics, its origins and its appeal; one which guarantees and legitimates the presence and power of evil in his rhetoric and in his world view, as well as providing a continuous link to what follows. It is not part of Rogin's story. Arguably it should be. This is the strength and pervasiveness of religious belief in American society.

The United States of America is, probably more than any other post-industrial society, God-fearing. This is ironic, not to say perverse, given the clarity and certainty with which its founding fathers insisted on the separation of church and state, and given its citizens' otherwise intense commitment to mammon.[9] The US is split. The current version of this increasingly visible fracture is framed through what are called the culture wars, the battles being fought between right and what passes for left in the US, between modernity and tradition, and between, most significantly, the Christians and the others, on a whole range of issues from the war in Iraq and America's role in the world, to abortion. gay marriage, intelligent design and the presence of the ten commandments on a courtroom wall.

Underlying these continuous and public conflicts is an unresolved tension in a society that has never fully come to terms with the modernity that it itself had a significant role in creating. In such a society religion can be seen as a reaction formation, a defence against the guilt of consumption. It can be seen as a compensation for the failures of the state to provide either moral or social support. Both possibly. But there is certainly religion there: on the screens and on the streets; in the mouths of babes and the speeches of presidents. And there is religion in multiple manifestations: from kabbalah to karma, and above all on the pulpits and television channels of the main churches and institutions of the faith.

Among the multiple expressions of individual and collective belief that define the distinctiveness of US public culture, it is arguably Evangelical Protestantism which dominates. Long established in the heartlands of the United States and well placed in the political hierarchies, particularly in the South and within the Republican party, Evangelical Protestantism brings with it a range of beliefs that have become increasingly politically influential.

There are a number of things to be said about this in the present context.

First, religious referencing and religious exhortation is simply part of the taken-for-granted rhetoric of American public culture. The eternal appeal to the 'American people' in speech after speech and commentary after commentary is an appeal to a community purportedly united in its focused and fundamental commitment to its nationhood and to its spiritual unity. It brooks no rebuke, and it acknowledges neither difference nor dissent. It is a version of populism uncompromised by history, belief or identity but it is an appeal grounded in a perception of the community as congregation, and as such deemed perfectly acceptable, from either pulpit or podium, as an expression of the authority of the singular.

Such authority is reinforced by the appeals to the Almighty at the end of almost all presidential speeches, certainly those that are addressed to the nation or deal with matters of substantial political import. President Bush rarely fails to ask God to bless America and/or his audience in his direct television addresses as well as those, also televised, which he gives to Congress. President Clinton was equally willing to call on the same benevolence, though less frequently, and he too was not averse to the identification of evil as the source of what might otherwise have been considered criminal behaviour, as for example in the aftermath of the Oklahoma bombing.[10] Indeed the latter's rhetoric was often preacherly in tone, content, and above all in performance. And once again it is this double singularity of incorporation and homogenization which is unproblematically presumed. All US citizens are assumed to be God-fearing, or at least to recognize his role in the pantheon. And notwithstanding the recent attempt to erase the reference to God from the daily pledge of allegiance, he remains firmly ensconced as a final arbiter in mediated public space.[11]

And his presence is rarely far away elsewhere in the media. Television shows such as *Angel* and *Buffy the Vampire Slayer* have him or his alter ego as a character. He is the dedicatee and principal of a number of cable channels and he is regularly referred to in appeals by celebrity after celebrity as the guiding light for their otherwise incomprehensible actions and as a key figure in their own attempts to stay viable in the world. Mel Gibson, the director of *The Passion of Christ*, stands, from this perspective, merely at the tip of a celestial iceberg.

The argument which I now intend to pursue is that this ground base of culture, this neo-spirituality of the social order, continually reinforced in daily media, provides fertile soil for the more particular narratives originating both from the religious tradition as well as from the more secular myths of the United States. And that it is the convergence and mutual reinforcement of these two dimensions of that culture which is precisely the point. What emerges from this interaction, one that is reinforced by the equally powerful interaction between the religious and the commercial in media and elsewhere, is a culture in which evil is no stranger. As I shall try and show, through discussion of particular arguments and cases, the willingness to accept the seamless transition from the spiritual to the material and from the religious to the political in the daily rhetoric of post-Cold War America, and especially in post-9/11 America, is not only one of its key defining features but one which has, in its mediation, the most profound consequences for an understanding of that culture's significance as a moral force in global society.

It was Reagan's presidency which, in the post-war period, most significantly enshrined Evangelical Protestantism in the framework of dominant public culture. A strong tradition of fundamentalist millennialism, grounded in the literal interpretation of biblical texts, not least the Book of Revelation, and an emerging theodicy, stretched from the early pilgrims through to the Millerite movement of 1830s' New England and to Hal Lindsey's apocalyptic politics of, and for, the American Christian Right in the 1980s. Lindsey's hugely influential text, *The 1980s: Countdown to Armageddon*, was published in 1981 and spent most of that year in the *New York Times* list of best-sellers. Reagan was caught in this web.

It was a web of storytelling and dire but certain prediction, in which evil was accounted for in narratives of redemption and resurrection. The presence of evil in the world was a given, but its elimination was just as certain, come the millennium and its apocalypse. Beliefs associated with such a firm conviction involved a version of global politics centred on the fall of the Soviet Union and the central significance of the state of Israel.

In tracing and analysing this particular strand of American cultural history, Stephen O'Leary (O'Leary 1994) distinguishes between two versions of this apocalyptic tale, one of which, the comic, 'conceives of evil in terms of error, misunderstanding, or ignorance; its mechanism of redemption is recognition, and its plot moves toward exposure of the evildoer's fallibility and his incorporation into society.' The tragic version, however, conceives of evil in terms of sin or guilt, 'its mechanism of redemption is victimage, and its plot moves toward the isolation of the evildoer in the "cult of the kill"'. Its temporality is progressive and predetermined (O'Leary 1994: 200–1). It will come as no surprise that it is the latter which dominates in the American apocalyptic tradition and, as

I shall argue, it does so because it fits so well with the established mythic narratives of popular film, television, comic books and, more recently, computer games.

Reagan's 1983 'empire of evil' speech, from which I have already quoted, is one of the clearest examples of this apocalyptic vision incorporated into a view of both domestic and international politics. The Soviet Union (the Magog of Ezekiel) was the source of all evil, and its fall would herald the beginning of the glorious end, from which Reagan seemed to believe that the US (in its Christian manifestation) would benefit. His views were not by any means uncontroversial. He was nevertheless re-elected in 1984 and O'Leary notes winsomely that 'it seems reasonable to conclude that, in this area as in so many others, Reagan gave voice to thoughts that, though unpalatable to liberal pundits, are shared by millions of Americans' (O'Leary 1994: 183).

Twenty or so years later, with shades of Armageddon now palpably in the air, his heir incarnate, President Bush, was still talking the talk (not to say walking the walk). Joshua Gunn (Gunn 2004) sees his post-9/11 rhetoric as mobilizing a version of exorcism, in which the naming of evil is a significant component of its eradication, with the assertion of the self-righteousness of the American nation both as its *deus ex machina* and as its consequence. Bush identifies the demons hidden within the wounded American body and then names those who lie hidden in the foxholes of the world body. The naming is the mystery, and in naming them the power to purge is enshrined. It is an invidious rhetoric which flows naturally off the tongue of someone whose adult conversion during a walk with Billy Graham (Fineman 2003; Singer 2004) is well known. But it is a rhetoric that owes its strength not just to the religious strand of American culture but to the increasing presence of exorcist imagery in popular culture (not least the neo-anamorphic presence of the smoke demon visible, at least to some, in Mark Phillips' photo of the clouds billowing from the World Trade Center).[12]

At stake was the mobilization of a population behind a symbolic struggle which in turn would legitimate a material one, and which in both guises reaffirms the righteousness of these two struggles and contains the anxieties which the original threat generated. As Gunn notes, thinking of Bush's rhetoric through the lens of exorcism 'helps us to see better the enthymemetic function of "evil", and how the use of evil in demon-making sets a civil pedagogy – a subtle form of discipline – in motion. By using a charged yet vague label, a speaker can demonize entire peoples and justify violence as a necessity. Describing the racial Other as 'evil' is a civil lesson in the intolerance of righteousness' (Gunn 2004). This is an argument which I have already begun and to which I will return.

The fusion of the religious and the popular in American culture is explored further by Robert Jewett and John Shelton Lawrence in their analysis of the Captain America complex. American popular culture, drawing on religious and national foundational myths in what amounts to an encompassing civil religion, has generally preferred, they suggest, the path of zealous nationalism offered in the Book of Revelation over the alternative, Jesus of Nazareth's prophetic realism: the one externalizing, the other internalizing responsibility for evil (Jewett and Lawrence 2003: 52).

The Captain America complex, sharing with Christian and Jewish zeal as well as Islamic Jihad a number of polarizing and demonizing characteristics, and in its vehement insistence on the lack of compromise and communication between self and other, seeks to protect democracy in its perceived weakness, and commits above all to defend democracy in its inability to identify and overcome the evil which constantly threatens it. And this is to be defence through attack; and defence ungoverned by the flabbiness of the rule of law. It is a belief powerfully embodied in Bush's post-9/11 foreign policy, particularly in his belief in the legitimacy of the pre-emptive strike, and it is one supported both by the popular press and, it would appear, by a substantial body of US public opinion:

> The story of superheroes who must bypass the restraints of law to redeem the nation and the world has become dominant in the past sixty years, and it should now be recognised as a major source of the crusading idealism that marks the American civil religion . . . That the ideas incorporated in these stories are indeed credible, not just to the fans of comic books, but even to political leaders, became evident in developments since the destruction of the World Trade Center and a portion of the Pentagon on September 11, 2001 . . . the fascist thinking lurking in the shadow side of the Captain America complex has roots in its religious foundations, and . . . these roots have always produced poisonous fruit. (Jewett and Lawrence 2003: 37–43).[13]

There is no sustainable, or even necessary, argument here about cause and effect, for it is clear that there is a constant interaction between mythic strands of thought and expression in American culture, at the very least throughout the twentieth century. Religion arguably was there first, but so too were the frontier myths of the hunter and his prey and the rites of passage, derived from the native Indian's own mythology that marked the emergence of the hero into a world of threat and terror.

Janice Hocker Rushing and Thomas S. Frentz (Rushing and Frentz 1995) take this argument into an analysis of the emergence of the cyborg, and above all in their discussion of *The Terminator*, link the struggle against a technological evil with both the warrior tradition and the now unsurprising narrative of redemption and regeneration. As they perhaps disingenuously point out, Christianity does not deal directly with the problem of technology, but it does address the problem of the shadow, 'that rejected part of us all which is projected onto an Other, a devil figure that carries the sins of humanity' (p. 180). And they suggest that technology has become our shadow. This is their reading of the core narrative of the first of the two *Terminator* films:

> John Connor, a modern day J.C., born of an 'ordinary' mother, is the warrior-king who is prophesied to reconstitute the world, to avert the apocalypse through a fight with a cyborgian devil. His birth is so important that it is foretold, and it must be secured by a warning from God (Kyle's message from the future) and a flight into Egypt (Sarah and Kyle's various hideouts). (Rushing and Frentz 1995: 179)[14]

And finally, I move from film to computer games. Lynn Schofield Clark (Clark 2003), in her study of teenage culture on television and on the computer screen, is clear about the mutual interaction between evangelical narratives and the contemporary media. Satan has emerged as a powerful character, not to say a celebrity, in a range of Hollywood films and computer games, an appearance which legitimates a perception of the world which accords well with the Evangelical Christian model where evil is to be defeated, and can be defeated, by the aggressive action of either the believer or the player of games. From *The Exorcist* (1973) and *Rosemary's Baby* (1968) via *The Omen* and through the genre of horror in both the 1970s and Reagan's 1980s, a genre which is paralleled by the films where evil comes in increasingly technological forms and where it is the future as well as the past which generates it, there is a consistent strand of evil-mongering and evil-resisting in Hollywood cinema. *The Lord of the Rings* and the various Harry Potter films reduce this to a play of neo-mythic narratives, but in so doing they still preserve both the metaphors and threats of evil as part of the culture of the times.

The spectacular framing of such Manichean struggle is the bread and butter of contemporary US cinema, as it has become in its wider public and popular culture. As such it sustains a version of that culture quite at home with the devil and apocalyptic threat, and quite at home with a representation of the world in which otherness is both the supreme threat and incomprehensibly beyond the pale.

While these narrative versions of the world continue interminably to bubble up to the surface of American culture, and provide the infrastructure for orientation and judgement in the world, from time to time eruptions occur: events, which as I have already suggested, become media events, which raise the level of demonization to a higher plane. These events have a double face. They involve both sacrifice and stereotyping. The events themselves become sites for memory and memorial, and sites in turn capable of structuring the next: preparing for it, framing it, licensing its representation.[15]

The attack on the US fleet in Pearl Harbor, perhaps archetypally, and I have already referred to it, has this status.[16] On the one hand it reinforces what Carolyn Marvin and David Ingle (Marvin and Ingle 1999) argue is the sacrificial thread within US culture, the 'blood rituals' supporting patriotism and culture, most of which centre on the symbolic power of the American flag (hence the significance of its burning). On the other hand they legitimate the pillory of the global stereotype, wherein first the Japanese then the Moslem becomes the threatening racial other. This punitive and paranoid space, once created (and preceded in turn through the construction and destruction of the native Indian), is preserved as if in a state of symbolic cryogenation. It sits on the shelf ready for the next moment, the next crisis, when the personification of an alien evil can resume its strategic place in the definition of what it is to be an American.

Pearl Harbor and 9/11, breaches of homeland security in both the symbolic as well as the material domains, are the events, the moral events, through which the American cultural psyche has been recently moulded. Their power is sustained and magnified through the mediated imagery and rituals that they inspire. Indeed the realities, significant though they might be in loss of life and loss of face, pale to insignificance when confronted by the long-term capacity of the media, sustained by both capitalism and evangelicism, the unholy alliance of cash and redemption, to create the nation's myths of origin, self-righteousness and imperial calling.

As Carolyn Marvin and David Ingle argue:

> The totem myth of blood sacrifice governs and organises media coverage . . . The biggest history is about the biggest hurt, which is sacrifice. Media witness sacrifice and model it. Though they cannot perform real sacrifice, they scratch the itch in small ways and at regular intervals. They provide maintenance and memory until a big sacrifice comes again. Then

they become the channel through which knowledge of sacrifice moves to the nation . . .

Media re-presentations keep a pool of useable models circulating and offer experimental arenas for new ones. Old models are refurbished; others drop out . . . the chain of mediated re-presentations is infinite, and re-presentation is a process of memory as well as a model of cultural maintenance . . . (Marvin and Ingle 1999: 141-5)

Consequences and questions

Evil is the signal expression of otherness, of the other as malevolent in a world governed by God. To ascribe evil to the thought, action or identity of the other is to put the other beyond the pale, to deny their rights of existence, as moral and as material beings. To ascribe evil to the other is to place him or her beyond the pale of understanding; the other is incomprehensible and, in a world supposedly governed by reason, the other is dispensable. Sometimes – but when? – and mostly, tragically, with the benefit of hindsight, the call is a good one, and through it humanity gains another life. To deny evil in oneself, however, is to refuse one's own otherness, and to put oneself beyond the pale of reason and responsibility, beyond humanity. Evil is in the eye of the beholder, but without its mirroring in the self the judgement is vulnerable, and the consequences of action based on that judgement are likely to be self-defeating.

As Hannah Arendt has argued there are actions in the world which go beyond the imagination of existing law to regulate them (and cf. Gaita 2004). At the same time to cast such actions as evil is to presume and possibly ensure that the law is unable to deal with them (cf. Klusmeyer and Suhrke 2002), and that those confronting what they see as evil can themselves eschew the law's procedures and constraints.

Evil is unequivocal. But its identification poses a dilemma rather than creates a certainty. Its presence in contemporary political discourse as well as in political action signals an absence of thought. But it arguably emerges as a vital category of judgement precisely because without it we will lack the judgement necessary to sustain our humanity. Can we do without a concept of evil? Can we have a concept of evil without a concept of God? Or the Good? As Hans Jonas notes, it is the *malum* which is the easier of the two to identify (Jonas 1984). Perhaps in an age where international law, albeit not without a struggle, defines certain crimes, as those crimes were defined for the first time at the Nuremberg trials, as crimes against humanity, we can do without it. Perhaps.[17]

These are fundamental questions, but ones which take me beyond my immediate and present concern as well as my competence. In my discussion of the category of evil in public, political and popular discourse, and especially in the United States of America, I have tried to indicate the conditions under which it has become so easy a notion, so easy a measure for the judgement of the world. And I have suggested that it is the convergence within American culture of the religious tradition, above all the strength and beliefs of evangelical Christianity, with the popular storytelling of Hollywood and the wider media which has provided the fertile ground for the Manichean seeds. The media are doubly involved as providing and legitimating the frameworks both for its rhetoric and its reception. Their storytelling constitutes the ground for a culture that is quick to find evil in the other, and to accept the self-righteousness of the imperial position. Yet it is a position which, it should now be quite clear, is not without its own violence and its own propensity to evil. As Jean Baudrillard has noted, 'Evil can only be dealt with by means of evil' (Baudrillard 1993: 85).

There are a number of things at stake. A recent book by David Frum and Richard Perle, written and published in the aftermath of the war in Iraq and at the height of its occupation, is called *An End to Evil*. Its first chapter ends with the following:

> For us, terrorism remains the great evil of our time, and the war against evil, our generation's greatest cause. We do not believe that Americans are fighting this evil to minimise it or to manage it. We believe they are fighting to win – to end this evil before it kills again and on a genocidal scale. There is no middle way for Americans; it is victory or holocaust. (Frum and Perle 2003: 9)

And Frum and Perle end the book as a whole with the following: 'Our vocation is to support justice with power. It is a vocation that has made us, at our best moments, the hope of the world' (p. 279). Frum and Perle at no point question the attribution of evil or its meaning. Nor do they appear to accept anything other than a polarized world in which America's destiny is clear. They understand neither difference nor ambiguity, neither reflection nor indeed the realities of any kind of freedom other than theirs. Note the use of the religious term vocation and the biblical conjunction of justice with power. Both the authors are, of course, very close personally and politically to the Bush administration. Their articulation of a policy for the American achievement of justice, indeed for the realization of the American century, is based on a rhetoric, and an analysis, of global politics which is now familiar. It is a rhetoric of violence and a rhetoric of pride. And it is a rhetoric which is at one with the strands of popular culture which are as distinct and decisive a part of US society as the more familiar and more benign apple pie.

In their present florid mode, the media prepare and perpetuate a view of the world in which the other is either to be incorporated or annihilated.[18] In their presumptions and narratives, but also in the unchallenged and unchallenging voices on their pages and screens, there is an ideology at work, which like all ideologies is difficult to disrupt but is yet radically contradictory. It is an ideology which depends, to a significant degree, on the substitution of the image for reality. It is an ideology in which the anamorphic is rarely visible as a caution against hubris and the misplaced innocence of evil. And it is an ideology which, notwithstanding marginal alternative and critical voices, seems unlikely to be vulnerable to immediate political change.

As Susan Sontag (Sontag 2004) notes, in a discussion of the Abu Ghraib photographs, those images of degradation and pleasure are more the focus of political recrimination than the action they represent. They also involve a kind of reversal, for now participants, in this case the prisoners' guardian soldiers with their own digital cameras, have recorded, appropriated and circulated photographs of what they could not, arguably, expect would be recognized as demonstrating their own capacity for evil.

Nothing perhaps manifests so radically Hannah Arendt's description of evil as a fungus than these images.

The presence of evil in contemporary American (but also British)[19] rhetoric has another connotation. It signals the failure of the Enlightenment project to disenchant the world. This may well have been always forlorn or misconceived (Latour 1993; Toulmin 1990), and once again I will have occasion to discuss it further, but it is nevertheless dramatically the case. As Lance Morrow suggests, without I believe too heavy a dose of irony, we are perhaps now beginning to live in a new age of 'endarkenment' (Morrow 2003).

I began this chapter by framing the problem of evil as a global one, and then went on to discuss it almost entirely as an issue in and for the US. Its global significance was always only a whisper away of course, not just in terms of the global consequences of the American preoccupation with the way in which the rest of the world is constructed, and therefore included or excluded in its imperial vision; but also insofar as the rhetoric of evil is generated by the other as well as against the other. The mirroring of this rhetoric within fundamentalist Islam and increasingly – though perhaps more cynically – within the rhetoric of the global left can hardly escape notice or attention. Its presence does not however absolve the US, or indeed the West, neither its politicians nor its media, from responsibility for it and its consequences.

Finally to my own ambiguity. And to the complexity of evil as a category of thought and judgement. That ambiguity revolves around the conflict between morality and politics, and the necessity but also the consequences of judgement. The failures of judgement, the consequences of past temptations to appease or to stand by, particularly but not exclusively in relation to fascism in Nazi Germany, still cast a formidable shadow on contemporary discourse. To walk away from judgements of the unacceptable and the inhuman in human conduct is unconscionable. Yet, and there is always a yet, as I have argued in this chapter, such judgements are powerfully double-edged. They can involve a discounting of evil, and they can lead to its doubling and its reproduction, as well as result in its confrontation and elimination. Richard Bernstein (Bernstein 2002: 2) argues that we cannot refuse to acknowledge and attempt to comprehend the problems of evil which come back to haunt us. And even though it is certain that such comprehension will – as it were by definition – prove elusive, the presence of evil as well as its work in the modern world require constant interrogation. Does evil exist, and does it corrupt those who perpetrate it, those who deny it, those who fail to challenge it and those who seek to eradicate it? The answer has to be, to all of these, almost certainly, yes.

The mediapolis has been a somewhat shadowy presence in the arguments of this chapter. Indeed my preoccupation has been with the context in which it might be seen to be operating rather than the operation itself. Likewise I have drawn much more on the popular media, the media of fiction rather than fact, and not sought to demonstrate in detail the ways in which the news media in the US and elsewhere collude or don't collude with the powers of government and other politically and culturally dominant institutions in the representation of the world. The latter is a big topic, though one well trodden in recent work.

My intention has been, however, to present what I obviously see as both malfunction and danger in one particular manifestation of the complexities of culture, politics and mediation. It was also to suggest how hard in given socio-political circumstances, both at national and global levels, it will be to free the media from the pressures of history and realpolitik. Whereas in the next chapter, in my discussion on the contrapuntal, I held out a model and a hope for the possibility of a plural mediapolis, my argument here was to address something of the difficulties embedded in, and the consequences of, the other way, not plural but polarized, not open but closed. The next four chapters are attempts to open up the agenda by considering the different dimensions of the mediapolis and to argue for a more critical and hopefully a more rigorous approach for the underpinning of its present and future. I begin with an argument about plurality.

4

Contrapuntal Cultures

Whereas the last chapter focused on the singular, this one will address the plural. It does so with one significant aim in mind. That is to explore the emergence of the mediapolis as a space for multiply mediated voices, as it appears in a specifically European context. Europe is the site for a new kind of cosmopolitanism, one to which Ulrich Beck has drawn our attention, one of inward and transmigration, one in which cultures sit side by side with each other, not always comfortably, and where the claims on individual identities come from both home and host societies. This is, at least embryonically, a both/and rather than an either/or kind of place. And the issue is the extent to which the presence of minority and majority voices, on the one hand, and the welcome of the one within the other, actually enables us to recognize something new and important: that is, a plural space for mediation.

There is no magic here. And I have no intention of romanticizing. European society, if such a thing exists at all, is far from harmonious, and far from coherent culturally. Most of the attempts to create a pan-European broadcast environment have failed, for obvious, most significantly linguistic, reasons. The media spaces in individual nations are still entirely dominated by the mainstream, national and transnational broadcasters, internet service providers and global search engines. Yet as a result of both technological change (digital and interactive media of various kinds) and societal change (migration and the lifestyle-driven fragmentation of cultures), the total media environment is being transformed. The major incumbents know about this well as they struggle to hold on to audiences and readers. But consumers of various kinds know about this well too as they flick between channels and find ways of downloading and communicating stuff (from gossip to news, however the latter is defined) on a minute-by-minute basis.

Within this cacophony of mediated voices, unheard and invisible in its totality for the most part, I see the possibility of a different kind of mediated environment, one which might one day lead to a version of the mediapolis which I am at pains to describe. Identifying the presence of the multiplicity of voices is, however, one thing. Finding a way of recognizing their value and creating a framework for their viability and integrity is clearly another. This chapter, as in the last one, focuses down in order to explore a bigger question. In both it is the same question. It is the question of how we might live together, and how the media in their capacity for hospitality and justice (which I discuss in more detail in chapter 6) can be enabling rather than disabling of that rather basic project.

Europe then, becomes a case in point, and the arguments in this chapter, the second of two which step back a little from the abstraction of chapter 2 to engage more directly with the mediated world, spring from two sources. The first is from a reading of the work of Edward Said, and in particular his intermittent but pervasive reflections on both his status as an exile and on his way of reading literature. The second is from some empirical research of my own, research on the presence and significance of minority media in European societies. Their mutual focus is on migration, diaspora and the experience and representation of otherness. In this case, as in so many, movement illuminates stasis. Said's experience of his own migration and my research on the role of the media in the increasingly diasporic late modern world is intended to throw some new light on how otherness and difference appear, or do not appear, on the pages and screens of the global media and to allow a modest measure of the consequences of such appearance and non-appearance.

What links these two sources together is the notion of counterpoint, the contrapuntal. And it is this idea, this way of seeing, which I want to develop and to draw into my discussion and definition of the present and future mediapolis. What also links them is a structural convergence between the social and symbolic world, a convergence constituted by mobility, fluidity, refraction and fracture. But also a world in which we are required to live, and to appear to live, side by side. One way or another this is a world of both lived and mediated experience.

The mediapolis needs to be understood, as I have begun to argue, as a space of appearance in which such appearance both reflects and constitutes the world. But in the momentary change of metaphors that I now propose, the shift is also one between senses. It involves a transition from the visual to the auditory. And with such a movement, and its metaphorical application, comes an orientation to the dynamics of mediation that addresses culture and cultures and their representation in the plural. It involves hearing, rather than seeing, the various manifestations and expressions of different cultures as intermingled and intertwined, as both present and absent, and as constantly shifting in their relations of dominance and subordination, In other words it involves seeing them as contrapuntal.

Both Said's own biography and my own empirical research highlight a fundamental dimension of life in the twenty-first century, one which while not novel is nevertheless increasingly significant both for an understanding of social change and, in my case, for an understanding of the changing nature of media and mediation. This is migration.

Migration involves something more than the physical, geographical, movement of populations, significant though such physical movements are. Migrations have long been part of the human condition. There has been constant movement of individuals, groups and cultures, movements prompted by economic, political, religious and environmental changes, movements both forced and voluntary, movements of the rich and the poor, movements seeking a better way of life, or at least a less worse one. Displacement and settlement; permanence and instability; the welcoming and the rejection; migration is marked by contradiction and not a little conflict. Migrants leave, arrive, stay and move on. They have few rights of passage. And their displacement, changing through the generations, leaves a trace across culture, like that of a snail on a wall.

The challenges that migrants pose both for their host societies and the societies they have left behind are increasingly visible, particularly in an era of economic migration. The educated of the underdeveloped world abandon their own societies and take their skills to where they can be better rewarded. The impoverished seek escape. The political refugees likewise. Their arrival in new societies is marked by problems of identity and community. The dilemma, as George Marcus (Marcus 1998) describes it, is that between routes and roots, that of passage and fixity. There is a dialectic between longing and belonging. Host societies, for the most part, seek assimilation and acculturation. The newly forming communities of migrants, sometimes called diasporas, seek security and the opportunity to preserve their identity and their way of life, in different ways of course and with different degrees of intensity, as the generations change. The politics of migration is a profoundly contentious one, both for the international community and for states and nations. It manifests itself in different ways in different societies, and the troubles when they come have different origins and are dealt with differently, as the 2005 riots in Paris and the 7th of July bombing in London in the same year illustrate. There is an invidious discourse of fear and threat, understandable perhaps in an age of global terror, but ultimately one which is self-defeating, perpetuating rather than ameliorating the challenge of difference, and creating a pervasive paranoia, not unfamiliar at least in the West, in relation to the presence of the stranger amongst us.

Migration, immigration, is therefore now a major concern in Europe, and elsewhere. And its consequences extend beyond the questions that dominate public discourse. For what such movements represent are a perceptible if not yet a conclusive change in the nature of national cultures and their capacity to sustain traditional boundaries and identities. We may not have quite reached the fluid, liquid society that many contemporary sociologists imagine we have; indeed the political frictions generated in these shifts are real and challenging enough. Nor indeed have we yet reached an age in which globalization is becoming a force significantly to undermine the nation. Yet, for all this, the struggles for community, identity and a place in the culture of region, nation and continent are becoming the central ones in the current century. It will be my contention, firstly, that these are being waged in many significant respects in the media; and secondly that how they are resolved, or not, within the media, in the mediapolis, will tell us much about the way in which public culture and civic space will emerge in a future age, a culture which whether we like it or not will be one of both diversity and difference. And finally I will be suggesting that the way in which we do or do not resolve these tensions within the mediapolis will have profound moral and ethical consequences.

There is some considerable pressure already building for new policies on minority media from within the European Union.[1] These policies would acknowledge, however contentiously, the rights of ethnic minorities to have media in their own languages, and would also acknowledge and promote, less contentiously, the central role of such minority media as mediators between mainstream culture and their own minority cultures, and consequently contributing directly to a multiethnic civil society within host nations.[2] So I will go further, and suggest that the European experience of diversity is significantly both reflected and constituted in its mediation. In short, I will argue that the perspective that a study of minority media generates is one that offers interesting and provocative challenges for how we might understand media culture as a whole for, and as, a mediapolis.

The contrapuntal turns on the issue of diversity, or a diversity of diversities. There is the diversity between, and necessarily within, the number of cultures, languages and ethnicities within (and beyond) Europe. There is the diversity in the relationships between dominant and subordinate media institutions; the diversity of technologies and platforms; the diversity amongst audiences and producers, and diversity in their location; the diversity in the patterns of inclusion and exclusion across and within nation-states and the diversity in those states' cultural and economic policies towards both established and recent migrants. But the contrapuntal also turns on the issue of integrity, that is on the need to recognize that these various strands of reporting, storytelling and representation need to be understood as part of a single media environment, some would call it a media ecology. This totality is constituted – notwithstanding the various strains to convergence, contradiction and conflict within them, the multiple and overlapping networks of local, national and global communication, and the manifest and persistent inequalities of power – as a single entity by its very presence, and increasingly by the ease with which all parts of it can be accessed. In the context of the arguments of this book as a whole the issue becomes one of the integrity of the processes of communication and mediation; the integrity of voice and response, and of the potential or actual mutuality of tolerance, reciprocity and responsibility in the communications we have with others and they with us. I will return to the question of media integrity at the end of this chapter.

Analytically the issue – hardly new for the social sciences – is that between the whole and its parts, and the expectation that we have a responsibility to make some sense of the complexities of the world in which we and others live alongside each other, a world in which mediated communication has become a *sine qua non* of everyday social life. Politically the issue – equally well trodden – is how to create and sustain a mediated public space in a world scarred by communication failure as well as, and ironically, by its very success. And morally and ethically the issue, one that I have already begun to try and address, is to clarify and communicate the criteria according to which that public space, the plural public space of the mediapolis, can both be enabled and sustained.

Hannah Arendt returns as a touchstone. She has tellingly observed that:

> To live together in the world means essentially that a world of things is between those who have it in common, as a table is located between those who sit around it; the world, like every in-between, relates and separates men at the same time.
>
> The public realm, as the common world, gathers us together and yet prevents our falling over each other. (Arendt 1998: 52).

At the core of this dialectic of relating and separating, indeed the axis on which the whole of mediated communication turns, is the stranger: that other whose presence or absence is crucial for our own sense of self and in relation to whom identities and communities are created and sustained. Arendt points to the possibility of the public space offering in turn the possibility of a shareable difference, an integrity which is premised on the commonness of our situation (the world in which we live), and at the same time on the distinctiveness of our place in it. Translated into the terms of the media, and in the context of the present discussion, this becomes the distinctiveness of voices, and the integrity of both the harmony and discord which both emerges and is presupposed by their coming together.

The contrapuntal

Edward Said (Said 1994; 2001), on a number of occasions and in a number of different contexts, refers to the contrapuntal as a metaphor for addressing the structured complexity both of his own experience of exile and of the nature, principally, of the novel in nineteenth-century, imperial, France and Britain. The fusing of both experience and cultural work in this one framing metaphor is instructive and enabling, for it brings together the two strands of my own analysis, and the two dimensions of the mediapolis. The contrapuntal speaks to the inevitable, continuous and significant juxtaposition of elements and threads in a life, a text, a history, and to the necessity for an analytic which confronts that juxtaposition and deconstructs it.

Counterpoint is defined in a fifteenth-century musical treatise as follows:

> Counterpoint is a moderate and reasonable concord which arises when one tone is placed opposite another, from which also the term *contrapunctus*, that is 'note against note', can be derived. Counterpoint is therefore a combination of tones. If this combination or mixture sounds sweetly to the ears, it is called *consonance*; if, on the other hand, it sounds harsh and unpleasant, it is called *dissonance* . . . (Tinctoris, *Liber de Arte Contrapuncti*, 1477, <http://www.contrapunctus.com/contrapunctus.htm>

This is obviously a term which emerges from the distinctiveness of western musical culture, and may have little relevance to others. Nevertheless the key idea is the presence in a single discourse of more than one voice. In such a musical discourse the individual tones or voices only gain meaning from their presence alongside each other. The relationship between these voices (or musical lines) is open, dynamic and fluid such that the dominant (the proper voice leading) is never singular or secure; it can become sub-dominant, fading and then reviving as the music progresses. Indeed the sub-dominant voice or voices can be present even in their inaudibility, and so they can, and do, shape the final musical score by their influence – a kind of dominance in absentia. The relationship is always in musical tension. The whole, that is the composition as a whole, does not exist without their co-presence, and each musical thread contributes to that whole and gains its specific significance only in its relationship to the other threads or themes within it. Indeed their interrelationship can create both consonance and dissonance, though which may well depend on the sensitivities of the listener, and dissonance may be either intended or pleasant, or both (Nicholls 1990).

The important thing is that every theme requires another in order to be meaningful, and that the relationship between such themes or elements creates the 'music' of the whole, its polyphony. In a more sociological or philosophical register, the contrapuntal signals the ever and necessary presence of the other, the stranger, in time and space, as a point of reference and as an irredeemable contribution to the significance of the present, of the here, the now and the self. It also signals both the presence of, and the necessity for, a multiplicity of voices, the mediapolis's own polyphony, its plurality. The relationship between themes within a contrapuntal text is always a political one. One theme will always be dominant, but it will not necessarily remain so; the play of sound depends on that of theme and variation. In the political culture of the mediapolis, such themes and variations constrained by the realities of economic and political power are nevertheless available and visible above all (but by no means exclusively) in the consumption of media, as audiences and users as participants in that culture shift their attention and interest from one voice to another. But they are also present in the changing balance of power between the dominant and sub-dominant media voices, a balance of power that, as I have already identified, comes with changing technologies and the changing cultures.

The contrapuntal appears in Said's work in a number of places and in a number of guises. So much so that it might appear to be, even in its inconsistencies (there are at least five or possibly six different ways in which he uses the term), an *idée fixe* in his work as a whole. There is an inevitable but productive tension between his sense of his life as contrapuntal, a life in exile, where the metaphor addresses a substantive reality, and the text as contrapuntal, where the metaphor addresses a critical approach, a way of seeing and analysing. In both cases the dialectic is between presence and absence, a familiar one by now in the context of mediation. And in both cases the dialectic is that between the part and the whole, the singular and the plural, as I have just tried to explain.

The starting point, then, is Said's description of his own status as an exile. Being in exile has some compensations, as well as its obvious pain. Both follow from the experience of seeing 'the entire world as a foreign land'. Exilic vision is always plural, generating an awareness of simultaneous dimensions of culture. Said's primary characterization of the contrapuntal is, therefore, experiential:

> For an exile, habits of life, expression, or activity in the new environment inevitably occur against the memory of these things in another environment. Thus both the new and the old environments are vivid, actual, occurring together contrapuntally. There is a unique pleasure in this sort of apprehension, especially if the exile is conscious of other contrapuntal juxtapositions that diminish orthodox judgement and elevate appreciative sympathy. There is also a particular sense of achievement in acting as if one were at home wherever one happens to be. . . .
>   . . . Exile is life led outside habitual order. It is nomadic, decentred, contrapuntal; but no sooner does one get accustomed to it than its unsettling force erupts anew. (Said 2001: 186)

The exile is in a constant state of suspension, now floating, now submerging, on the sea of culture, and the contrapuntal expresses that state of suspension and dispersion. But this metaphor for the specific experience of exile extends into his substantive analyses of culture and text. And it does so in a number of dimensions, all of which can be found in his *Culture and Imperialism* (Said 1994; Said 2003).

The first is the dimension of culture as such in which the contrapuntal appears as a way of identifying both identity and history as ensembles. 'No identity,' he argues, 'can ever exist by itself and without an array of opposites' (Said 1994: xxviii), and histories are similarly coeval and co-existing even in their differences and discrepancies. However it is his literary theory and his analyses of the text, above all the novel, which provide the most direct application of the idea of the contrapuntal, both as a claim about the real world and as a way of seeing that world.

One further quote, therefore, from him:

> As we look back at the cultural archive, we begin to reread it not univocally, but *contrapuntally*, with a simultaneous awareness both of the metropolitan history that is narrated and of those histories against which

(and altogether with which) the dominating discourse acts. In the counterpoint of Western classical music, various themes play off one another, with only a provisional privilege being given to any particular one; yet in the resulting polyphony there is concert and order, an organized interplay that derives from the themes, not from a rigorous melodic or formal principle outside the work. In the same way we can read and interpret English novels, for example, whose engagement (usually suppressed for the most part) with the West Indies or India, say, is shaped and perhaps even determined by the specific history of colonization resistance, and finally native nationalism. At this point alternative or new narratives emerge, and they become institutionalised or discursively stable entities (Said 1994: 59).

The generic argument is that literary texts both are, and therefore must be read as, contrapuntal. And indeed contrapuntality, if there is such a word, emerges as a product of the reading rather than writing, since the writer might not be aware of the otherness against which she is writing.[3] The contrapuntal appears to exist in three dimensions of such texts. It first of all consists in the sociologically identifiable subtexts present, even in their absence, in the novels, for example, of the late eighteenth, nineteenth and even twentieth century (Jane Austen, Joseph Conrad and Albert Camus are key figures in his canon, and imperialism is the key subtext). A contrapuntal reading, for example, would bring to light the significance of the barely concealed imperial trade that sustains the wealth and comfort in, for example, Jane Austen's *Mansfield Park* or *Persuasion*.[4]

But the contrapuntal also consists in the presence of oppositional and resistant writing, which in a colonial and post-colonial environment appears against but also alongside that of the mainstream.[5] And finally the contrapuntal appears as a way of characterizing the process of reading in which novels are read again and read differently as time passes and cultures change. The significance of the contrapuntal lies in its doubling (or trebling or quadrupling), and the presumption is made that there is an identifiable integrity which is constituted, but at the same time disturbed, by that doubling.

Each of these various manifestations of the way in which a literary text can be read constitutes a political act. The reader reads both with and against the grain of the text, and as such it is that both writing and reading, but not always in the same way, are contrapuntal: the manifest text which is itself always the product of a not always audible or visible political context is informed and changed by the location and the activity of reading it. So too in our current mediated environment, where its texts – the news reports, the game shows, reality television, the mainstream, the niche and the alternative – each offer an account of the world, both serious and playful, which makes a claim on the world's attention. They contribute, both in relation to each other, and in the product of the audience's more or less literate response to them, a mediated environment which requires a degree of media literacy for that environment, the mediapolis, both to work well and to generate a recognition of its value. I return to the importance of media literacy in the last chapter.

So there is clearly an epistemology at work here. It is constituted against various kinds of essentialism, and depends, to a degree, on the absence as Said puts it, of an 'Archimedean point' (Said 1994) outside culture, some vantage point from which to observe without being a participant. This is all relatively familiar (Hannah Arendt makes the same point), though still important, and has a very specific relevance in the context of the analysis of media culture from which none of us can escape. Most significant, however, is the assertion of the distinctiveness of the contrapuntal as a way of approaching questions of cultural difference and cultural process which in turn avoids the essentializing fusions of hybridity theory and the inevitability of synthesis and resolution embodied in many notions of Marxian dialectic.

Each of these latter interventions in cultural and social theory addresses the problematic of difference and contradiction, both in the realms of everyday life and in reflections on those realms or against them in literature or art or music (or in the case of Hegel and Marx in the dynamics of history and the socio-economic system as a whole). Each recognizes something of the dialogical, but each presumes some kind of resolution: hybridity in the emergence of a new cultural entity, fusing elements of previously discrete cultural identities; dialectic in a new synthesis formed through the clash of contradiction between elements of the old.[6]

Mikhail Bakhtin (Bakhtin 1984), on the other hand, in his analysis of Rabelaisian culture and the social significance of the carnival as a dialogue of difference, perhaps comes closest to the idea of the contrapuntal, insofar as he neither presupposes nor insists on a resolution of cultural difference and conflict, on the emergence of a new whole. And he also constructs a space for complex cultural interactions visible both in the texts and in the practices of reading them. This is not too far removed, albeit in a different register, from Said's approach to literature, one which, I have just suggested, insists on a constancy of interaction between text and reader, between what is written and what is disguised or invisible in the text, and between presence and absence in both texts and the reading of them.

Thinking about the contrapuntal in its various manifestations, in the literary text, in reading, and as I now wish to do, as a structural component of contemporary culture and its mediation, involves the recognition of a dynamic of representation and reading (of media production and consumption) which is both plural and singular. If we do not recognize the plural we significantly distort the reality of the present-day media world. If we do not recognize its singularity we lose sight of the media's significance. The presence in one social or cultural space of hundreds and thousands of individual voices does not imply dialogue between them. And we know well that the mediapolis is a space of both (one to many) dissemination and (interactive) dialogue (Peters 1999). We also know well how unequal and how unjust it is: with freedoms to speak and above all to be heard being denied to many. Yet, and there has to be a yet, a recognition of the presence and increasing accessibility of its multiple threads (broadcast programmes, websites, home pages) and of the importance of this multiplicity for the quality of both private (individual) and public life is a precondition for any enlightened approach to the significance of global media.

Some of these quite abstract arguments can be illustrated and explored through a discussion of some recent research on minority media in Europe.[7]

Media and minorities in Europe

This research offers an empirical approach to the study of mediation, in which the media (print, broadcast, computer, and various network technologies) intervene in the processes of individual and institutional communication and provide a framework for the transmission and reception, and appropriation, of meanings in public and private, local, national and global settings (Silverstone 1999; Silverstone 2005). It addresses both components of mediation, that of production and reception, in their necessary interrelationship. And it says, hopefully, some new things about mediation as it involves audiences and users as participants, in this case as members of migrant and minority groups, making and communicating meaning as they engage with the endless flow of images and texts that are a significant component of their everyday lives.

The research is therefore a study of mediation in the everyday lives of these producers and users of media, and it is pursued in relation to contemporary, principally ethnic, minorities' engagement with local, national and transnational media in the nation states of the European Union and in relation to those states' policies on multiculturalism (Georgiou 2005).

We identify and discuss the minorities themselves through a series of national mapping exercises and individual case studies, and we find some 75 distinct groups or communities among recent as well as well established minorities with populations of over 1000 in the 15 member states of the EU.[8] We discuss and analyse their media and their media practices. The groups themselves vary significantly in size, composition, culture and history. The focus of the research is on the presence of distinct media in these groups' everyday lives and on the consequences of their engagement with those media, as well as with mainstream national and global media, for an understanding of their inclusion and exclusion in their host society. The focus is also on the ways in which the full range of media to which they had access (from their own press and radio, to national broadcasting, satellite television from their countries of recent or distant origin, and the World Wide Web) enable or disable their efforts to build identity and community within and also beyond the boundaries of national culture and contribute to, or ameliorate, their experiences of exclusion.

Perhaps the most important thing to indicate is that mediation is contextualized and that minorities engage with their media in ways that are more complex and more layered than one might imagine. So from the point of view of these groups, minorities outside the social and cultural mainstream, their media are not just national, and not even then simply so but also local and transnational.[9]

The first of the *local* contexts is that of the city. It involves accessing and participating in media and communication via the use of neighbourhood telephone, internet or video hire centres. These environments, which are sometimes more or less exclusive to specific ethnic groups, for example neighbourhood internet cafés, and sometimes local authority-provided urban facilities heavily used by minorities (for example public access internet in libraries or community centres), provide both mediated and lived social and cultural resources in what might otherwise be (and probably for many would still be) denied to them because they would be seen to be beyond reach or appropriateness.

The second of the local media contexts is provided by cultural and multicultural media outlets and projects, the first of which are quite specific, linguistically and culturally. They might comprise, though often ephemerally and with extremely limited circulations, print (newspaper and journal) publications, and sometimes also radio and cable television. One version of this localism in media production and consumption, though normally the product of a national broadcasting initiative, involves the presence of multicultural broadcasting, which brings together on a single spectrum and often as the result of national or at least top-down policy making, an integrated 'public service' of multiple ethnic programming. Examples include Couleur Locale in Belgium, Radio Multikulti in Germany, Colourful Radio in the Netherlands and Sesam in Sweden). Here of course the local is linked directly to national initiatives.

Indeed the presence of such integrated minority-oriented media, particularly in broadcasting, is hugely dependent on the national policy context in which the presence of minorities is or is not recognized, and where minorities' desire for mediated cultural expression is or is not supported. There are substantial variations in the ways in which governments provide such support, and these variations are reflected in the number and intensity of minority media in their countries, though such variations are, of course, also a reflection of the economic, political and numerical strength of each of the individual minorities. So, for example, the Netherlands and Sweden, the two countries with the most developed multicultural policy framework in relation to the media, had at the time of the research the richest array of minority media. In a world where minorities have limited financial resources and political influence, this should hardly come as a surprise. It should also be pointed out that many of the most recent of the refugee communities in Europe have no media of their own, their media invisibility both reflecting and reinforcing their marginality or exclusion in the societies in which they find themselves.

There is a second national context, of course, that provided by the mainstream press and media, where, in the ordinary course of events, minorities are unlikely to find themselves satisfactorily represented, either as subjects or participants. This relative invisibility is often the catalyst for efforts to generate both an increased presence in the mainstream but also to encourage governments to recognize and support minority media in such a way as to provide greater access for them on national spectra and frequencies. There are different ways in which such national presence can be claimed.

The first is through direct visibility, both in the presence of members of ethnic groups in mainstream media as journalists, as well as soap opera characters and in the transmission of ethnically distinctive situation comedies and other programming; or through the presence, for example in the weekly *Perşembe* supplement in the German daily *Die Tageszeitung* during 2000, of a discrete culturally specific mediated communication within that same mainstream. The second is through a mediated communication, for example the website New Vision, which was run (it seems now to have disappeared) by members of the Ethiopian community in Britain both for their own community and for the wider group of nation-based refugees and refugee rights activists across the country, and which sought, from the bottom-up as it were, a wider audience than that defined by the ethnicity of its producers. The final expression of this kind of national local hybrid, also in the UK, might be that of London Greek Radio which offers, in Greek, information for a national Greek audience on rights and social services available to them (and others) across the nation. The BBC Asian Network in the UK, it should also be noted, currently broadcasts a 24-hour radio schedule, including programmes in Bengali, Gujarati, Hindi, Urdu, Punjabi and Mirpuri, as well as in (and predominantly) English.

It is clear, however, that minority media are not exhausted either by the local or the national and indeed it is the transnational that provides an increasingly compelling context for media consumption, particularly for relatively recent migrants. There are two dimensions to this relatively recent globalization. The first is the presence of satellite television transmitted from, for want of a better term, the homeland. Once again the availability of such channels varies hugely across cultures, as does their significance for those displaced.[10] There were, for example, at the time of the study some thirty Arabic satellite channels available across Europe (not including those from North Africa), some thirty-six Turkish channels, and an increasing number of channels from Russia, Poland and the ex-Soviet states, as well as some eight Hindu channels and twenty Spanish and Portuguese channels originating in South America, a smaller number of Western European Channels, though few, other than Arabic channels, from Africa. There are indications, however, that communities, especially those with limited resources and from countries which are likewise economically weak and with limited or no access to transnational television, are increasingly using the internet as an alternative medium for the connection with home as well as with others from their communities similarly globally dispersed.

Indeed, the internet is fast becoming a distinct and significant choice for communication within diasporic communities. Low costs of access and maintenance enable the rapid growth of on-line diasporic news and information sites, hosted by the displaced as well as by those in home societies. These are supplemented by specific search engines, for example the one dedicated to Spanish and Latin American websites hosted in Belgium. The information and news sites are remarkably convergent across cultures, and most are bilingual. Sites are also sometimes positioned as oppositional not so much to the mainstream media of the host country, but to the established voices emanating from their homeland or regions of origin. There are a number of Arabic sites that conform to this description, but they are not unique.

There are, then, a number of general points to be made arising from this study.

The first, I hope now obviously, is the need to recognize the diversity of minority media available to minority audiences in Europe, that is media produced specifically with the minority as the principal addressee. This diversity is of course neither uniform nor consistent. And it is certainly vulnerable to the exigencies of changing policy, the collapse of even the minimal amounts of financial support that individual minority media need to survive, and to other eventualities. These media do not often have a very long shelf-life and their availability varies significantly between communities, depending on their political clout, the money they can raise and their cultural confidence.

It needs to be clear that the availability of such media, their own media, does not imply that these are the only media that minorities will access. Choices are made, often in an intensely iterative way, as users switch between mainstream media and their own, especially at times of national or cultural crisis (Matar 2005). Choices in media use can be and are made, constrained as they will always be by language and culture. Such variations in access and participation, such variations in the individual pattern of media use are also the result of the differences in gender and in generation. In many minority cultures the women are still more tied, both by culture and language, to the domestic and consequently have a stronger attachment to traditional culture and therefore to whatever they can find of their own media. In almost all minority communities the shift across the generations, as those born in the host society have to manage the borders between the culture of their parents and the culture of their peers, suggests that for them too the patterns of media consumption and production will be radically different. It will be much more closely aligned to their mainstream, in either a kind of contrapuntal (that is a switching between cultures) or hybrid (that is a fusing of cultures) way.

The presence and availability of national mainstream media, the national mainstream media of the host society, is crucial.

They define empirically, that is through the experiences and practices of minority audiences, and conceptually, as I intend to argue, the context within which minority media have to be understood. Minorities with distinct languages and cultures, pasts and presents, have access to a wider range of media than those of a more sedentary or linguistically challenged cast. Indeed they are not only addressed by their own media and by the generic broadcast mainstream, but have access too to what is left of the old 'imperial' media, the BBC World Service, Die Welt, Voice of America and in another mode the English language Al Jazeera and Al Hurra (the US channel broadcasting in Arabic to the Middle East).

In the same way, though obviously in an asymmetrical way, the presence of minority media in a given society now has to be seen as a context for understanding the mainstream, even for those audiences or institutions who are not aware of the presence of minority media in their national (or transnational) media cultures or in their own patterns of consumption. Minority media may be relatively invisible within a national media culture, just as minorities themselves may be invisible on the screens of the mainstream (other than, as so often, in negative representations), but that invisibility does not erode, and cannot deny, their presence. Both minorities and their media exist as a continuous subtext, occasionally appearing in, and being acknowledged by, occasionally challenging, occasionally defining and transcending, the dominance of the mainstream: Al Jazeera and other Arab stations, given the context of the present polarization around Islam, are, once again, perhaps the most significant cases in point. The presence of minority media and the participation of minority audiences and users with them signals the significantly diverse integrity of contemporary media culture, whether this is constructed at a local, national or global level.

Two further issues follow from these observations. The first has to do with the role of the media in the diasporic experience, the second has to do with how we might come to understand European media culture or perhaps more realistically the media cultures of the nation-states within Europe.[11]

It is easy to romanticize the role of the media in the lives of migrants, just as it is easy to reify notions of diaspora (Anthias 1998). The everyday lives of displaced minorities suffer, in a great many respects, the strains of displacement, the consequences of their experience of forced or voluntary mobility, or usually a complex and sometimes tragic mixture of both. The everyday lives of minorities are also marked by significant differences, not just between the well established and the recently arrived, the wealthy and the poor, the politically free and the politically repressed, but also within themselves between the traditionalists and the modernizers and, as I have just discussed, between the genders and the generations.

Their everyday lives also reveal how limited a role, often, the media have in those lives, given the material challenges of finding home, work and education (though for many, especially first-generation immigrant women, the media are very likely to play a very significant role).

Media do have, however, a double and sometimes contrary significance, offering to diasporic groups various competing cultural spaces and alternative imaginaries, which are constructed in relation both to the national host-land and, in many cases, the national homeland.[12] To talk of identity and community in this context is perhaps premature, for processes of identification are continuous, contradictory and unstable both within and across gender and generation; and community-building, for the most part, remains at the level of the imagined.[13]

Minority media, both in the form of the culturally specific and the national mainstream, provide alternate and interwoven resources for sharing experiences across time and space. In their consumption dislocation shades into location-seeking and the challenging experience of the present connects into memories of the past and dreams of the future. Media, particularly those of the country of settlement, provide continuous challenges to the integrity and dignity of minority cultures, both in their failure to include positive images, their reluctance to employ minority personnel, or simply in terms of the minority's complete invisibility. Though it is of course the case these mainstream media too, both broadcast and on-line, provide much in the way of practical resources, in the form of information, support and shareable commentary, in news, soap opera or talk show, on the containing minutiae of everyday life in a strange land.

It is perhaps worth pausing briefly to consider some of the implications of these observations for the present and future of public service broadcasting, particularly, but by no means exclusively, in the UK. It is clear that the conditions under which such broadcasting operates are changing. These conditions are both social and technological. And the two, for the most part, are, unsurprisingly, moving in the same direction. Their convergence is enabling a world of increasing geographical mobility, increasing social differentiation, increasing media connectivity, increasing religious polarization, increasing fluidity of culture and identity, increasing alienation from dominant institutions, increasing individuality, increasing globalization, increasing parochiality. One primary consequence of all these developments is that what constitutes the national bit of British Broadcasting is no longer what it was. Above all what follows is that any notion of Britishness can no longer be contained or understood without its contextualization in something that might be called, contra-puntally, non-Britishness.

Of course diversity, difference and mobility are not new. And the BBC in its early years and throughout the twentieth century, as other public broadcasters elsewhere would also have done, saw its role as providing a cultural, civic and political space in which that diversity, pre-eminently of class and region (the BBC's first major crisis was the General Strike), could be restructured into a national and unified culture. In doing so it offered an *umbrella* for the nation. It protected those underneath it from the storms of difference and, during wartime especially, from the storms generated by other societies and other values. Sheltering under it the British people recognized something of their commonness, their com-munity and at least in theory (and to a degree also in practice) they put aside many of their differences.

There is, I would suggest, no longer any possibility of this kind of shelter. The high winds of social, cultural and technological change have blown the umbrella inside out, and the BBC can no longer keep out the rain. What is required now is something much more like a *raft*: a raft which provides safety and connectivity on a stormy sea; a raft which can move with the political and economic tides and the currents; and a raft which essentially (with its various bits and pieces) provides the resources necessary for those on it to survive and ultimately prosper culturally, civically and civilly. Being on a raft rather than under an umbrella forces those involved to recognize their shared predicament, their need to come to terms with their differences as well as their similarities, but places responsibility much more in their own hands.

The challenge, arguably, for the BBC and for other media oriented towards public service or national readership is how to construct this raft. British audiences, and of course not just ethnic minority audiences, as consumers or as citizens or indeed as both, have already begun to make the distancing cultural choices, and engaging with a rapidly diversifying media environment in ways that have broken away from their depend-ence on even a small number of broadcasters, though arguably towards an increased dependence on the media as a whole. Such cultural, but not technological, independence inevitably leads to disengagement. What audiences and media users appear therefore to need (even if they don't realize it – and it is unlikely that the population of the United Kingdom in 1922 realized they needed the BBC then either) is a range of mediated cultural supports and above all resources which will re-engage their active participation in their society, a society which is no longer bounded by the shoreline, and which will enable the recognition of their shared condition and their shared future.[14] There is a salient difference here between what is shared and what is common, and possibly too, between an orientation to the future as opposed to the past. A shared future is, plausibly, a more appropriate foundation for this civic culture, and indeed for the mediapolis, than a common past.

Mediating the contrapuntal

This brings me back to the contrapuntal. And I have a number of points to make.

To start with the nature of the experience of migration, which is where I believe Said starts too. Migration is a process that unfolds in space. The *here I am* is always connected to and made meaningful by, especially, the presence of the elsewhere, the somewhere else, especially by the present absence of home. In this, the experience of diasporic space is arguably contrapuntal. Migration is also a process that unfolds in time. The time of the here and now is always connected to, and made meaningful by, the presence of the past; perhaps, at least for first generations, the time of home, the time of origins, but also the time of the future. The experience of diasporic time is therefore also contrapuntal. My life as a first- or second- or third-generation immigrant, my own relationship to the others in the face-to-face and the mediated worlds which I now inhabit gains its significance in its relationship to the cultures that I have both left and perhaps aspire to. Biography and history co-exist in an often uneasy contrapuntal relationship.[15] Diasporic cultures can only be understood in their relationship to the multiple contexts of cultures that are both present and absent (Ganguly 2001).

But this relationship of integrity and difference is also visible in the realm of media culture, and insofar as mediated culture is a *sine qua non* of culture, in relation to the nature of our distinctly contemporary culture as a whole. Perhaps, as I have been at pains to argue in this chapter, this is most clearly evident in the relationship between mainstream and minority media (but it is also present in the relationship between different minority media). Here the point is quite a simple one too; it is that the two cannot be understood apart from each other. Minority media claim their space and gain their significance in relation to, against or alongside, the mainstream; but equally (though much more contentiously) the mainstream media themselves will have to be understood in their increasingly visible and contested (political and economic as well as cultural) relationships with minority media.

There is a technological dimension to this of course. As I have already noted, the new media technologies are offering in various guises the possibility of both creating alternate if not alternative media spaces, on-line and in the telephonic exchange of speech, texts, still images and video. They are also offering a degree, indeed a high degree, of personal mobility, in such a way as that, for these groups at least, the mobility of migration is reinforced by the capacity to be on the move not just between countries but between territories.

Released from the fixed lines and solitary domestic screen, media culture is fracturing and distancing itself from the singularity of the mainstream, but it is also finding new ways of engaging with that mainstream, in its interactivity with it, in the form of textual choices, on-line purchasing, or perhaps most significantly, especially in times of crisis, in the submission of video and still images gathered on the mobile phone and submitted to news agencies and broadcasters for their immediate onward 'live' transmission. There is a political and economic dimension to this fragmentation and diversification too, of course. The convergence of the personal and the political, once the banner of feminism, has now become a reality, which has meant what many would suggest is the decline of the political, especially a withdrawal from the established and still modestly potent spaces of official politics and public discourse. There is a weakening, too, in the confidence which established media can feel in relation to their hold on the market as new entrants continue to challenge their twentieth-century security as dominant players (this goes for the established mainstream in press and broadcasting as it does for the established transnational enterprises in the new media marketplace).

This is, to a significant extent, a global story. And it is perhaps even more consistently a European one. And given this I am suggesting that the mediapolis as it is expressed in Europe and in European states is contrapuntal. Its component parts, the distinct, as well as the relatively indistinct, mediated voices and presences within the European media together define an often unstable and contested territory, where relations of domination and subordination seem, for the most part, clearly defined and well entrenched. Yet those relationships are constantly changing, and in their changes – in relation to their relative audibility, visibility and their different audiences – they constitute a whole.[16]

More specifically, we can only grasp the meaning of a particular minority media initiative, and assess its significance, in its relationship to the presence of other media and media texts which it either addresses, contradicts or seeks to bypass. And, likewise, we can only grasp the meaning of dominant mainstream media insofar as we register their contrapuntal relationship to the experiences, voices and practices of both the included and excluded (but still present) minorities. These will, as often as not, draw on and in the sounds, images and values from outside the boundaries of the national. And in so doing, of course, they draw on, or deny, other mainstreams. The emergent mediapolis within Europe is a diverse but integrated space, both discordant and concordant, and one in which voices are still repressed and denied. Yet it is, already, a very different one from what it was as little as twenty years ago. The metaphor of the contrapuntal enables us to recognize the significance of those changes and, arguably, devise those policies, in the development of new forms of literacy as well as new forms of regulation, which will enable more voices to be spoken and heard.

There are two points, finally, I want to make about the generality of both national and European mediated environments. The first is that they are both fluid and contested. They are a commons, even if much of the commons is enclosed by the dominant media players. Indeed they are potentially a global, cosmopolitan, commons, a commons which no longer has clear boundaries although one which is not evenly or indeed fairly, or justly, available to all.

In such an environment voices are heard but so is silence, and indeed some voices are actually, consistently and unacceptably silenced. Minority media are increasingly central to that environment, even in their present marginality, and their capacity (and willingness) both to address their own communities but also to speak to the majority is a core, and will become an increasingly fundamental, part of public culture. But likewise, and even more fundamentally, are the responsibilities of the mainstream media, in their capacity to recognize cultural difference and to create the space for it to be heard. Such recognition would involve, if it is to have any meaning, a commitment to offering media hospitality to the stranger, and to make available a portion of time and spectrum for his or her voice. I discuss the issue of hospitality in chapter 6.

The second point follows, and it is merely to draw attention to the hopefully creative novelty in framing this discussion through auditory metaphors rather than visual ones. I have been talking sound and music, though not necessarily harmony. The contrapuntal invites us to listen, and to listen differently, attentively, sympathetically, but also critically, to the play of voices, to a mediated soundscape that expresses, in its simultaneity, a constant and unresolved play of discourse, narrative and expression. There is harmony in this soundscape; but there is also discord; we need both even if we long only for the former: the 'sounds and sweet airs, that give delight, and hurt not'. I will have more to say about the justice of being heard also in chapter 6.

This discussion is not of course one that stops with an understanding of institutional relationships, nor is it one that can in any way be divorced from a concern with the political, with the relationships of power between the various institutionalized or semi-institutionalized voices. Media are only significant insofar as they generate meaning. And meanings are constructed in representational space, and through the presence and absence of distinct images and narratives. It is in these images and narratives, as well as in their exclusion from them, that media are inscribed into the hegemonic struggle (perhaps the bottom line, ground base of the contrapuntal) that cultures always manifest and mask. But it is also in these images and narratives that the significance of the other as the defining reference for an understanding of contemporary mediated culture emerges. It is to this issue and to some of the wider implications of my discussion of minority media, that I now, finally, wish to turn and to return.

Informing the moral agenda

The contrapuntal speaks to both an empirical reality, the presence in a given social and cultural space of many voices, and an epistemological position, a way of seeing that world as defined and only understandable through the interrelationship of self and other, of similarity and difference. Said's contrapuntal occupies similar intellectual territory to the less specific but equally insistent arguments in favour of pluralism with which this book began.

The stress on otherness, its presence, its absence and its character, is crucial. But the contrapuntal as a metaphor and a heuristic for the analysis of contemporary mediated culture, and as a precondition of an effective mediapolis, has a further significance: one that goes beyond substance and epistemology. Our relation to the other, to the stranger, is the principal determinant of our moral worth and our status as human beings. Since, as I have already argued, our media provide the most pervasive and persuasive perceptual frameworks, in an increasingly global society, for the way in which meanings, representations and relationships to the other are offered and defined; since these media representations, in their consistency and in their power, tend to delegitimate and marginalize other kinds of framings; and since, in so doing, they define the asymmetries, hierarchies, presences and absences of public space, then the contrapuntal relationships of self and other, of minority and majority, of minority and mainstream, and of the distant and the close at hand, become increasingly material as the foundation for contemporary public life and for the articulation of its moral order and disorder.

To a degree the media both reflect as well as represent something of the cosmopolitan in which, as I suggested in my opening chapter, the other is no longer just beyond but is alongside and within us. Indeed this is a world (which for Ulrich Beck is something of a brave new one) in which Europe seems to be in the vanguard:

> For one thing [it is impossible] to deny the reality of the roughly seventeen million people living in the EU who are unable to accept [an] ethnocultural definition of European-ness on account of being Muslims and/or people of colour, but who nonetheless understand and organise themselves culturally and politically, as Europeans. For another it is [impossible not to] to recognise Europe as a microcosm of global society . . . In the face of growing transnational interconnections and obligations, Europe is turning into an open network with blurring boundaries, where the outside is always already inside (Beck 2003: 238).

Beck's vision is appealing. It may even be accurate. But it underestimates the dark side, not just of prejudice, but of the hardship of what I have called elsewhere minor cosmopolitanism (Silverstone 1999). And it is of course yet to appear fully in the mediapolis. However, I would argue, notwithstanding all the qualifications in the world, that the contrapuntal pluralism that I have been discussing in this chapter is a reality, if still an embryonic one. But it is a precondition for the future of the mediapolis and in turn for the future of civil society in Europe.

The ways in which the media present and represent the other are central, now, to the formation of the morality of the world. They are crucial to the future of the human condition. The images and voices of the other are routinely present (but just as often absent) in both the detail of nightly news reporting and constant advertising and, more visibly and intensively, in the reporting of wars and catastrophes. They are also present in, and significantly result from, the media's national and international institutional arrangements and in the politics surrounding minority media and minorities in media. In this context the contrapuntal shifts from an analytic to a normative category, with the result that we are encouraged to question, but required also to judge, the ways, and the consequences of the ways, in which the stranger appears or disappears in contemporary media.

But it is not just a question of appearance or disappearance. I have been arguing, both implicitly and explicitly, given the musical metaphor, for the importance of being heard. And being heard requires not just sound but meaning. It requires understanding.

Charles Husband makes this case eloquently (Husband 2000). Husband's argument is solidly grounded within liberal theory, and he accepts the inevitability and desirability of differentiated citizenship. His position extends that of Jürgen Habermas in order to construct a claim for the establishment of a multicultural public sphere in which a right to communicate is replaced by what he suggests is *a right to be understood*. He draws too on Stuart Hall's use of the term *différance*, which proposes a weaving of cultural similarities and differences which are constantly changing, with no single origin, and only recognizable in the shifting and unstable, but mutually defining, interrelationships of self and other. The presence of such a plurality of voices is, in his view, substantially meaningless, unless they are heard and understood.

In making these arguments Husband also specifies, and endorses, a wider range of new responsibilities that citizens as well as states need to accept in a complex mediated space. He finds in the new media, as well as in the survival of public service broadcasting, enough to sustain a hope that the future will enable ethnic minorities to find a voice in this mediated public sphere, notwithstanding the pain of any transition from a politics of singular national culture to a politics of the recognition of diversity, and the correlative refusal of both universalism and multiculturalism as the bases for public culture. Husband believes that what he proposes as a multiethnic public sphere may be utopian but that it is not futile. What it lacks in his own account of it, however, is a clear sense of how it might be structured. It misses an analysis of how communication across difference might take place, and how such a sphere might be understood as reaching beyond the rationalities of liberal and post-liberal theory, to encompass the tensions between global and local action and ethnic and national identity, as well as their representation in local, national, regional and global media.

These are questions that I try and address in the last three chapters of this book, in the discussions of the centrality of media in everyday life and the possibilities for active response by audiences and users; in the search for media justice and hospitality and, finally, in the role that both regulation and literacy might play in enabling the maturation of the mediapolis.

The mediapolis, however embryonically, is now emerging as a complex moral space of presence and absence; distance and closeness; but also responsibility, reciprocity, dignity and trust. These are the dimensions of media that will now assume their place as central for an understanding of mediation and the exercise of media power in late modernity.

My continued gnawing at the normative is not without its significant, but obvious, dangers, of course. But it is required by the increasing globalization of mediated representations and the increasing salience of, and dependence on, these mediated representations in the everyday life of those otherwise distanced (and that is most of us most of the time) from the everyday life of others.

Perhaps I can return to the quotation from Hannah Arendt's *The Human Condition* that I cited at the beginning of this chapter. It continues as follows:

> What makes mass society so difficult to bear is not the number of people involved, or at least not primarily, but the fact that the world between them has lost its power to gather them together, to relate and to separate them. The weirdness of this situation resembles a spiritualistic séance where a number of people gathered around a table might suddenly, through some magic trick, see the table vanish from their midst, so that two persons sitting opposite each other were no longer separated but also would be entirely unrelated to each other by anything tangible. (Arendt 1998: 52–3)

Arendt's disappearing table destroys the necessary and proper distance between self and other (Silverstone 2003). It is, though she does not refer directly to it as such, a mediated table (indeed séances are media, and someone who conducts a séance is referred to as a medium). The counterpoint of relating and separating, so crucial for the operation for an effective and humane public space is, in Arendt's formulation, dependent on the presence of a technology, material and objective, which provides a framework for publicness which is common, but shared by those, and indeed can only be effectively shared by those, who at the same time acknowledge and respect each other's difference. Such a public world must, in her view, have a life beyond the generations. The challenge she poses is that of being able to confront present media through an analysis which privileges, if not an ideal world, at least a world from whose perspective the present one falls short. But it is also one which highlights something perhaps we know already, but now must address in earnest: the capacity of media both to undermine, as well as constitute the possibility of, communication.

The contrapuntal provides a way of approaching the emergent structure of the mediapolis, an infrastructure of parallel, separate but connecting threads of expression and identity, which in their occupation of a common space, at the very least, define some of the parameters of the space of appearance, of an ultimately global civic space. The mediated space of appearance is becoming, and indeed must become, a space for audience: both for listening and for the expectation of being called into public presence to be heard. The mediapolis, in its contrapuntal manifestation, grants that audience. Or at least this is how we should see its future.

From this perspective, the notion of integrity, of the whole as perhaps more than the sum of its parts, appears as significant. For without an idea of the whole there can be no examination of the relations of its parts, and without a shared understanding of what might constitute publicness there is no possibility of adequately recognizing the politics and dynamics of consociation which the media both represent and enable but also misrepresent and disable. But there is another sense of the notion of integrity which is also material to the discussion of mediation and the mediapolis. It is the sense of integrity as honesty and truthfulness: of integrity as the absence of corruption.

These are the issues which are now on my table. They will be developed in the chapters that follow.

The Mediapolis and Everyday Life

On the 2nd we were at the Wenglers in the afternoon. It once again made an enormous impression on me when they put on the wireless and leapt from London to Rome, from Rome to Moscow etc. The concepts of time and space are annihilated. One must become a mystic. For me radio destroys every form of religion and at the same time gives rise to religion. Gives rise to it twice over: (a) because such a miracle exists; (b) because the human intellect invests, explains, makes use of it. But this same human intellect puts up with the Hitler government.

Klemperer, *The Klemperer Diaries*[1]

Victor Klemperer, in his remarkable account of life under the Nazi regime, an account which charts the progressive erosion, as a Jew, even as a Jew converted to Christianity, of his everyday life in Dresden, points with wonder at the significance of radio not just as an instrument of propaganda (it was key of course to the Hitler regime, and listened to both in public and private settings), but also a moral force. Radio destroys religion, he observes, and at the same time recreates it. It is both transcending and eroding of the limits of ordinary understanding and it is perplexing in its relationship to a society that both has the sophistication to create and sustain such an extraordinary medium and at the same time to collude with a monstrous regime that would seem to be opposed to all that radio would otherwise enable. Radio's erosion of conventional notions of time and space, and the capacity to extend beyond the immediate, are profoundly disturbing of the moral order of life, both demystifying and remystifying the world. Klemperer points to the intimate interrelationship between the presence of the mass media and the quality and character of everyday life; their interdependence, their contradictions, the capacities of revelation and dissemblance; the complicity of otherwise thoughtful and intelligent individuals with the messages received through this novel and powerful medium, and through it with a tyrannical and murderous regime.

Klemperer's prescient observations will continue to inform my own thinking in this chapter. My perspective here will be predominantly that of the audience, the media user, of the individual in his or her daily round, and with that individual's engaging with the increasing press of mediated sounds, images and stories. It is a perspective on the emergent mediapolis principally from below: from the perspective of the everyday. And it is a perspective on the morality of the relationships to those mediated images as well as to the world which they claim to represent, which are offered, and accepted or resisted, eternally, in the endless broadcast and on-line accessibility of the present age.

There is an initial question to be resolved, however. It is terminological but also substantive. What are we to call this person, this individual who listens and watches and e-mails and texts and seeks information on-line, and who talks about what has been seen or heard and learned or understood or who, alternatively, resists or ignores it? An audience member? A spectator? A user? A communicator? A consumer? A producer? A 'prosumer'? A citizen? A player? And how are we to assess such an individual's power in this mediated world? As a nonentity passively and impotently on the receiving end of the continuous stream of communications, or as an active, and more or less skilled, participant in the management of her or his own media culture?

One is tempted to answer that the individual in the mediapolis is all of these things. And perhaps the temptation for the indiscriminate should not be resisted, since it is indeed manifestly the case that we are all of these things now and then, and perhaps always. I am not therefore looking for a neologism, but for a sense, encapsulated in a word or phrase, that requires us to remember the dynamics of the mediapolis as it invites our constant attention and as it intervenes in the structuring of our everyday lives. So I will, perhaps banally and cumbrously, talk of *audiences and users as participants:*[2] addressing those who live in the world in which the media are central and whose everyday life is perpetually but always unevenly interconnected with the mediapolis in its various (active, passive, benevolent or malevolent, challenging or collusive) manifestations. We cannot but be participants in this world of mediated appearance, and in our participation, we commit something of ourselves to the mediated world which is offered to us on an hourly basis.

There is, however, a catch to the notion of participation, for it implies and requires something else. One way or another any kind of participation involves agency. Those who engage with the media must be understood, however minimally, to be taking some kind of decision so to do.

Even switching on the television. I want to understand participation as something active, and therefore, and this is of course crucial, and the pervasive thread running through this chapter, is that such activity, such agency, implies some kind of responsibility. Participants in media culture (all of us at some time or another and mostly all of us all of the time) must be understood to be taking responsibility for their own participation in it. Anything less reduces the individual to the level of a zombie, and while popular versions of the couch potato and its derivatives indeed make just such a judgement, such a judgement seems to me impossible to sustain (even, ironically, in its truth). For the refusal of responsibility is itself an act for which one has to take responsibility. Our humanity depends on this being the case.

The mediapolis, therefore, does not exist without our participation in it. And the work of mediation, as I have argued and will reaffirm shortly, does not stop with the appearance of the world on the screen. It crucially and definitively depends on the work of the participant: minimally perhaps in the consistencies and inconsistencies of programme choice; and maximally in the capacity directly to produce media content in one form or another, as well as in the social or political responses to what has been seen or heard – that is through participant talk and action which engages directly not merely with the mediated images but with the world that those mediated images have sought to represent.

Let me turn to the dynamics of the mediapolis from the perspective of everyday life. And to the dynamics of everyday life from the perspective of its mediation.

The mediation of everyday life

Everyday life is the realm of experience. It is where lives are led, where bodies are born and die, where humanity is constructed: identity, community, connectivity, the relationships between self and other. The everyday is the common ground. It is where the social emerges, where values are tested, and beliefs fought over. It is where action takes place. It is where the struggles for existence, both material and symbolic, are waged, where certainties are sought and securities protected. The everyday is suffused with memory and hope, both individual and collective. There is difference and there is sameness. Things to be shared and things to be refused. Stories to be told, images to be framed, words to be spoken and heard. The everyday is where normality, ordinariness, the taken-for-granted, is to be found; yet it is the kind of normality and ordinariness which is always at risk, always vulnerable to crisis, catastrophe, disappointment or disillusion. Everyday life is sensuous and contentious. It is ambiguous. It answers back. Everyday life is constrained by the interests and the power of others, by resistant structures, both physical and social. Everyday life is where individuals can be free, creative, but also where they can be exploited, excluded and repressed. There is nowhere else. Everyday life is a moral space. It is unsustainable without trust and truthfulness: without reciprocity and responsibility for others.

And now the everyday includes media. And the media's presence in everyday life, as I have been consistently arguing, is not neutral. The modern world has witnessed, and in significant degrees has been defined by, a progressive technological intrusion into the conduct of everyday life, of which the most recent and arguably the most significant manifestations have been our media technologies. These technologies, principally in the twentieth century broadcast technologies, and now the internet and the mobile phone, have become increasingly central to the ways in which individuals manage their everyday lives: central in their capacity, in broadcast schedules and the consistencies of genre, to create a framework for the ordering of the everyday, central in the infrastructure they provide for instant communication and information finding, and central too in their capacity to provide the symbolic resources and tools for making sense of the complexities of the everyday.

These technologically enabled processes of communication and meaning construction are processes of what I have already defined as mediation. Mediation, in the sense in which I am using the term, describes the fundamentally, but unevenly, dialectical process in which institutionalized media of communication are involved in the general circulation of symbols in social life. That circulation no longer requires face-to-face communication, though it does not exclude it (Silverstone 1999).

Mediation is dialectical because while it is perfectly possible to privilege those mass and digital media as defining and perhaps even determining social meanings, such privileging would miss the continuous and often creative engagement that participants have with their products. And it is uneven precisely because the power to work with, or against, the dominant or deeply entrenched meanings that the media provide is unevenly distributed across and within societies.

Mediation is both technological and social. It is also increasingly pervasive, as social actors become progressively dependent on the supply of public meanings and accounts of the world in attempting to make sense of their own. As such, mediation has significant consequences for the way in which the world appears in and to everyday life, and as such this mediated appearance in turn provides a framework for the definition and conduct of our relationships to the other, and especially the distant other, the other who only appears to us within the media. This much I hope is by now clear, given the arguments of the preceding chapters.

Now I want to pursue the discussion more deeply into the realms of everyday life itself, and from the perspective of those who, for the most part, are mostly, or most significantly still, on the receiving end of mass-mediated communications. In this chapter I argue that there are profound moral and ethical issues to be addressed in confronting the mediation of everyday life and that these issues revolve around the issues of action and responsibility. What kind of claims do the media make on their audiences and what kinds of claims can, or should, audiences be making on their media? What kinds of action are possible in a mediated world in which images and narratives transcend distance; what kind of responsibility can or should be taken by audiences for the world they will only see on pages and screens, and for the media which provide those images and stories?

My argument juxtaposes the media and everyday life while at the same time arguing that the media and everyday life are in significant ways inseparable. It presupposes that one can no longer conceive of the everyday without acknowledging the central role that increasingly the electronic media (but also books and the press) have in defining its ways of seeing, being and acting. It also presupposes that the media take as their paramount reality, in terms of their orientation and indeed the grounds of their very possibility and justification, the everyday life world of its audiences, readers and users. Of course neither the media nor everyday life are unitary phenomena, nor do they have a singular relationship to each other. Notwithstanding these differences of individual and institutional practice, as well as differential possibilities for both resistance and transcendence, the media are becoming a second-order paramount reality, fully equivalent to what would otherwise be understood as the world of the tangible face-to-face.

This second order paramount reality, what I am calling the mediapolis, does not replace the world of lived experience, as Jean Baudrillard (Baudrillard 1983) imagined with his notion of the simulacrum it did, but it runs through that experiential world, constantly engaged with it, eternally intertwined. The lived and the represented consequently become the warp and the weft of the everyday, and what is at stake in any investigation of their interrelationship is the historical and sociological specificity of the ensuing fabric, its strengths and its weaknesses, its coincidences and its contradictions: the touch and the feel of culture – the ethics and aesthetics of experience. From this perspective mediation is already a crucial constituent of everyday life. And from this perspective everyday life is a weave of the real and the symbolic, of the directly experienced and the mediated. One cannot enquire into one without simultaneously enquiring into the other.

The mediapolis, therefore, signals the presence in everyday life, both empirically and potentially, of that mediated space within which as participants we confront the world, and where, as citizens, we might confront each other. Of course the move from participant to citizen, and from a mediated space to a civic space, is very much the issue. It is by no means pre-given. It is, as I will be arguing, however, increasingly necessary to think how it might be realized.

Everyday life has a history, though mostly an invisible one. It also has a sociology. It emerged, as a concept, empirically in the analysis of both the social conditions of the poor (in nineteenth-century Britain) and of the urban (in Chicago and in the work of Mass-Observation in mid-twentieth-century Britain respectively). The underclasses, at least, had an everyday life worth studying. Many observers saw the everyday as the location for the authentic, the creative, the transcendent, but also where such impulses and possibilities were increasingly (under capitalism as well as in totalitarian regimes) repressed.

Out of these tensions and paradoxes everyday life emerges in its full-blown kaleidoscopic intensity. In that intensity, the struggles of the day as well as of a lifetime are together material, social and ethical. And so it is that in each of these domains, the media are players, shifting expectations, both tools and troubles in the management of life in the world.

Everyday life is therefore full of struggle and full of paradox. Recent critical accounts of everyday life have come to see such paradox as the defining characteristic of a mode of being in the world, one which is both creative, playful and political, and at the same time constrained by an increasingly dominant and strategic system of technological rationality, administrative order and capitalist commodification. In this possibly over-romantic view everyday life is consequently a site for the ambiguous, the unpredictable and the tactical. It may be so, as one looks down on it, but it is probably not quite like that when seen from the perspective of the lives of those who live it.

Indeed life as it is lived is rather less than a succumbing to paradox and rather more a struggle against the uncertainties and disturbances that would otherwise be seen as the consequences of paradox. Paradox, like history, is a luxury of the elite. Paradox comes from critique, not from life.[3] For most of us, most of the time, ambiguities are threats not comforts in the material struggles of the everyday. Indeed it is arguably the case that everyday life within modernity, but also earlier, consists in a continuous battle against uncertainty and for clarity and confidence in the conduct of daily existence. Even Mikhail Bakhtin's carnival, with its famous refusal of the singular orderings of dominant culture and its playful celebration of the disorder of the popular, nevertheless gains its meaning from its own precise and predictable order (Bakhtin 1984). In this sense it cannot escape the ritual frames that are a central dimension of popular, even more perhaps than of high, culture. So insofar as paradox and ambiguity persist within the lived cultures of everyday life, as opposed to the representations or the imposed aesthetics of everyday life, then it might be suggested that they express a degree of failure, failure to control the contradictory demands of daily life in modernity.

At one crucial and substantive level the media are implicated in this refusal of paradox, for in their own forms of ordering, in their narratives and in their schedules above all, they provide a framework for the resolution of ambiguity, the reduction of insecurity and the creation of a degree of comfort. Thus the predominant genres and modes of broadcast representation (news, chat show, soap opera) meet the needs and the desires for order of, and in, the everyday, and even in those areas of media production and consumption where it may be suggested that there is scope for both resistance and ambiguity, as well as the expression of the uniqueness of the individual (in popular music culture, blogging, messaging, file sharing and so on and in some on-line networks where this is the case), it could still be argued that what is at stake is not the embrace of ambiguity and paradox but the search, perhaps the impossible search, for different kinds of order and a struggle for power and control over one's immediate material and symbolic space and time.

It is an order in which the ordinary and the taken-for-granted is constantly interrupted by crisis, both personal and political. In the context of the mediation of everyday life, such a rhythm is one which the media are crucially involved in managing or seeking to manage, and indeed which provides the resources for participants in the mediapolis to attempt its daily management. The imposition of structures of media talk and representation on the one hand, in the framing of news and documentary accounts, as well as in the reflections that fictional representations offer on the world of lived experience, and on the other hand in the endless iteration of comment, both informed and misinformed, which the 24-

hour news now provides, together provide a kind of seamless security blanket for the conduct of everyday life. Its puncturing by the reporting of acts of terror, or natural disaster, of famine and human malevolence, is constant too, though as I have long argued such potentially dramatic disturbances are mediated and contained, mostly, both through the familiarities of narrative and generic convention, and the media's chronically short span of attention (Silverstone 1988).

This structuring of knowledge and experience is further developed and expanded in the frequent explosion of communications on-line and on-phone following a major event. What is involved in all these forms of communication is the mediation of risk, or at least the mediation of its perception and representation. Despite the constant tension between creativity and repression, between ambiguity and certainty, and between the ordinary and the exceptional, all of which together define the quality of everyday life for most people most of the time, the media offer a framework for its ordering, an opportunity, as I will discuss later, for a kind of complicity or collusion with the dominant forms of representation.

The order at the heart of everyday life, or at least the search for it, is an order grounded in the body. Everyday life is still grounded in the face-to-face, in physical presence and in the physical present. Everyday life is bodily life: life that is gendered, sexed and aged; life both enabled and limited by material resources, by circumstance and by fate. The everyday has its own smells, its own desires, and in its refusals of the antiseptic orderings of high culture, the everyday also refuses the Cartesian dualism in which bodies and minds are separated, and where bodies come a distinct second in the creation of social value.

The viability, as well as the value, of everyday life consists in our physical, intellectual and moral capacity fully to engage with what the system throws at us, and indeed our capacity to construct, if we can, our own reality, albeit from a position of structural weakness. In everyday life we seek, within the limits of our resources, to transform the abstract structures of language into the vivid discourses of daily speech, or to convert the alienating spaces and times of the city into something like home (de Certeau 1984). We try to take some kind of command of the world with which we engage every minute of the day. The world of the everyday is above all a vivid world, and that vividness is grounded in bodily experience and sensibility. And it is through the vivid face-to-face that socially meaningful and robust relations are sustained: in places and across generations, reproduced through time. And in this process it is the body which is central.

Bodies, however, require comfort and security, both material and symbolic. It is in the repetitiveness of the everyday, its very familiarity and predictability, that such securities are sought and sometimes found. So much is taken for granted but so little can be guaranteed. Amongst the disturbances caused during the modern period are disturbances that have affected the body mightily. It has been subject to increased and often terrifying risk. It has been incorporated into the technological, a cyborg fusion that many argue is transformative of our capacity to act in the world. The body, finally, is also seen to be the site of the exercise of power, inscribed, as Nikolas Rose (Rose 1990; 1999) has argued in his work on governmentality, with the ink of states and nations. Risk, technological dependence and the intrusion of the state and its agents into the pores of everyday life are each made manifest through, as well as becoming dependent upon, their mediation. The mediapolis is not just a space of appearance, but a space for control, and of course, resistance.

So the experience of everyday life is no longer obviously containable within physical space, even if it ever was. The media have provided an increasingly available and increasingly insistent alternative, one which provides both support and through identifications with characters, the seductions of narrative, obsessional gaming or internet chat, the possibility of bodily transcendence. Though the media do this, of course, at a price. In the palpable dematerialization of the body, our own but crucially that of the other, the media have created a space in which the lack of physical contact undermines a sense of meaningful difference between bodies. Of course this is not new. It is a constant in all forms of imaginative and aesthetic experience. But in the electronic media it is disguised, and in some ways denied, in the constant presence of the other in the images and voices of mediated representation and interaction. The immediacy and the liveness of so much of what is seen on television, on the internet, or in the voices and images instantly transmitted via the mobile phone are easily mistaken for life itself.

Such connections and disconnections have, of course, consequences for the social dynamics of everyday life, indeed for the way in which individuals relate to each other on a daily basis. And here again we face contradictory impulses and pressures, in all of which in one way or another the media are involved.

Modernity as mediated now, and our experience of it and of its variously and variously mediated others – family, neighbour, stranger – is itself premised on the kind of communications that emerge and flourish, and in their flourishing define and determine the way in which everyday lives are conducted. We have seen huge changes in the way in which everyday life is lived in those societies and amongst those populations touched by media technology and, without being overly determinist, it is hard to argue against both the direct and indirect consequences of technological changes on the way in which everyday life is lived: the mobile phone, following hard on the heels of the internet, is only the latest significant communication technology whose emerging patterns of use are beginning to transform the nature of the relationship between public and private spheres, and which are creating a kind of perpetual contactability that marks a fundamental shift in our status as individuals in social and virtual space (Katz and Aakhus 2002).

There is a certain kind of symbiosis between social and technological change, particularly when it comes to media and communications. To say this of course is not to deny the tensions and the lack of synchronicity between them, Nor is it to imply that such changes are necessarily or uniformly benevolent in their consequences. On the contrary. However, both Raymond Williams (Williams 2003) and Manuel Castells (Castells 2000) have pointed to this kind of mutuality. Williams's argument, in the first case in relation to radio, is that it enabled, in its secondary emergence as a broadcasting technology (it was originally of course a two-way interactive technology) the connection of an increasingly dispersing and suburbanizing population into a framework of national culture and mutual connectedness. And in some ways quite similarly Manuel Castells points to the internet as being a technology which has become appropriately fitted to the increasing individualism and the further, global, dispersal of late modernity.

Castells suggests that while this emergence keeps nodes and participants separate it also simultaneously links them together in intense forms of sociability. On the one hand he points to the triumph of the individual, on the other to the possibility that this triumph will in turn lead, with technologically enabled mediation, to the creation of a new kind of network society. What he does not question is the quality of this new kind of sociability, its strengths and its weaknesses, and its capacity to sustain a world which will accept responsibility for this relatively new condition, a condition in which the difference between presence and absence, and distance and proximity, is no longer secure; a world in which technological connection does not necessarily mean social connection.

The quality of everyday life is often seen to be threatened by modernity, above all by the relentless rise of individualism, as both ideology and reality. Both capitalism and industrialism are believed to have undermined those otherwise primary social groups: family, church, community, and the possibility for solidarity and the sharing of common experience, which they offered. These institutions and groupings were once seen to have enabled a shared body of common-sense beliefs and assumptions, unquestioning though they may have been, which in turn enabled and sustained traditional forms of collective life with (and without being too romantic about it) their sense of mutual care and responsibility. The discipline of sociology is grounded in the analysis of the transitions and tensions between pre-modern and modern ways of life. It is not too foolhardy to suggest that the study of media and communications needs to be grounded in the study of the equivalent tensions and transitions as we move into something that increasingly justifiably, at least from the point of its social and cultural dynamics, we can call post-modernity; a transition which would be inconceivable without the liberating constraints of both broadcast and interactive media.

I am, however, arguing that mediated late modernity can also be seen to have generated the conditions for the sharing of a multiplicity of perspectives and positions which in turn has enabled, at least the opportunity for, a new kind of publicness. This is the potential of the mediapolis. It depends on a primary, but only superficially paradoxical, observation that it is individuality which is what is actually shared. And if we can recognize that commonality, one which is available to inspection and contemplation on a daily basis in the mediapolis, then we can begin to glimpse how the everyday is already changing and how those changes might be mobilized for the global better rather than the global worse.

It is hard not to return to Hannah Arendt at this point, who compares the value of public and private spaces through an observation of the centrality of difference. Let me record again her crucial insight:

> For though the common world is the common meeting ground of all, those who are present have different locations in it, and the location of one can no more coincide with the location of another than the location of two objects. Being seen and being heard by others derive their significance from the fact that everybody sees and hears from a different position. This is the meaning of public life, compared to which even the richest and most satisfying family life can offer only the prolongation or multiplication of one's own position with its attending aspects and perspectives. (Arendt 1998: 57)

Arendt is bewailing the loss of public life. I, however, want to take what she says is a starting point for the suggestion that there might be a possibility of its re-emergence. Such a re-emergence from the increasing privatization of the everyday becomes a possibility precisely because the boundaries between the public and the private are actually undermined by the presence, on television screens still above all, of mediated public-ness in the front room. While the world, as it appears on those screens, is sucked into, and domesticated by, its presence in the private spaces of cosy suburbs, it is at the same there, visible, from time to time demand-ing, and almost impossible to exclude.

Such observations have implications for how we understand connectiv-ity in an increasingly networked age, and what the moral and ethical consequences of this particular but core dimension of mediation are. Indeed there is an increasing amount of scholarly work purporting to show how forms of on-line connectivity, chat and the sharing of enthusi-asms or anxieties can and do provide meaningful contact, sufficient for participants to feel engaged and supported, to make friends and even to transfer their virtual mutuality into the real world (cf. Baym 2000). Some-times these new connectivities are seen as providing compensating alter-natives to the weakening infrastructures of everyday life, patching the thinning ozone layer of sociability in the daily round. On the other hand, such on-line sociability is decried for its limited singularity, a mono-chrome of lifestyles and interests, and unsustainable beyond the narrow confines of mutual identification (Calhoun 1998). On-line relationships are consequently seen to be provisional and essentially voluntaristic; they can, and do, break down under the slightest pressure.

At best, therefore, one can arguably see these networks as involving the privatization of sociability: an until-further-notice, rather than a taken-for-granted, kind of thing. This is the kind of privatization, albeit in another mode, which Arendt herself decried as one of modernity's major downsides. And notwithstanding her perverse refusal to find almost any value in private life (a position which did not, and still does not, endear her to her feminist critics), there is little question that the with-drawal into the private realm, one now arguably to be seen in otherwise public cyberspace, is telling.

It may be telling but is it inevitable?

The network society, if that is what we have to call it, is not a singular entity, any more than any other social formation is. Not only is it marked by conflict, inequality and exploitation, but it has generated its own con-tradictions, contradictions which go to the heart of the contemporary experience of everyday life, at least in those societies most touched by digital media. Two at least impress me. The first is that between the voluntarism which I have already indicated as being at the heart of the connecting disconnectivity of the mediapolis and the anxiety generated by the absence of connection: anxiety that comes both with technological dependence and with the horror of being on one's own in a world in which identity depends precisely on not being alone. The second is that between the involuntary connectivity that above all broadcast media offer, and the capacity, voluntarily, to resist, deny or disown the presence of the other who is offered to us in this way. Both of these contradictions turn on the possibility, but the consequent pain, of either switching off or being switched off.

I have been arguing in this book that at the heart of any enquiry into the ethics of everyday life must be a concern with our relationships to each other. And these relationships need to be premised on a recognition of difference, on the legitimate and indelible differences between us. Such difference is what constitutes the basis for what we have in common. *What we have in common is our difference.* This is, I believe, what Arendt is arguing in the quotation already cited above, and it is, of course, the core of the ethical position taken by Emmanuel Levinas.[4]

In the broadly philosophical mode, the argument is based on the issue of otherness, perhaps in the abstract, but as the baseline for a singular and compelling approach to morality. In the no less broadly sociological mode, the question is the more empirical one, of the nature of our relationships to those who share the world with us, and with those of whose continued or intermittent mediated presence we are being asked, and sometimes required, to take account. What does such accounting involve, and what are its consequences? How far and how deeply can we insist that the conduct of everyday life can only be meaningfully and morally sustained on the basis of an ethic of care for our immediate fellows, care for those who are present but also distant in space, and care for those yet born, whose lives nevertheless will be affected by our own? What is the role, if any, of the media, of the mediapolis, in this awesome but basic undertaking?

I would like to approach these questions by considering four dimensions of the mediation of everyday life: distance; trust; complicity; and responsibility.

Distance

Communication and mediation are both means to transcend distance. The distance that separates one being from another in the face-to-face encounter is arguably as significant, profound, and as ultimately unbridgeable as that which separates two cultures across differences of global space and fundamental belief. Yet we are prone, in both domains, to believe that such distance can be crossed, and that in the spoken language and touch of the face-to-face encounter, as well as in the instantaneity and immediacy of the mediated one, connections are real and genuine – which of course, if we believe that they are, they are.

These beliefs, however, in the context of the mediapolis, have significant consequences for how we approach the world as it appears to us in its mediation, and how we might position ourselves both in relation to the representations and the realities which emerge in that mediation.

Distance remains a huge problem in this mediated world and for our management of everyday life, above all because the persistence of distance is of such moral import. As Kevin Robins has noted in his discussion of the psychodynamics of the representation of the Gulf War, 'the screen exposes the ordinary viewer to harsh realities, but it screens out the harshness of those realities. It has a certain moral weightlessness: it grants sensation without demanding responsibility, and it involves us in a spectacle without engaging us in the complexity of its reality' (Robins 1994: 313). This observation is both familiar and unfamiliar. It is familiar insofar as spectacle has, at least since Guy Debord (Debord 1977), been seen as a major component of the media's totalitarian occupation of the spaces of the everyday; but it is less familiar insofar as it provides the basis for taking an ethical position, one which engages the problem of mediated distance as being a crucial component of the morality of the everyday.

I have argued, in chapter 2, and contrarily, that the global media provide, in both the real and an ideal world, resources for judgement. Their invitation, in news and current affairs principally, but also on blogs and in chat rooms, is an invitation to engage. Such an invitation is for those who come forward as participants, users, audiences, lurkers even, and who seek, or find without seeking, information, ideas, or fantasies which may be of use to them as they make their way through their everyday lives. And it is also an invitation, of course, and of course much more problematically, to enlarge their lives by incorporating, if only for a moment, something else, someone else, some otherness otherwise beyond reach. The construction of what I have called proper distance, the capacity to enlarge one's perspective, and the willingness to recognize the other in her sameness and difference, are challenges effectively that the mediapolis poses on a minute-by-minute basis to all its participants.

However the rhetoric of the mediapolis, the invitation to engage, is hardly straightforward. It is, indeed, replete with ambiguity: disclosure and dissemblance are bedfellows. On the one hand a visible and trenchant expectation of truthfulness and disinterest in the reporting of the world. On the other a barely hidden gloss of at best disingenuousness and most often an absence of context, an overdependence on the immediate, a collusive oversimplification of the complexity of the event. The resources being offered for judgement themselves require judgement – an issue to be dealt with in the final chapter. But there is a further, perhaps obvious, complication. It is that news, the most categorical media genre in its necessary claims for truthfulness, is not just a matter of report. It seeks to engage, to please, to shock: it tells stories; it offers explanations. Its rules of engagement, always evolving, and currently evolving in ways that many see as self-defeating, nevertheless embody forms of discourse that at one level both depend on, and at the same time undermine, its claims for objectivity and truth, but on another play within the shared conventions of public communication in popular culture. And who is to say that the latter is not just as much a key to credibility as sober reporting? The mediapolis is constituted by a culture of the yellow press and the tabloid as well as the serious weekly; a culture of public service broadcasting as well as the commercial; and a culture of powerful browsers and search engines as well as autochthonous weblogs, a thousand flowers blooming, and fading, minute by minute, on the global internet. It is also constituted by sceptical as well as gullible publics.

The simplicity of the news report masks, therefore, a huge complexity, not just in its relationship to the world and the events to which it refers, but in its relationship to its audiences and users as participants without whom the communication would be stillborn. It also masks another, occasional and arguably functional, characteristic: that of anamorphosis, which I discussed in chapter 3; a not-infrequently visible reminder, though partially masked and not always either coherent or intended, of the vulnerability of the world of men and women, and of the institutions and ideologies that sustain that world.

Each of these components of news and factual reporting contributes to the complexity of the appeal that is made to the audience and user as participant. Each indicates, too, the extraordinary difficulty of creating some kind of proper distance between subject and mediator and between mediator and audience in such a way as effectively to enable the engaging of the latter with the distant world in its troubles and, though perhaps more rarely, its joys.

The global media are never short of examples which would help to illustrate some of these arguments. During the course of 2004 and 2005, three, at least to me, stand out, in different ways, as significant in the context of these discussions.

The first was the release of the footage produced by the hostage-takers themselves in the catastrophe of Beslan in September 2004. The footage reportedly was shot in order to inform the authorities during the siege of what was taking place within the building, and the realities of its dangers. The British media, for the most part, reproduced components of the footage, though in some cases with more extensive coverage than others. We are bound to ask what was served by such reproduction, and whether the appearance of these images constituted an acceptable propriety (this maybe is the word) in the distance it introduced between audience and subjects. The invitation to the viewer is inevitably a challenging one for, above all, what these images showed in almost real time (and not the delayed time, for example, of holocaust imagery) were the bodies and faces, the immediate and compromised lives, of those who were about to die, and in the short time between the bombing and the appearance of the images on the screen, had died. Children mostly, and parents and teachers, killed. Three hundred and thirty-one of them. These images were like those of someone in the condemned cell: an intrusion into the privacy of their imminent death. There is an issue of dignity here, something that easily gets lost in the rush for immediacy.

Yet it is not possible to be definitive about this. These are images shocking in their uniqueness and prescient tragedy, but also familiar and dulled by the context of their representation: screen- or page-based, momentary, singular and quickly eclipsed. But here were also images of those with whom one could identify: people like us, children like ours, and enemies like ones that we could recognize and increasingly, in the UK and the US, are being taught to fear. What were we supposed to think? What were we supposed to do?

Proper distance requires context as well as imagination. And here the singular context was terrorism, the context was our impotence in the face of it, the context was that this was taking place far away and until that moment beyond our imagination, the context was the impossibility of our making a difference. The context was also of course intensely political, polarized, and for the most part unyielding, a context in which the framework of terror crowded out any other possible accounts or explanations for what was being seen. The context was the screen. The invitation clearly was to identify with the victims, notwithstanding that distance: to recognize in them the same as well as the different. Would that be possible?

The specific as well as the generic invitation in this sequence and story has to be to try and understand, to make sense of it, and to invite some kind of response, in thought, judgement or action. The media cannot do this for us: they can facilitate it but they can also get in the way. Perhaps this was one moment when the harshness and horror of the images, and their appearance in the mediapolis, was justified, but it is difficult to see how and in what ways it was constructive.

The second set of images was equally dramatic. They were those first significantly made public on the evening of 28 April 2004 when the US television channel CBS broadcast an episode of their regular show *60 Minutes II*. It included images of US soldiers and their prisoners in what was, not long before, Saddam Hussein's most notorious prison, Abu Ghraib. The pictures caused a sensation. And they may well be remembered as the defining images of the invasion and subsequent occupation of Iraq. The storm that was provoked was as complex and as polarized as one might imagine. Here, arguably, the response, at least in the West and especially in the US itself, was one which invited rejection rather than identification: these were people like us but with whom it was difficult if not impossible to identify, from whom we had to become distanced.[5] Here was the private erupting into public space. Secrets were broken and the underbelly of western imperial power displayed.

This was a different move from the one embodied in the Beslan reports, but on the same axis of proximity and distance. Here the immediacy of the closeness of recognition would have to be managed if somehow a position of responsibility was to be achieved. The soldiers were identifiable. They belonged to the world of the viewer, one way or another. But what of their victims, hooded, naked, threatened, humiliated and perhaps above all unnamed (Butler 2004)? Did they appear to us as the animals they manifestly had become in the eyes of their persecutors? Without their presence on the television and computer screens in the West, the question would not even be poseable, never mind answerable. Yet, even with it, these images were far from unambiguous. They were certainly anamorphic. They provided a barely coded reminder of the vulnerability, and arguably also the capacity for evil, within ourselves: they were too close to home.

The third example is perhaps less equivocal, and also one which may have had as significant a consequence for the media in the US as it has had for the country's political culture and social structure. The reporting of the aftermath of Hurricane Katrina, by almost all accounts, provided not just a narrative of political ineptitude but an almost involuntary stripping of the country's illusions about itself. The hidden injuries of race, class, poverty – systemic, exploited, denied – appeared in all their depth and horror as the flood waters rose and as the intensity of both national and global reporting gathered pace. In the UK, the main channels were quick to pick this up, to dwell on it and to question it. In the US, perhaps slower on the uptake, the consequences of ultimately having to recognize the same thing became increasingly irresistible: the presence of the other in their midst, and the sore of it. The distance between image and reality in the US had been breached just like the New Orleans dykes. The media, both local and national, found themselves for the first time in years (certainly since before 9/11) having to report and to analyse the deep troubles at the core of American society. There was to be, at least for the moment, no more distance.

The challenge of proper distance begins in the preparation of the images for their appearance on the screen or page, and their manifestation in the world in the mediapolis, but it has to be resolved finally in the minds and actions of those who, in one way or another, find themselves confronting them. There is no single position from which the world can be seen and represented, and the determination of proper distance has to be decided in each case.

But the mediapolis is in constant tension with respect to its position in relation to its participants and to the management of distance. The moral consequences of such tension are played out in the everyday lives of those who watch and listen. And such consequences are themselves dependent on other dimensions of the relationship that individuals have, or don't have, with their media. Perhaps the most significant dimension of that relationship is that of trust.

Trust

Trust is a way of managing, that is reducing, distance.

Luc Boltanski (Boltanski 1999), in a related discussion of the mediated representation of suffering, argues that one of the central components of distancing in mediated communication is the inability of the receiver to know about, or interrogate, the context or the intention of those who initiate the communication:

> The media situation, by not only distancing the spectator from the unfortunate but also from the person who presents the unfortunate's suffering to him (without necessarily having witnessed them), makes more exacting the necessary conditions of trust which, as many experimental studies

have shown, are broadly dependent upon an effect of presence. (Boltanski 1999: 151)

Trust, and trustworthiness, is as crucial a component in the mediation of everyday life as it is in other dimensions of social life. But here, if recent commentators are to be believed, it is in increasingly short supply. While it is obviously the case that the everyday in modern and late modern societies is unsustainable unless we trust in abstract systems, the media, as one of those abstract systems, have once again a double significance, since not only have they to be trusted in themselves, but they are the key to our capacity to trust the world. The decline in support for, and trust in, the democratic process in such societies can be seen to be, at least in part, as Onora O'Neill (O'Neill 2002) argues, a consequence of our increasing lack of trust in the media's representation of that process.

However the media, like all those involved in relations of trust, operate in a doubly skewed economy. To start with, while it is rarely difficult to find evidence of untrustworthiness, it is virtually impossible to prove its opposite: I cannot prove that you are trustworthy, only, should the case arise, that you have broken that trust. And once broken it is difficult, often impossible, to rebuild. And then it might be worth observing that trust is asymmetrical and, in this context non-reciprocal. For the media to be viable they have to be trusted by their addressees. Yet there is no equivalent requirement for those addressees to be trusted by the media.

Trust then is a slippery thing; it is always conditional, requiring continuous maintenance and evidence of fulfilment. There is yet another paradox, however, in the mediation of trust, and in the creation and sustaining of our trust in the media, for such trust is beset with ambiguity. Much of our media has palpably an unstable, not to say from time to time an exploitative, relationship to reality and to truth (I return to the notion of truth in the next chapter). The boundaries are daily crossed between the so-called purity of information and the impurity of entertainment. The blurring of the distinction between descriptive and analytic reporting and the 'op. ed.' has become a feature of the world's press. Reality TV and docu-soaps visibly and playfully massage the boundary between reality and fiction. Spontaneous chat shows are rehearsed. Live transmissions from the world's hot-spots are pre-recorded. How can we trust in a fake, especially one we know to be a fake? Or to put it another way, the question is not so much about the absence of trust within the processes of mediation, but our acceptance of those absences, our willing refusal to challenge their manifest breaches. How come we don't seem to mind? How come trust appears to be deferred, as in some way (for those who are other than constitutionally sceptical), actually irrelevant to the continuing participation in media culture?

Max Horkheimer and Theodor Adorno end their critique of the cultural industries with an observation on the power of advertising. Consumers, they say, 'feel compelled to buy and use its products even though they see through them' (Horkheimer and Adorno 1972: 167). They indicate that the cultural industry is omnipotent, and that we have no choice but to collude with the devil.

Tempting though it sometimes is to endorse such pessimism, my own argument differs from theirs in one key respect. While it acknowledges the representational power that the media wield, it nevertheless suggests that if we are to maintain an intellectual but also a political position which insists on our capacity for agency, then we have to recognize that this kind of media power can and must be challenged. If we are to be acknowledged as active, that is as willing, participants in mediated culture then there has to be some meaning in the notion of *willing*.

Therefore the question of our acceptance of such dominant forms of mediation is a real one, and much more complex than contemporary claims of media irresponsibility and dumbing-down tend to assume. One way of addressing this question might be to indicate how both the everyday and its manifestation in popular culture has consistently refused to take the mediated representation of the world entirely at face value.

The serious-minded do not recognize the profound centrality of play at the heart of media culture, a playfulness accepted and indulged in by both parties to the communication. Play offers a different and distinct basis for the exercise (or breach) of trust. Instead of a betrayal of the facts, what counts in play is essentially a betrayal of the rules. Instead of the liar, the cheat. The conventions and rules of playfulness define a set of limits and practices which are only challenged, and distrusted, in their breach. Media representation, of the so-called popular kind, plays, by and large, according to rules, though the rules are not always clear cut; they are neither fixed, nor are they unregulated by states. The playfulness of popular culture to which mediated culture is heir has always been misunderstood, distrusted and also quite often feared by those in authority. The history of Victorian Britain was certainly in part a history of the struggle to regulate and contain the playfulness of the popular, seeking to constrain its anarchic streak and bringing it safely into the confines of, increasingly, commodified culture. Yet, in many of the strands of popular television, as well as in the tabloid and yellow press, these forms of play live on. The playfulness of mediated culture is not simply, then, a post-modern invention. It has a history, and a logic.[6]

There is a difference between trust in a narrative or a report, that is trust in factual accuracy, and trust in the media's enabling structures, where accuracy might take second place, even in factual reporting, to aesthetics and to the authority of genre. In the former there is a concern with content, and with the singularity of a representational claim. In the latter there is a concern with the quality and reliability of the enabling structures, and the rules which govern them. Pleasure, maybe, rather than truth.

The mediapolis consists of both of these, often contradictory, kinds of textuality and both of these kinds of claims on audiences and viewers. The literal and the playful overlay and complicate the relationship between the factual and the fictional. The knowingness that audiences can bring to their media consumption is a crucial part of the trust that is generated in their relationship to what they see and hear, though it would of course be wrong to suggest that such knowingness is uniform or invulnerable. Audiences and users as participants in the mediapolis can make mistakes, just as media can, wittingly or otherwise, lead them astray. Audiences and users as participants, however, secure in the rules of the game (and trusting in them, by virtue of their familiarity) can avoid the confrontation, for example, with factuality. Such familiarity does not matter, or it matters less, than the known and accepted playfulness or position-taking of, for example, the British tabloid newspaper *The Sun*, or Fox News in the US.[7] Trust in this context is not necessarily trust in the capacity of the newspaper or the channel to tell the truth, but trust in the newspaper or channel to be what it is and is expected to be. Of course such playing is also about the absence of challenge and the sharing of perspectives and prejudice. I'll come to some of these issues shortly.

So it can be argued that seeing media consumption, at least in part, as play, has interesting implications for media ethics, for in play there is a significant displacement of responsibility. While there is no game without our participation, the game itself, as play, inoculates its players against accepting responsibility for anything other than what takes place within its own clearly bounded framework. 'It's only a game.' We trust in the other within the game to play fairly, but we do not take responsibility for the game itself. We leave that to others. On the other hand notions of trust based on play have to involve a shared responsibility, for there is no game without all participants. Mediation, too, is a shared activity, involving reciprocity and mutuality, albeit in a highly skewed political infrastructure. We, the audience and user as participant, cannot walk away if the game is to continue; the game cannot continue without us.

It is therefore no surprise to suggest that trust is terribly troublesome, since it begs the question of both ends and means. We cannot but trust in the media, for the media, despite their manifest weaknesses, have to be trusted for social life to continue. But such trust cannot be blind: it has to be sceptical, it has to be informed; it has to be part of the responsibility that is taken in everyday life by audiences: a demand for accountability, but also a demand for respect. Though when we talk of accountability we need to be careful in insisting that accountability cannot be vouchsafed simply or only to the regulatory apparatus. This may be necessary but it will never be sufficient. Accountability must be systemic, and as such dependent on the work of audiences and media users as participants, who are media literate enough to make their own judgements on what is being presented to them or in what they are participating. Our trust therefore must be conditional, critical. Our participation must be knowing participation: proper distance must be informed by proper scepticism. Trust can neither be blind nor passive. The media are both institutions and discourses. Both need to be trustworthy.

Indeed there is an important distinction to be made, which I have implicitly been making, between trust and trustworthiness, such that the focus should be on the prior conditions which need to be in place for trust to be possible. These issues too connect to questions of justice and truth which I discuss in the next chapter, and these too need to be addressed as matters both of policy and literacy, which I discuss in my conclusion.

However before doing so there is one further issue that needs some discussion. It follows from the perception of the media as play. And it concerns the question, the familiar and basic question, at the heart of the book which is about the media's capacity to engage its audiences and participants in the world of others, particularly, now, in their suffering.

Complicity and collusion

Recent media research has been at pains to demonstrate the degree to which audiences for a wide range of broadcast material must be considered active. Choices are made between programmes, and meanings are not pre-defined either by producers or texts. An understanding of the reader–text relationship requires the recognition that both at the point of impact, and in subsequent social and cultural discourses, that audiences are at work, actively engaged with the significant continuities (and the continuous significance) of otherwise one-way communication. Such activity, of course, becomes interactivity in the world of the computer and the network with, consequently, a sense of even stronger kinds of participation.

I have already suggested that such notions of activity necessarily have a moral consequence. If audiences are active and if the notion of activity has any meaning at all, then they must be presumed to have to take responsibility for those actions. If audiences refuse to take that responsibility, then they are morally culpable. And we are all audiences and users as participants now.

I have also already suggested that the weaknesses of our media, which are both structural and circumstantial, do not just impinge on everyday life, imposed on our daily values and practices as if from Mars. They emerge and are accepted as components of a shared culture. Without challenge, without interrogation, and above all without our willingness to take responsibility for them, they fail us, and crucially, we them.

In a sophisticated and challenging essay on the relationship between the anthropologist and his or her subject in a post-colonial global world, George Marcus (Marcus 1998) finds in complicity the figure with which to address both the ethical dilemmas within the practice of ethnographic fieldwork and the means to move beyond the limits of the singularly local as its container. Complicity, 'being an accomplice', 'partnership in an evil action' (OED) emerges when both partners in the ethnographic project are in some senses aware of, but do not fully acknowledge or question, those aspects of the world which are material to that relationship and to the two mingling cultures which sustain it. Both parties privately know that an explanation for the reality in front of them depends on moving outside it, to other sites and settings in time and space. They are complicit in a project of knowledge-generation which both know is inadequate, but which both are willing to accept.

From one perspective this kind of complicity is a terminally disabling dimension of the anthropological project, ethically and morally. However, rather than seeing complicity as the death-knell of ethnography Marcus argues that it provides, once recognized and understood, a route into a new kind of multi-sited ethnography, an ethnography which requires the anthropologist, at least, to follow the trails and explore the contexts necessary to engage properly with the other.

Discussions of media and everyday life can learn from this dilemma in anthropological practice and the kinds of reflexivity it requires. In the context of the present discussion the notion of complicity turns on questions of distance and of representation. Complicity figures as an irony of position, in which none of the participants in the interaction (the journalist and his subject, in this case) quite know enough about the other, quite understand enough about each other's power, to create a secure collaborative relationship, but nevertheless proceed on the basis that they actually do know enough. Together they share knowledge of a material absence, but in the half-light of their inevitably time-limited interaction, they leave well alone.

However, the anthropological critique, perhaps for understandable reasons, stops one step short, for it does not consider the third party to this interaction, the party who reads the anthropologist's text. To include the audience, and to include it in its plurality and in the context of the everyday, infinitely complicates the complicity of mediation, which involves, always, not two but three parties: the represented, the representing, the witnesses to the representation. Each of these, notwithstanding differences and formal responsibility, are participants in, and party to, the process of mediation.

Documentary film-making and news reporting, indeed any attempt within the media to claim a reality and thereby claim a truth, involves a complicity in which all involved participate; a refusal to recognize that the process in which they are all engaged – albeit from different positions of power – is inadequate and compromised by its own contradictions. Audiences, producers and, increasingly, the subjects of representation are complicit in this representational practice when they fail to challenge it, and when they fail to reflect on those of its aspects, which, by default, risk betraying the world. Subjects are complicit when they play according to the rules, when they accept the limitations of genre, when they fail to recognize the impossibility, and partiality, of representation.[8] Producers are complicit likewise when they fail to reflect on the limitations of their practice, and fail to communicate these both to their subjects and their audiences. Audiences and users as participants in the mediapolis are complicit both insofar as they uncritically accept the media's representational claims, and insofar as their knowing acknowledgement of its limitations remains tacit.

There is, then, a close link between this dimension of complicity in everyday life and the will to power in mediation, that is the need to believe in our ability fully to know the other, and our need to believe in the reality and authority of the facts about her or him. Participants in media culture are complicit insofar as they accept the media both as necessary for our understanding of the world and our capacity to value the other, as indeed they are; but also as sufficient, which they can never be.

Our complicity relies on this mutual misrecognition and of course it sustains it too. It provides us with comfort, at least until such time as events in the world break through the tissue of representation. That comfort, in turn, inoculates us against the challenges of the real, and against our need ever, fully, to take responsibility for the other.

The boundary between complicity and collusion is a permeable one. But whereas I have argued that complicity is a kind of substrate in the relationship we have both to the other and to our media, and to the other through our media, collusion can be seen to be more direct in its moral consequences.[9] This is particularly the case where we are confronted by images and narratives of suffering and pain. Stan Cohen, in reflecting on the process of mediation in his recent trenchant account of denial in the face of human suffering, notes an important paradox. It is worth quoting him at length:

> Television is the primary channel through which the agonies of distant others reach the consciences of the more privileged, safe and comfortable . . . These images belong to a hyper-reality, a continuous set of paradoxes about the observer's view of what is 'really' happening . . . But there is also a fathomless distance, not just the geographical distance from the event, but the unimaginability of this happening to you or your loved ones. . . . On the one hand, immediacy breaks down the older barriers to knowledge and compassion, the TV news becoming 'a hopeful example of the internationalisation of conscience'. But, on the other, its selectivity, promiscuity and short attention time span make viewers into 'voyeurs of the suffering of others, tourists amidst their landscapes of anguish' (Cohen 2001: 168–9).[10]

Whereas one can read the ambivalence of this as a sign of hope, and indeed increasing international responsiveness to distant suffering is certainly hopeful, it would be a mistake to ignore its negative. For it is the intransigence of the distant and the ephemeral which provides the raw material for collusive denial. If the as-if of representation brings tragedy and trauma onto the threshold it nevertheless also makes it easy to deposit them both outside the back door.

Collusion, therefore, involves such shared denial. Indeed, as Cohen notes, denials draw on shared cultural vocabularies to be credible. Collusions, 'mutually reinforcing denials that allow no meta-comment, work best when we are unaware of them' (Cohen 2001: 64). Just as families can deny the presence of an alcoholic member, because it would be too painful to acknowledge, so too can societies deny the presence of problems and traumas that they would otherwise have to confront. Media images enable a collusive illusion that the appearance of the other in crisis on the screen is sufficient for us to believe that we are fully engaged with him or her in that crisis. The post-Katarina reporting in the US, briefly at least, as I have suggested, challenged this collusion, as did the global reporting of the tsunami in the Indian Ocean at the end of 2004. So it can be done.

However, for the most part in the contemporary mediapolis, in this crucial matter of our relationship to the other, and our capacity to care, we are confronted by the sharing of, and our complicity and collusion with, two kinds of cultural vocabularies. The first is that between us and our media: the vocabulary and discourse of representation, narrative and report. The second is that amongst ourselves: the related vocabularies and discourses of everyday life – its talk, its memories and its imaginings. Complicity depends on our willing acceptance of the media's capacity to translate the properly challenging other both into the comforting frames of the familiar and into excommunicated banishment. Collusive denial depends on our capacity, and our desire, both to ignore and to forget the reality and pain of the other's everyday life.

These arguments have implications for an understanding of compassion and its possibility in modern society. Compassion relies on identification with the plight of another. It is personal, and individual. Compassion takes place in private. Pity, on the other hand, is public, political and generalizable.

In this context Susan Moeller writes of 'compassion fatigue' which involves a judgement of the media's responsibility for our failures fully to engage with the suffering of the other as being the consequence of the bludgeoning of bottom-line led journalism, a problem to be solved by better, more honest, more professional, less compromised journalism (Moeller 1999: 322). This is probably too singular an argument. The media's direct representation of the suffering of others in times of war, crises or environmental disaster is, actually, by no means homogeneous, as Lilie Chouliaraki (Chouliaraki 2006) has convincingly shown. And there is clearly evidence of their role, still, in mobilizing support from individuals and collectivities for distant disaster.

However, I have just noted that it is possible to suggest that compassion, which Hannah Arendt among others argues is a private rather than a public matter, is less important than what should be emerging from the media's representation of suffering, and that is a (public, of course) politics of pity.[11] The problem, at least in her view, and as we have seen, is the privatization of public life, for which we can now acknowledge the media as being signally responsible.

Privatization is certainly a problem, since it arguably leads to withdrawal or, at best, to symptomatic rather than structural responses. Yet distance is clearly another, and arguably a prior, one. Luc Boltanski confronts this issue in the context of his analysis of the media's representation of distant suffering. Boltanski is more optimistic about a politics of pity than Arendt. He is also content to accept speech as a form of action, to recognize both its limits and its necessity, but also to acknowledge the centrality of emotion to the media's attempts to transcend distance:

> . . . emotion staged by the media occupies an unstable position between real emotion and fictional emotion. It is attached to real emotions inasmuch as the suffering of unfortunates put on view is given as real, assigned to a form of support arising from existential belief . . . But the spectator is sheltered. He is not in the same situation as the unfortunate; he is not by his side during his agony or torture . . . To prevent the unacceptable drift of emotions towards the fictional we must maintain an orientation towards action, a disposition to act, even if this is only by speaking out in support of the unfortunate. But also there must not be too much doubt about the real existence of the unfortunate represented, or about the intentions or desires of the presenters and spectators. (Boltanski 1999: 152–3)

For Boltanski the media are the inevitable bearers of the images which require both private and public responses, but he has few illusions as to how those responses can be turned into effective political action. It is clear, however, that such a politics, if it is effectively to emerge at all, must take what is seen and understood from the screen into the world. Individual compassion needs public pity and the organizations to mobilize it and to turn it into account, but it depends on trust in the messenger.

There are two arguments, then, to be made with respect to compassion. The first is its privatization, the consequence of the media's progressive erosion of the boundaries between public and private realms. This encourages an erosion of the possibility of a politics of pity and its replacement by an economics of compassion, and, worse, by indifference. The second, notwithstanding the problems of conducting action at a distance, is the vital and contrary possibility of acknowledging, as Boltanski suggests, the necessity of thinking and speaking at a distance, and consequently of imagining the imagining which brings the pain of others into mind and into a framework of care, responsibility and, possibly, of action.

In the meantime, the domestic, our entirely understandable desire for simplicity, comfort and order in our everyday lives, has a lot to answer for. The media, in their collusion with that desire, do too. But our complicity and collusion lie even deeper than this, for they lie at the heart of the media's mediation of the realities of the world, and in the as-if of its representational practices. The mediated symbolic is not imposed upon us as a space of no escape. It is one, historically, we have chosen, one that we choose on a daily basis, and one whose choice we have chosen to deny. Choice involves agency. Agency involves the possibility of challenge and refusal. This is not to say that we can walk away from our media-saturated culture. Manifestly we cannot. But we can begin to understand it and in that understanding take responsibility for it. We can then, perhaps, begin to challenge and change it.

Our mediapolis allows us to frame, represent and see the other in his or her own world. It does not often, in its distancing, invite us to engage with the other, nor to accept the challenge of the other in sustainable ways. In effect, and this is its primary weakness, it provides a sanctuary for everyday life, a bounded space of safety and identity, both within and around it. But sanctuaries insulate and isolate as well as protect.

Responsibility

There is clearly a crisis of responsibility to be confronted: a double crisis, which involves responsibility for the media and responsibility for the world that the media represent. Neither are easy to accept, yet both lie at the heart of the relationship between media and morality, and its appropriation into the realms of everyday life.

Both Emmanuel Levinas (Levinas 1969) and Zygmunt Bauman (Bauman 1993) argue for responsibility as a prior condition of the social and for our status as human beings in the world. Responsibility in turn requires proximity, the caress, the duty of care, the immediacy of the face. Levinas's face is not a material object, but it implies its presence, and without it we can neither see nor acknowledge, nor accept the significance of the other in our world. Hence the requirement, my requirement, to confront media in terms of proper distance, the bringing into cognitive and emotional, and therefore moral, reach the subjects otherwise removed from us, beyond the horizon. The other is present for us, whether we like it or know it or see it, or not. And by virtue of our own status as subjects in the world, we cannot refuse the other's claims on us. Yet we can, and do. And one way we do is precisely to create and maintain distance (or a kind of closeness that results in distance), the result of which is the inevitable emergence of indifference.

The kind of responsibility enshrined in these abstract arguments is not one easily amenable to life in the world, since, in a sense, it is primordial, and in its essentialism it seems very much beyond application, never mind understanding. Yet what it signifies is a primary and defining characteristic, a condition for the possibility of life, and even everyday life, in the world. To deny it is to deny the possibility of morality and ethics. Such a denial would be the ultimate in humanity's self-defeat.

There can, of course, be no reasonable and sustainable expectation that audiences and users as participants in the mediapolis can or should take responsibility for everything they see and hear on television or which they access on the internet. This would be both absurd and crippling. Yet to expect that they should *never* take any responsibility for what they see and hear in the mediapolis would be equally crippling. News really would then become merely spectacle, and the world would disappear into the realms of fantasy.

Each of the principal players in the process of mediation carries some of this responsibility. The first, and perhaps the primary, group is the one comprising those who are responsible for the production and transmission of the images and narratives that inform us about the world: the proprietors, editors, producers, journalists of the world's media. They have to be responsible for their responsibility. The current talk is of transparency and accountability: but the first is meaningless without a prior commitment to truth, or honesty, or justice, and the latter risks undermining precisely what it is designed to enhance – individual responsibility for actions taken in the world in relation to, and on behalf of, others. Neither of course are unreasonable, neither can be simply discarded, but without a prior commitment to, and framework of, ultimately individual responsibility neither have any meaning.

The second group comprises those who appear as subjects in the media. Their dependence on, and vulnerability in relation to, producers and other intermediaries is known and recognized, but it does not excuse an equally primary commitment to be responsible for their own appearance and for their own speech. As subject, and as mediated subject, I am still responsible for the other, the other whom I address, who in this case will see and hear me even if I am absent.

And finally there is the responsibility of audiences and users as participants – the hardest of all. How can they take responsibility without
power? Levinas's argument is clear on this point. We have it, it commands
us, we have no choice. But in practice, as I have argued, we are complicit,
we collude, we are often active without being agents, and thinkers without
thought. This position of passivity is part of the deal struck with our
media for the order and comfort they create for us, perhaps even in
moments of high drama and disaster. We need, perhaps, to demand a
modicum of discomfort, a willingness to be troubled and an expectation
that the media might help us in those expectations. But we also, and crucially, need to be more critical and more alert. For our ultimate responsibility as citizens goes wider than the media's representation of the world:
it reaches to the world which the media represent.

These are themes that I discuss further in the next two chapters.

6

Hospitality and Justice

If justice is the first virtue of social institutions, as John Rawls suggests (Rawls 1999: 3), and truth that of systems of thought, then hospitality, I want to argue in this chapter, is the first virtue of the mediapolis. Hospitality as an obligation to welcome the stranger. Hospitality as a right not just to the freedom of speech but as an obligation to listen and to hear. Hospitality, in Kant's sense, as a right of visitation in which '. . . *the right to visit,* to associate, belongs to all men by virtue of their common ownership of the earth's surface; for since the earth is a globe, they cannot scatter themselves infinitely, but must, finally, tolerate living in close proximity, because originally no one had a greater right to any region of the earth than anyone else' (Kant 1983: 118).[1]

This right of hospitality, and the obligation to provide it; what might it mean in the mediapolis? We are confronted these days with a global media system of great complexity and in profound transition. Technologies and commerce going one way. Politics and cultures going in others. The national systems of broadcasting are breaking down, and doubly so. They are being undermined by the fracturing and fragmenting of audiences and the weakening integrity of national identities. They are being transcended by the digital revolution's opening up of the spaces of the internet, and by the transformation of the singular exercise of broadcast power as a communication of the one to the many. They are also being distorted, and in their distortion exploited, by terror whose impact depends, significantly, but necessarily, on its global mediation.

In many respects the whole process of globalization has been both led and determined by the globalization of communication. And if it can be said that we live in a global world, *if,* that is, then it is because we can see and hear that global world on our screens and speakers on a daily basis. And to a significant degree it exists, for most of us, only in its mediation. Global satellite television and radio, but above all the internet, are creating a virtual space which, in principle, is a common possession, and within which, in practice, we live side by side with each other.

Let us not be too quickly seduced by Kant's utopian cosmopolitanism. But let us not walk away from it too quickly either. His insistence on the rights of presentation can properly be translated, in the context of mediation, into rights of representation. His insistence, later on in the same section of his essay, *To Perpetual Peace*, on what he calls the 'public right of men in general', and in which he argues 'that a transgression of rights in *one* place of the earth is felt *everywhere*' (Kant 1983: 119) (an appeal to feeling which perhaps calls the lie to those who only see in him the arch rationalist), is one that in a world of political and religious polarization, of hate speech and censorship, of the intrusion of private mobile communications into public spaces, and public communications into private ones, and the cheek-by-jowl-ness which is the mediapolis's defining characteristic, can hardly be ignored. For in the obligation to provide media hospitality to the stranger and the visitor, in the obligation not to distort the system of communication so much that the visitor cannot be heard, lies the possibility that the present pollution of the mediapolis can be seen for what it is and, albeit perhaps less confidently, reversed.

In these terms, media hospitality is intimately linked with issues of justice and with truthfulness, or so I propose to argue. And likewise such obligations, to hear and to listen and to create the space for effective communication, obligations which are to be imposed both on the media-weak as well as the media-powerful, are primary ones in any attempt to construct a mediated world in which the claimed freedoms to communicate can be made meaningful, sustainable, and where we can expect them to make a difference.

Present failures are easy to determine. What Jürgen Habermas would label as the refeudalization of the public sphere manifests itself in the various political and commercial appropriations and infiltrations of the dominant means of mass communication. And in times of trouble, global trouble, which as the new century begins to show its colours seem to be constant, the disappearance of any real and tangible awareness of the mediated presence and value of the stranger, the other, on his or her own terms, is both symptomatic and self-defeating.

Present opportunities are also easy to determine. For there is no action without a reaction, if not, in this context, exactly an equal and opposite one. For running parallel to the dominant and traditional media's refeudalization is another strand of global mediation, superficially though not simply libertarian, and still hugely vulnerable to the same forces of appropriation and infiltration suffered by the dominant, as well as to other threats peculiar to itself. The internet is coming of age, and in its troubled adolescence it is throwing up significant alternatives to established forms of media practice, ones that are beginning to stand on their own terms, and perhaps more significantly to threaten both the authority and integrity of the dominant media institutions and their platforms.

Chat rooms and bulletin boards have, relatively speaking, long become the semi-public, semi-private spaces for a kind of intimacy and a kind of politics, where the otherwise invisible and unheard can claim an audience, different in quality perhaps but not always in significance, from the fifteen minutes of celebrity offered by the chat shows and the tabloid press. The strengths of such on-line spaces, ease of access, speed and intensity of connection, are also their weaknesses, in the fragility and ephemerality of that intimacy, and in the self-reinforcing move towards the singularity rather than the plurality of voice. In this context the stranger emerges as an individual, but she or he is increasingly and effortlessly vulnerable to exclusion if the voice does not fit or if it does not match: exclusion or self-exclusion comes with the click of a mouse or the instant judgements of a web-master.

But despite these structural weaknesses alternative networks are emerging to occupy the public and the political spaces of the global media world. And in crucial areas this is not a matter of a parallel universe, but of a directly challenging one, above all perhaps in the emergence of the web-log as a phenomenon to contest the already weakening stranglehold of the national press and broadcasting systems. Web-logs offer a potentially radical contribution in the emergence of contemporary mediapolis, by taking for themselves the time and space for communication, and in at least a number of significant cases (both as projections of the private and the personal, and in the more self-consciously and deliberately political) they are beginning to have an impact on the global mainstream.

In the example of the web-log, perhaps above all, the internet can be argued as being already a hospitable space in ways that the broadcasting media could never, nor were never intended to, be; or at least it has the potential to become so. The internet is, from this perspective, a media space of global proportions with still an extant commons, but one constantly at risk both of its self-violation (paedophile and terrorist networks) and its enclosure (by transnational corporations and political controls). The fulfilment of this potential, or so I will argue, depends on a number of factors, and they are not unique to the particularity of this kind of communication. The baseline questions concern the nature, status and role of the audience and user, the kinds of regulation that might or might not be imposed, and the emergence of media publicity and literacy as practices of expression and critique within the mediapolis as a whole. Some of these issues will emerge for discussion in the present chapter. Others will have to wait to the next and final one.

Let me begin by considering what I mean by media hospitality.

Hospitality

> Hospitality is culture itself and not simply one ethic amongst others. Insofar as it has to do with the *ethos*, that is, the residence, one's home, the familiar place of dwelling, inasmuch as it is a manner of being there, the manner in which we relate to ourselves and to others, to others as our own or as forgiveness, *ethics is hospitality*; ethics is so thoroughly coextensive with the experience of hospitality.
>
> Derrida, *On Cosmopolitanism and Forgiveness*

Jacques Derrida's elision – ethics-hospitality – is hugely suggestive in the present context. Hospitality, an obligation, principally, rather than a right, is a primary ethic in a cosmopolitan world. It goes to the heart of our relationships with others. Indeed it is constitutive of such relations. The capacity, indeed the expectation, of welcoming the other in one's space, with or without any expectation of reciprocity, is a particular and irreducible component of what it means to be human. Hospitality is the mark of the interface we have with the stranger. It speaks of the long relationship between the sedentary and the nomad. It is inscribed into the cultures of most of the world religions as an ethic beyond the political, an ethic of humility and generosity, which bypasses differences of power and the inequalities of wealth and status. Hospitality is, in these terms, a primary moment of morality.

I want to argue, in this section of the chapter, that an ethics of hospitality has also to be a primary requirement in the constitution of the mediapolis. Indeed I will go as far as to suggest that the obligation to offer hospitality to the stranger in the symbolic space of media representation is a precondition for media justice. I will discuss what might be meant by media justice in the next section. Hospitality then becomes intertwined with the requirement not just to let the other speak but the requirement that the stranger should be heard. Hospitality is neither tolerance nor toleration. It has nothing to do with sufferance, or with the patronage of the powerful. Tolerance, Derrida suggests, is 'a scrutinised hospitality, always under surveillance, parsimonious and protective of its sovereignty' (Derrida in Borradori 2003: 128). In principle and in its ideal and unconditional form hospitality is entirely innocent, and ignorant, of judgement, of discrimination. The requirement is uniform and universal. And it stands as an obligation wherever one stands in the social or symbolic hierarchy. The rich will welcome the poor, and the poor the rich; the powerful the weak and the weak the powerful. In this it sits comfortably, quite comfortably, as we will see, with John Rawls's account of justice. Indeed one might want to suggest that hospitality is a core component of justice: and its absence, correlatively, a sign of injustice, in the lived as well as the mediated world.

Hospitality, I will also suggest, is an imperfect obligation. In the mediapolis such an obligation already exists in the requirement to make space for clear, free, non-sexist, non-racist communication. But as I will also go on to argue, the presence of such forms of communication may be a necessary, but will not of themselves be a sufficient, guarantee of media justice.

Of course, there are big questions to be answered in the implementation of these obligations. Derrida, also drawing on Kant's discussion of hospitality in *Perpetual Peace*, distinguishes between unconditional and conditional hospitality, the first beyond, the second within, the law. True hospitality, in the context of city and state, for Derrida is the former, breaking all bounds, unconstrained by the forces of law and urban and national self-interest. For true hospitality has to be, just as he argues true forgiveness has to be, beyond constraint. To give hospitality to the terrorist, let us say: to forgive the unforgivable: these are the true expressions of the primary ethic, this moral principle. Hospitality, in its pure and unconditional form, does not involve, nor is it dependent on, an invitation. It is only when someone enters our lives, and is welcomed, without having been invited, that we can truly accept the otherness of the other: his or her implacable difference from us, and his or her immeasurable sameness to us. The law, of course, sets limits on who will be welcome and under what terms. And it could be said that in some sense the law is by definition inhospitable. Yet, perhaps somewhat reluctantly, Derrida accepts the necessity for law, and its rule in these matters, notwithstanding his earnest desire always to improve it.[2]

Hospitality is dangerous. It is not without risk. If it was not then it would not be true hospitality. But its risk is part of the cosmopolitanism of which it is a condition. And this is of course true for the symbolic spaces of the mediapolis, where hospitality can be, and is sometimes, abused, though where its consequences may not, at least directly, be as threatening as in the material world. Perhaps this banal observation is instructive and reassuring, in the sense that it moderates the horror of hospitality's abuse. Yet in the political realities of today's mediapolis, never mind its future, hospitality which is abused will be hard to accept.[3] And like so much else in the management of our relationships with the other, such abuse, or fear of it, will easily threaten to undermine the commitment to be the otherwise haspitable and generous host. The disinterested, or fair, reporting of terrorism in a society recently terrorized is perhaps the test case. What kinds of distance are appropriate in such representation? Do we listen to the terrorists on their own terms? Can we hear what they may have to say? And likewise how are we to deal with those (those other than in the claimed legitimacy of the State), whose only aim is retribution: the threat to society posed by those claiming revenge: the eye for the eye, the ear for the ear?

It could be said that the primary condition of existing media, in democratic societies at least, and in their most liberal manifestations, is already one of conditional hospitality. The news of the world, as well as documentary accounts of it, invite the stranger onto page and screen. However, the invitation is always conditional on good behaviour; on the acceptance, by those who do so appear, of the editorial controls exercised by those constructing the texts. Even when such hospitality is extended to allow the nominally unconstrained voices of the other to be heard, those editorial controls remain in place. They work to constrain those speaking either by marginalizing them in the schedule (the late night or early afternoon show) or on the page (in the letters column, or in the form of a half-hidden editorial apology for misrepresentation), or by limiting the rights of access to the relatively safe or ordinary (that is, to those who are unlikely to challenge the hospitality so cautiously granted).

And we should acknowledge that in all forms of mediated representation except perhaps in the limiting case of entirely free self-representation, mediation, as translation, always involves a constrained, a limited, restricted form of hospitality. Since, at least within the dominant forms of media, and above all within the press and broadcast forms, the welcoming process is compromised by the edit, and by its exercise of symbolic power: you are entering my text, always, always, on my terms. This would be just as true of the letters page in a national newspaper, as it would be of a posting to a well-run website.

So unconditional hospitality, operating at the level of the channel, in the context of the media as publisher, which it is increasingly becoming, as well as at the level of the individual item of reportage, is not just a tough call, particularly in the latter. It might be reasonably said to be an impossibility. Yet without acknowledging its call on us we will, at best, have no sense of the limits of what we are doing editorially and politically in the conditional mode of media hospitality, nor be able to conceive of how to transcend those limits. In media terms, as well as in material terms, there is a difference, then, between the hospitality of invitation (which might also involve an idea of hospitality as reciprocity)[4] and what Derrida calls the hospitality of visitation. And it is the latter which is increasingly required in a truly cosmopolitan society. There has to be space for the unbidden and the uninvited, both in the material as well as the mediated world. The journey towards unconditional hospitality involves respect for those who speak in public space, and a willingness to grant, without qualification, a right of audience to those who would otherwise be beyond the pale. And indeed, the mediation in real time of, and in the endless discourses that follow, acts of terror is from this perspective both evidence of the acceptance of the obligation to grant such hospitality (though it is not seen in these terms, of course), and of its palpable abuse.

And on another platform, too, the principle of hospitality within the mediapolis is already in operation. The internet is often seen as offering such a space. Yet the internet even in its openness is not necessarily a space of hospitality, for if it is hospitality it is hospitality, and this is its contradiction in terms, without a host. It is interesting, and perhaps ironic, to note that the defining discourse of the internet generically includes such terms: host, home-page, visitor, which are equally those of the discourse of hospitality. It is ironic principally because of the substitution of the human by the technological, a de-anthropomorphization, which fundamentally undercuts the humanity of the relationship of self and other, without which hospitality in any of its forms cannot be considered as effective.[5] Yet the internet can be seen, and is often seen, as unconditionally open. In what is that openness constituted? And without a meaningful host, one who takes responsibility for the welcome, can it ever provide, at its most general global level, as opposed to on a particular site, the proper location of the kind of hospitality the mediapolis should provide?

As Derrida argues there can be no hospitality without a home, a place of welcome and in it someone who welcomes. I would want to suggest that the internet generically is not, securely or consistently, a home, and individual sites, the home pages, are just as likely, perhaps even more likely, to reject the unbidden visitor as unwelcome as many of the more established broadcast media channels. The mediapolis cannot, therefore, depend on the internet, though it will include it, and the requirements for media hospitality in a globalizing world are still premised on the continuing importance of some form of broadcasting, some mode or modes of dissemination; some meaningful and effective exercise of individual and institutional responsibility. The possibility of dialogue, interactivity and other forms of mediated intimacy, if they are to extend beyond the excluding private, depends on the priority of the disseminative, essentially broadcast, mode and on the presence and accessibility of a shared communicative space (though it is of course acknowledged that net-based communications are also disseminative as well as dialogical).

The mediapolis, in any and all its forms, must be shareable even if it is not always or often shared. And as I have argued in chapter 4, such shareability is contrapuntal. It is the continued co-presence of multiple voices that defines, both actually and potentially, the possibility of spaces of mutual hospitality in the mediapolis. For hospitality begins in the recognition of the other and in the sound of his or her voice. It is the hospitality of a cosmopolitan society and of an intensely mediated culture. It involves sharing that space and taking responsibility for it. And it involves all parties accepting the obligation to open their space to the stranger irrespective of their position in the media hierarchy.

In practice this might mean a number of different things, but the baseline expectation is a willingness to ensure that the digital and analogue spectrum is available for minorities, the disadvantaged and for non-national transmission; that individual channels provide programme time for the otherwise excluded; and that within news and current affairs the bodies and voices of those who might equally be otherwise marginalized will be seen and heard on their own terms. These obligations are also expected of the minority channels and programmes. The stranger needs everywhere to be welcome in the media spaces of home and hearth.

In practice, of course, this is a huge expectation, one which is neither immediately likely nor ever likely to be free from the risks of abuse. It is however, as I shall now go on to argue, a necessary principle of media justice. For without the presence of the other – the presence of the other, once again, on his or her own terms in our media space – there is no possibility of an audience. And without an audience, without an acceptance of the other's voice, there can be no understanding of the other in his or her difference, and as part of our world.

And, finally, without an acknowledgement of the other's moral standing (O'Neill 1990), of the right to be in the world which we share, and a recognition that his or her presence in such a world presumes a right to act on and in it, then once again hospitality loses its meaning. In this sense, though with a different inflection, Onora O'Neill's (O'Neill 2000)

Kantian description of what she calls moral cosmopolitanism, the possibility of the responsibility for the other in an unbounded world, fits quite well with Derrida's grounding of hospitality and culture, and the arguments which I am also trying to make in relation to the particular challenges of media representation.

Two, at least two, related questions are raised by this. The first is that of hospitality's abuse, and the second is that of its regulation. The first is relatively easily dealt with, at least in principle. If those accorded hospitality abuse it by denying it to others in their own space then they forfeit their right to it.[6] The second is much more complex, since it raises significant questions about the nature, the scale and the location of regulation in an increasingly global media space. All regulation inevitably limits the rights to media hospitality and the obligations to provide it. All regulation inhibits the rights of passage. Yet the mediapolis, if it is to be a genuinely cosmopolitan space (in whatever terms this is defined), has also to be a hospitable space. How do we square the circle?

Perhaps by entering the difficult spaces of justice, responsibility and obligation, which I now propose to do.

Justice

Media are institutions. And as institutions they can, and do, act both justly and unjustly. There are many ways in which they can act unjustly: by denying or distorting the voices of others; by refusing airspace to the indigenous, the diasporic, the marginal and the minority; by systematically foreclosing, for commercial or political reasons, on the alternative or the critical, or more simply on the uneconomic, the unpopular, or the ideologically offensive. As the media globalize, such injustices as these become more insidious: for the consequences of repression, the enforced silences or absences, still in evidence in many states even in the post-Cold War age, they increasingly become more significant as the size of an audience who might be available to hear but cannot, increases. But such injustices as these can also be mitigated: above all perhaps in the minority appropriation of the still effectively free airspace of the internet and the ease and speed of its access and connectivity, with the result that at least some will listen, some will know, some will react. Such injustices can also be mitigated, at the margins, in the occasional flowering of community radio stations. In a world that cannot continue to exist without the free passage of information, nor survive without communication across borders and cultures, such injustices are tangible and real, such mitigations are all the more important. But if we cannot speak; if we cannot hear; if distortion outweighs translation, we are condemned at best to silence and at worst to the disasters of misrepresentation and misunderstanding.

The institutions with most power carry the greatest risk of injustice. And injustice is easier to recognize than justice, just as evil is easier to recognize than goodness. If we are to identify and condemn the injustices of others, we need somehow to agree on what counts as justice, as its value, as its good. I have spoken of hospitality as a principal good of global media, and as such a core component of media justice. But we need to secure it. And we need to secure it both because of, and despite, the differences of, and the inequalities within, the world in which we live.

Let me turn to John Rawls.

John Rawls (Rawls 1999) is well known for constructing an elaborate theory of justice as, initially and significantly, a counter to utilitarian theories which, he argues, cannot be sustained if one has the well-being of all members of a society at heart. Utilitarianism's insistence on the greatest good for the greatest number systematically denies the rights of the minority. It is Rawls's intention to devise a theory which insists on the generality of the good, and on a presumption that no principle of justice can be applied if as a result the interests and expectations of the vulnerable are reduced, even in favour of this greater good. 'Injustice,' he suggests, 'is simply inequalities that are not to the benefit of all' (Rawls 1999: 54).

Rawls describes the basic social conditions for his theory as follows:

> In justice as fairness society is interpreted as a cooperative venture for mutual advantage. The basic structure is a public system of rules defining a scheme of activities that leads men to act together so as to produce a greater sum of benefits and assigns to each certain recognised claims to a share in the proceeds. What a person does depends upon what the public rules say he will be entitled to, and what a person is entitled to depends on what he does. (Rawls 1999: 73–4)

The first point to be made is that this basic structure characterizes the necessary equivalence and equality which must inform any attempt to provide an approach to justice in the mediapolis. This is particularly appropriate in a media context where the most familiar argument is the general but self-serving and perniciously utilitarian one that an increase in choice offered by the major providers of content is for the general good, notwithstanding its consequences for the capacity of minority and alternative providers to gain a rightful share of the audience. For it is the case that arguments for the value of choice, when made by an incumbent or by a dominant media provider, systematically constrain the range of choice to be within what they themselves see fit to provide. And as such it masks the consequences of such an extension for the capacity of others to contribute to it.

The second is that justice, as Rawls accounts for it, is both principled and procedural. It begins with a presumption of a clean slate, a level playing field, or as he defines it, a veil of ignorance. The rationality at the heart of his theory of justice requires that judgements which are to result in agreement on the principles of justice must be grounded in circumstances where the parties involved cannot mobilize their special interests and expectations, and where the outcome therefore is not dependent either on the circumstances of social status, or the arbitrariness of natural chance. This is the veil of ignorance. It is hypothetical. No one involved is to know their own social or cultural status. No one involved can have an idea of what constitutes their own good. Only under these conditions, therefore, can rational argument produce a fair account of justice, and it is this procedure which Rawls adopts as the ground for his position.

He proposes, in what he calls the original position, two principles of justice. First, each person is to have an equal right to the most extensive scheme of equal basic liberties compatible with a similar scheme of liberties for others. Second, social and economic inequalities are to be arranged so that they are reasonably expected to be to everyone's advantage and attached to positions and offices open to all (1999: 53). He then goes on to argue that because there is no independent evaluation of what might constitute a just result in the establishment of justice, such agreement as does occur can only be the result of a fair procedure properly followed. Ends therefore do not overrule means.

These Kantian principles of universal rationality are both presumed and defended. Human beings have a system of primary goods which it is rational for each and everyone of them to desire. The definition of what constitutes primary goods, as Rawls explains in the preface to the second edition of the book, is dependent on the judgement of the human as a moral rather than as a physical or psychological being, and as such primary goods are characterized as 'what persons need in their status as free and equal citizens, and as normal and fully co-operating members of society over a complete life' (Rawls 1999: xiii). And as pluralist as well as rationalist thinkers have argued, it is hard to deny, notwithstanding profound cultural differences in their realization as well as their denial, a common need and desire for such things as rights, liberties and opportunities.

My argument here is that access to, and participation in, a global system of mediated communication is a substantive good and a precondition for full membership of society, and that the distribution of such a right must be fair and just. Let me develop this further.

There are a number of points to make. The first is that media justice, with hospitality as its first principle, is built on an equivalent presumption about the nature of communicative space as Rawls makes in relation to society as a whole. It is that full participation in the social life of the society in which one lives, an increasingly global society for larger and larger numbers of people around the world, is a primary good. And that such participation is increasingly coming to depend on access to, and competence within, a media culture in which the capacity to gain the information required, and the capacity to participate in free and effective mediated communication, are in turn primary. This makes both the traditional requirement for freedom of speech, as the beginning and end of a human right in this context, insufficient on its own terms. For such freedoms cannot to be vouchsafed in a world of intense inequality without the expectation of equivalence between those with and those without the basic resources to do so, and without the expectation that the exercise of freedom to speak by the powerful does not restrict the capacities of the powerless to exercise their own equal rights (O'Neill 1990).

But secondly, and once again this is inscribed in the principle of media hospitality, there is the expectation not just of the freedom of speech, but of the freedom to be heard. Speaking into the air is therefore necessary but it is also not sufficient. Media justice requires there to be no distortions in a global system of communication which result in the systematic exclusion of any group and that the conditions for effective speech require in turn and in practice the effective distribution of, once again in principle, all that is spoken.

If we apply, procedurally, the veil of ignorance to the definition of justice in the mediapolis, we would have to discount completely the differences between the large and the small, the powerful and the powerless, the national, the local and the global media producers and distributors, for in accepting the universal relevance of the expectation of hospitality as a first principle of media justice, we would need to understand that its claims would not discriminate. In accepting it we accept it without knowing where we are in the media hierarchy. And in accepting it we agree to act in accordance with it, likewise.

And it follows, further, that if we apply such principles of media justice, that we are going to need to presume, and to ensure, something we might want to call *the universal audience*: universal rather than global, since it is a philosophical rather than an empirical concept; and universal because it is based on the presumption that to be a member of an audience is a right. No one should expect to be excluded, even if in practice (of course) complete inclusion is an impossibility. But this is a universal audience in another sense, too. For it is becoming increasingly clear that as digital technologies evolve, the boundary between production and consumption is being eroded above all in the emergence of the audience as producer, in peer-to-peer, internet, mobile phone- and pod-based cultures. In all these various activities, invisibly and naively, all those who engage in such practices are inscribed into the moral space of the mediapolis, where their participation will need to be both regulated and defended, and to be governed by the same principles of justice as I have been arguing apply to the established players.

There is an irony, of course, in my argument here, that the promise of a universal audience emerges at a time when, at least in some sectors of some societies, the boundaries around such a thing as an audience are beginning to erode more or less completely. While one can argue for the principle of universality, and the practice of open participation and access, one is also forced to recognize that the latter involves subverting the traditional category of the audience as receiver in a fundamental way. Yet perhaps the way to think of these changes is in terms of extension rather than subversion. In which case we will have to consider what audiences are (and might be) these days. I have discussed some aspects of this situation in chapter 5, though there is much more to be said.[7]

Indeed the much, and easily, criticized universalism in the Rawlsian position is declared and is arguably defensible, too, in these presumptions. For it would have to be argued that such rights, as well as their equivalent obligations (of which more later) such as the freedom to participate in global media culture, either as speaker or as audience, or as both, are something that would have to be *not* seen as a good, would have to be seen as *not* a good, by some cultures or members of cultures. In other words to suggest that, for indigenously sustainable reasons, the distortion of, and the exclusion from, media culture would be seen as preferable. One can of course imagine groups (Trappist monks) and whole cultures (traditional Korean society where silence is valued above all) where such expectations are not likely to be high on the list. One can more than imagine situations where those who claim the right to speak would not want everything they say to be heard by everyone. But equally one can argue, and must argue I believe, in the context of the intensely mediated global world in which we now live, and in the manifestation of the mediapolis as I have defined it, that such principles of justice – the right to speak and an obligation to listen – are demonstrably, logically and empirically, universal in their claims, and sustainable as such.

There is no ultimate defence against such abstract universalism, but there is no escape either. Certainly there is no escape if the intellectual and institutional aim is to ensure a measure of justice between those who otherwise share nothing, or little, else. One might suggest that it survives as a defensible position as long as no opponent emerges successfully to argue that under certain social or cultural conditions the basic claims for, say, equality or fairness in communication are inappropriate or unsustainable. Yet, by the same token, the consequences of its defeat are incalculable.

Media justice requires, therefore, the creation of a system of institutions of global reach, which can in their very working guarantee to maximize the basic freedoms of mediated communication, without which the mediapolis would remain unjust. But media justice also requires something else, something more than procedure, and something more than the creation of institutions and institutional processes. And what this is, is in significant ways often seen as contrary to the rational logic of procedure which informs Rawls's version of justice. It is responsibility.

Responsibility

The achievement of a measure of justice is, in Rawls's view, the product of following the correct, that is a fair, procedure. I take procedure to have two referents here, one in the determination of principles, that is as a logical procedure, and the other in its implementation, that is as an institutional procedure. There is no objection to the first, as should now be clear. But the second could be seen to be unduly restrictive insofar as it seems to require a primary, if not even an exclusive, commitment to institutionalized processes of regulation. I would argue, however, as I will indeed do both in this and in the next chapter, that in the empirical reality of globally mediated mass communication, there needs to be space for other, albeit parallel, responses and practices[8] if the notion of procedure is to have any *political* value.

To make such an argument I need to shift sociological and philosophical register, and to address an approach to morality that depends less, if at all, on a theory of justice, but rather more on a theory of responsibility.

The two approaches, on the face of it, are radically opposed. For justice, in Rawls's sense, and indeed in mine thus far, depends on the abstract rationality of a commitment to procedure, one in which ends do not trump means. The implication of this position is that the moral order of the world we live in or desire to create does not depend on the individual's actions or the primary engagement of individuals with each other and their duty of care, their responsibility, for those actions and for those others. Indeed the appeal to the procedural as a measure of the legitimation of action is one that can and has been used by the most immoral and murderous of regimes. It is an appeal which can systematically and fundamentally undermine the responsibility of the individual for their own actions and also deny the humanity of those excluded from its process.

This is, at least, how it appears to Zygmunt Bauman. Why is this important in the present context of the morality of the mediapolis? Because, as I want to argue, the mediapolis needs a morality that is grounded in *both* procedure and responsibility. This is hardly shattering news. However, it has significant implications not just for the integrity of global media culture as such, but for how it can be enabled. So I will be arguing for the need to hold both to account and to recognize that effective procedures and equally effective acceptance of responsibility are together preconditions for a moral mediapolis at every level of its operation, in which the first is a matter of regulation, and the second a matter of literacy. Neither on its own will suffice.

Zygmunt Bauman's book *Postmodern Ethics* (Bauman 1993) can be understood as a defence of responsibility rather than, and contrary to, justice, and justice as a term barely makes an appearance in it. His argument is that modernity's appropriation of reason, its institutionalization of process and procedure, its embodiment of reciprocity as a principle of social life, indeed its very sociality, has systematically undermined the possibility of moral action and responsible behaviour. This is because morality can only be the property of the individual, the individual who takes command. Morality can only genuinely emerge from the refusal of social order, as order. The moral individual is one who takes responsibility for his or her own actions, and indeed for a primary duty of care for the other. Society, certainly modern society, society as mass society, society as rules, society as codes and deference and denial, society as such, gets in the way. And since justice is social, it too, perversely enough, gets in the way. His position is itself a classic inversion of Enlightenment thinking on these matters, of course, wherein justice and morality were seen to be the products of social life, as property and propriety. And of course it puts him at the opposite pole to Rawls.

For Bauman, indeed, morality precedes society. We enter society as moral beings only to be seduced away from moral responsibility. And we come to be seduced into the belief that, rather than having to accept a duty of care, society will care. For Bauman, as for these others, the challenge of post- or late modernity is to find some way back to the individual as a thinking, sentient, caring being, for it is only in responsibility, and by this he means personal responsibility, that humanity can be saved from its own self-destruction. And he concludes:

> Contrary to one of the most uncritically accepted philosophical axioms, there is no contradiction between the rejection of (or scepticism towards) the ethics of socially conventionalised and rationally 'founded' norms, and the insistence that it does matter, and *matter morally*, what we do and from what we desist . . . Moral responsibility does not look for reassurance for its right to be or for excuses for its right not to be. It is there before any reassurance or proof and after any excuse or absolution. (Bauman 1993: 250)

The point about moral responsibility is that it is, and has to be, the property of the individual, and not of the collective, nor of the procedural.

This is a similar argument to the one I have just made about hospitality. I have suggested that the challenge is to see it as a matter for the individual, and his or her obligations to the other. Once these become displaced onto the institution, onto procedure, into regulation, then the connection between person and person becomes disturbed and attenuated, and it loses its force. This is the argument behind my sense that the internet cannot in an uncompromised way be a host, and it is the argument behind Derrida's notion that the law will equally and inevitably compromise the possibility of pure hospitality. In each case this is not just a matter of the inevitability of loss, the impossibility of perfection, but the intervention of technology and procedural rationality into the process, and its capacity to undermine what it protests it is protecting. And above all it is the problem of distance and distancing: the material distance of spatial separation and the political distancing of procedural rationality.

And I have already suggested that the particular challenge of the mediapolis is that of distance, some aspects of which I discussed in the last chapter. For if the account of responsibility presumes the enabling primacy of the face-to-face, then the question becomes how we can effectively translate that obligation into a world in which distance is no longer a barrier, and where the other, albeit through his or her mediation, is always within reach.

The philosopher Emmanuel Levinas, whose work I have already cited and who has profoundly influenced Bauman, also argues for responsibility as a prior condition of the social and as a precondition of our status as human beings in the world. Responsibility in turn requires proximity, the caress, the duty of care, the immediacy of what he calls the face. Levinas's face is not a material object, but it implies its presence as a command; that is, the other is seen always to be with us, even if we cannot see him or her. And therefore without the face we can neither see nor acknowledge, nor accept the significance of the other in our world. And if this is the case, and we instinctively know it to be the case, since our concerns and cares are most easily and most often devoted to those close to us, the problem of course is how, or whether, to extend this duty of care to those distant from us materially, to those who are separated from us in space, even though we can see and hear them only in their mediated appearance; or through (the mists of) time, since we know that they will follow us in the next and subsequent generations.

There are two aspects to this problem of mediated distance. The first is one that I have already discussed on a number of occasions in this book in my elaboration of the idea of proper distance. The second concerns the practical capacity of the individual to act responsibly.

Let me deal with the first, first.

Hans Jonas (Jonas 1984), whose principal concern is the exercise of responsibility over time rather than space, distinguishes between formal and substantive responsibility. Both are relevant to the present discussion. The first is the responsibility I have for my own acts, those aspects of life and deed for which I can be held accountable. The second is responsibility for the condition of the other – paradigmatically in some sense the responsibility of a parent for a child, as long as they both shall live. It is also the responsibility of the statesman. This, very different kind of, responsibility is an expression of power, and extends with the extent of the power that I have. Substantive responsibility is non-reciprocal. And underlying it, in Jonas's terms is the responsibility that we all have to ensure the continuing existence of mankind. As he argues: '. . . the *existence* of mankind comes first, whether deserved on its past record *and* its likely continuation or not. It is the ever-transcendent *possibility*, obligatory in itself, which must be kept open by the continued existence. To preserve this possibility is a cosmic responsibility – hence the duty of man to exist' (Jonas 1984: 99).

Even if this is an argument, as Richard Bernstein (Bernstein 2002) in turn argues, that cannot bear the weight of rational justification, it is far from being unreasonable and is no different epistemologically from that of Rawls's commitment to justice. Yet it is clear that the global media are both the product of, and the stimulus for, both kinds of responsibility: the formal in which I must take responsibility for my own actions within the mediapolis – I, the proprietor; I, the producer; I the editor; I, the subject; I, the interlocutor; I, the reader, the audience, the user; I, the participant; and the substantive where I can be also held accountable by virtue of my existence in this planet and because I am an agent, albeit proportionate to my power, and as such I bear a responsibility for its continuing existence.

But central to both Jonas's discussion, and to mine, is the role of modern technology in enhancing and extending the reach of human action, both in time and space. His preoccupation with the future, and the manifestation of his concern for that future, is now of course embodied in the environmental movement and in the thinking and action of those concerned with the consequences of current science's engagement with the genetic. Jonas's, ultimately unanswerable, question is that of how to deal with the new temporal distance introduced into human affairs by the power that technology has given us. My different, related, but equally possibly unanswerable, question is that of how to deal with the new spatial distance introduced into human affairs by the power that media and communications technology has given us.[9]

The establishment of proper distance, a notion I am discussing in its different inflections at a number of points in this book, is a matter for individual action, but it is also a product of the collective process of mediation. In this sense it has both formal and substantive dimensions, and individual and procedural components.

The requirement of proper distance is to bring into cognitive and emotional, and therefore moral, reach the subjects otherwise removed from us, beyond the horizon. In an intensely and extensively mediated global world the other, the stranger, is present for us, whether we like it or know it or see it, or not. And by virtue of our own status as subjects in the world, as well as by virtue of the strangers' equal and equivalent status as subjects in the world, we cannot refuse their claims upon us. Yet we can, and often do. And one way we do refuse such claims is precisely to create and maintain distance (or a kind of closeness that results in distance), the result of which is the inevitable eruption of amorality and indifference. Jonas's argument is a variation on this theme. Indeed for him the emergence of technology reinforces the requirement for responsibility because it increases human power, above all to affect what will happen in the future. My argument is a parallel one in relation to space, both global and civic. The achievement of proper distance as a moral position is both the product of effective procedures and indeed the management of media hospitality. And it is also a product of individual action and the taking of responsibility for those actions.

So the second aspect of the problem of responsibility in the mediapolis concerns its practice, its application. And here we have to confront the individual, and indeed the continuing significance of the face-to-face. For it is in reality in the face-to-face that much, if not all, of the work of media is done. It is done in the direction and production of news and documentary, where journalists, reporters and researchers confront their subjects in the one-to-one if not always strictly speaking in the face-to-face (because so much is done on the telephone or on-line). It is also done by the editors of those communications insofar as their decisions on inclusion and framing rely on the face-work done with colleagues. And it is done by the non-professional participants, the audiences and media users, in the context of their communications and discussions around the TV set or on-line, where judgements of truthfulness, authenticity, value and relevance are made. In the mediapolis responsibility is cellular. And it cannot be avoided.

So there are principles. There are procedures. And there are decisions to be made minute by minute, day by day, by individuals whose principal responsibility is the reporting of the world and making it understandable. And by individuals whose obligation it is to undertake this without undermining the dignity of those who are their subjects and without deliberately or ignorantly distorting the meaning of events. Equally there are decisions to be made by the receivers of those communications: to respond, to seek understanding and to complete the communication without surrendering to prejudice or fear.

And such acts of responsibility are on the one hand embodied, but also perhaps both masked and muddied, in codes of professional practice. But they also emerge, or should emerge, also as I will go on to argue, in the need for greater competence in the various kinds of literacy that any and all engagement with the media now requires. All of those involved, at whatever level, and according to their power, must take their own responsibility for their actions in the mediapolis. Perhaps we already know and understand this. Perhaps.

One final point about responsibility. It is that it signals a shift in the discourse on the morality of media from one of rights to one of obligations. This shift has been implicit in much of what I have written so far in this chapter, especially in the discussion of hospitality and responsibility. Justice, it might be said, could be considered both a right and an obligation.

Obligation and truthfulness

There is, arguably, a difference between an obligation and a right. Rights-based approaches to communication take as their starting point the question of how we are entitled to express ourselves (rights to freedom of expression or freedom of assembly). They start from the perspective of the agent as claimant; they involve a demand. An obligation-based approach starts from the question of how we ought to communicate and it starts with the agent as provider. The issue is not how we should be treated but how we should act. Rights-based approaches to communication are unable to judge which kinds of communication are to be judged acceptable, since rights-based approaches will approve of any communication as long as it does not infringe the rights of someone else. An obligation-based approach to communication requires more active and deliberate attention to the circumstances and conditions within which free and genuine communication can be established and preserved.

Once again, I have a mentor in this discussion. Onora O'Neill (O'Neill 1990) argues, in a brilliant essay, that rights-based approaches to communication cannot decide on which rights are maximal: disputes about the freedom of expression that take rights as their starting point are certain to be inconclusive. Rights are important, of course, but they need a framework of obligations, of what one ought to do, of a conception of the good or of virtue, in order to be meaningful and decidable. Communication can be wrong, perhaps even bad, even if it does not affect or challenge rights.

So obligations place responsibility as the primary condition of morality. They are based on a presumption of a good. They require a focus on the agent and the action, the subject and not the recipient of communication. Whereas a rights-based approach is geared to those on the receiving end of communication, an obligations-based approach concerns the agent, and both individuals' and institutions' capacity to act.[10]

Every right might be seen to have a corresponding obligation, but there are some obligations without equivalent rights. These are called in classical ethical theory imperfect obligations. In traditional societies there are often obligations to provide the stranger with hospitality, but it could not be said that the stranger had rights to it. In mediated communication, arguably, obligations to provide the provision of clear, free, non-sexist communication precede any claims for individual rights to receive only such communications. And although it will never ultimately be possible to agree a perfect set of imperfect obligations in global communication, it is essential to be able to ask the question of how we ought 'to speak, publish and program, and what sorts of practices of representation and communication ought to be prized and fostered' (O'Neill 1990: 165). And as I have been arguing I would regard media hospitality as such a primary good, the basis for just such an obligation in the mediapolis.

Rights-based approaches to speech are essentially that. They protect the individual's rights to express an opinion but not necessarily to communicate. They do not require an audience, do not address the conditions under which someone who speaks can be heard. This is the nub of the issue. The rights to self-expression, vital though they are, do not need to take into account the social context which may or may not make them possible; they are only concerned with not violating someone else's similar right to freedom of communication. But:

> Those who aim to *communicate*, and who do not pre-empt others' acting on like principles, must do more than refrain from violating others' rights. They must also communicate in ways that do not destroy or erode linguistic, social, and technical conditions of communication. Toleration of *expression* may need only non-interference; toleration of *communication* must also sustain conditions of communication. (O'Neill 1990: 167)

I have suggested hospitality instead of toleration, but the point still stands. And as such the obligation to provide it requires attention to the conditions, the historically and sociologically specific conditions, under which the prospects of free communication can be enhanced. The specific principles and practices of hospitality will need to adjust to changes in the means of communication, as those means extend not just to changing technological conditions but also to the changing skills and literacies that are required to make communication meaningful. Imperfect communicative obligations, that is those obligations which have no commensurate rights (whereas for example non-deception and non-coercion are both obligations and rights), address those conditions of communication that need to be in place to ensure that languages are preserved, literacies are inculcated and that technologies are not introduced and institutionalized which destroy or undermine the possibilities of communication as such.

Communication is always, in principle, a two-way process, and even in those circumstances, the dominant ones in a broadcast world, where the technology precludes immediate audience response and interaction, such a principle requires a recognition that all involved must adopt a certain view both of their own activity as communicator and of their audience:

> In particular they must treat their own communication, as well as the communication of others whom they report as *particular voices among many*, as voices that are subject to challenge and error and not as the oracles of truth or authorities beyond question. Second, they must *respect the voices of their audiences*. They must be committed to communicating only in ways that neither *mislead* by assuming bogus authority nor *silence* others by undermining their standing and capacities to respond. Neither obligation is easily met. (O'Neill 1990: 171)

Such obligations are consistent with the pluralist position that I have already indicated as being essential in the context of global communication. Above all, that position, and now the obligations that it presupposes, addresses the centrality of not just respect for the other's voice, but of the obligation to ensure that such a voice is not only present in the mediapolis but is entitled to claim an audience, and is *capable* of being heard.[11]

This is of course a terribly challenging demand. It requires attention not just to the regulatory infrastructure of national and international communication networks, but to a degree of reflexive attention to the nature of communication, its limits and possibilities, in any given setting. For without understanding both the politics and the power of mediated communication, and without addressing the norms of professional practice, such obligations will be stillborn. There are two dimensions to this. The dominant players in the mediapolis must not only be prepared actively to tolerate the presence of others within it, but should seek interaction with them. This cannot be effected, merely if at all, through regulation, however sensitive and facilitative. And there are obligations in relation to audiences. For members of the (universal) audience require the skills and literacies which will help to ensure their adequate, that is to say their critical, participation in global media culture. These are issues which I address in the next and final chapter.

But before providing a summary of, and a conclusion to this one, I want to consider one further obligation, albeit briefly. It is the obligation to the truth. Such brevity needs to be explained. The presumption of truth and truthfulness in matters of public discourse in the mediapolis, and in the broadly liberal society which both sustains and is sustained by it, has been implicit in all my arguments thus far. If I turn directly to a discussion of truth only now, it is merely to ensure both its presence, its importance and a sense of its difficulty. But the brevity is also justified by the complexity and longevity of the philosophical issues and my limited competence in dealing with them. It is not in any way intended to reduce truth's significance in the mediapolis; on the contrary.

Yet it is often said that there is no such thing as truth in the mediapolis, and that, to suggest that there is, is both hubristic and wrong. This is because in matters of significance, in the accounts that any given mediator will offer of the complexity of the world, as exceptional or indeed in its ordinariness, what is reported will inevitably be partial (it comes from a single perspective however inclusive of the perspectives of others), provisional (it is always subject to change, and as a news story unfolds, it is bound to do so) and incomplete (there is no end to the narration of the world in its claims for truth, though it can possibly be suggested that falsehood is finite). Only in the simplest and most literal claims can truth be said to be plain, and the claims for it to be justified, sustainable. Otherwise, in matters of global and national report, in a distorting marketplace and a pressurizing political culture, such claims to truth are increasingly seen as being unsustainable and effectively only claimed by those who believe in their power to report it.

In such truth claims, for example, that 'I was there and this is what I saw,' (what can be called 'positional advantage'), both statements can be considered, relatively unproblematically, as true, but then what follows by way of accounting for what is seen, and the presumption that the seeing, the physical presence, the fact of being there, is sufficient to sustain those claims, this cannot be so easily secured. Yet in offering such scepticism and an effective disbelief in the possibility of truth, we nevertheless expect our media to be truthful, for without that expectation they have no value – they become mere noise.

This is an argument made much more elegantly than I can ever hope to do by Bernard Williams. He suggests that an expression of scepticism that truth in any given circumstance is possible nevertheless depends on a notion of truth not only being possible but necessary; for without such an idea the claims for its absence cannot be sustained. He also points out, in another version of the same argument, that while we reasonably can accept, and often do, the argument that truth is a chimera we nevertheless still value and are committed to truthfulness, and by that he means 'a pervasive suspiciousness, a readiness against being fooled, an eagerness to see through appearances to the real structures that lie behind them' (Williams 2002: 1). However the more fully we endorse this commitment to truthfulness, the more it becomes clear that there is little if anything confidently we can call true.

These paradoxes, equivalent, perhaps, though in a different register, to the paradox of trust in the media that I discussed in the previous chapter, in which our trust in the media seems to decline as our dependence on them grows, are not easy to resolve, but they do have significant consequences, in Williams's context for the writing of history; and in mine, of course, in the production of, principally, news and current affairs.

This is not going to be a philosophical argument. At stake however, within the interstices of Williams's paradox, is the nature of the expectation that the media are, and must be, truthful, if we are to depend on them for their accounts of the world, and even if we know that they can never fully tell the truth. And at stake is the obligation to tell the truth, or perhaps more strictly, to be truthful. This is the third obligation: the other two are hospitality and the construction of proper distance, which we need to establish at the moral core of the mediapolis.

Communication of any kind is, of course, impossible without a commitment to truthfulness. Mediated communication cannot be an exception. Its role in a global world is both to express its own truthfulness and to challenge the claims of others. Fulfilling such a role, and the justification for so fulfilling it, depends significantly on a presumption of the qualities of a liberal/democratic society, which cannot be imagined, either, without such a commitment. And at the same time such a society cannot be imagined without the institutional frameworks for enabling the emergence of truth not only in the literal marketplace of ideas (a marketplace that Williams is not alone in recognizing as being potentially and actually substantially flawed in this respect) but in what he calls the idealized marketplace of ideas, where public communications can be tested against each other, according to criteria adduced for their evaluation.

As he says:

> No liberal democracy can afford to be too discouraging of expressive, disorderly, and even prejudicial speech, or too fussy about who publishes it and how, and it cannot force people to think about public or political matters. At the same time, the basic rights of liberal society and democratic freedoms themselves depend on the development and protection of methods for discovering and transmitting the truth, and this requires that public debate embody in some form an approximation to an idealised market. Squaring this circle must be a prime aim of institutional intervention in liberal states. (Williams 2002: 219)

The production of truth is a matter of both accuracy and sincerity.[12] It involves a commitment to make sense of the world, and notwithstanding the cultural variation between what that might mean, as well as cultural differences between what truth itself might mean as well as might be, this making sense is a common, perhaps universal, component of truth telling. Making sense, as an ideal, involves an expectation that the media should tell us the truth, 'in the sense that they should not lie or mislead, what we need them for is not to tell us something called "the truth about [the past]". We need them to be truthful, and to make sense of [the past] – to us' (Williams 2002: 258). The practice of making sense, one indeed in which, I would insist, all parties to the communication are involved, recognizes that the search can never be for a single truth about the other in time or space, but a practice of interpretation which must be responsive to the demands of truthfulness, however those demands are interpreted in any given society or setting.

Williams is himself pretty dismissive and despairing of the current state of truthfulness in today's media, including the internet. Of the media, he cites approvingly R. H. Tawney's comment that they only exist to sell pieces of paper with nonsense printed on one side and advertisements on the other. And when it comes to the internet the challenge is the familiar one of how to distinguish truth from falsehood, to separate sincere and accurate reporting from gossip, and how to break free from the solipsism of the private conversation.

This is not a position I would, of course, completely endorse. Nor, it could be said, can Williams either unless he is willing to dismiss the media entirely as potential and actual contributors to democratic society (he acknowledges the historical consistency of course with which all media continue to address only, or principally, an elite). On the contrary, for it is precisely because the media have that role, whether we like it or not, that the concern for their well-being is so closely linked, in my account, to the well-being of global civil society and the future of liberal democracies.

Truthfulness in the mediapolis is therefore a matter both for institutions and their regulation, and a matter for the individual who speaks, and has to take responsibility for, his or her words. But it is also a matter of interrogation and critique, the reflexivity of the professional and the critical skills of the readers and listeners, those who might or might not be, or become, one day, society's citizens.

The time has come to take these abstract arguments into the vital space of the mediapolis and to enquire into the kinds of responses that they might require, as I confront the conditions under which it, the global space of mediated appearance, could fulfil some of its potential, and enable the formation and the sustaining of a civil society both within and beyond the territory of nations.

I do not underestimate the difficulties. My book, so far, is testament to the dynamic complexity of the media in creating and sustaining an effective public space for understanding, debate and deliberation. Yet there has to be a way to consider the issues: to till the ground perhaps, so that it becomes more fertile and so that the seeds of political action and professional judgement have greater likelihood of germinating. There is a sense, which I take from Habermas, that this public project is ultimately, but neither slavishly nor entirely, a rational one; indeed it is one of 'more or less good reasons' (Habermas in Borradori 2003: 35). And that this acceptance of the inevitable compromises that one needs to make in the sphere of public communication is both productive and necessary. We need to know what the foundations for policy or ethics in the mediapolis are for before we can make sense of how to develop them. It is my task in the next and final chapter to explore these issues and, if not to make specific recommendations, at least to clarify their terms of reference and their terms of trade.

7

Regulation and Literacy

And so to some of the implications and consequences of what I have been saying.

I have been arguing that the mediapolis is a moral space, and insofar as it can be so considered then it assumes central importance in any discussion of the future of humankind. Big claims, I know, but not, I hope, unreasonable ones. The morality of the media within the environment in which they function is grounded in their singular capacity to represent, to re-present, the world, and in our everyday dependence on that capacity. There are other forces in play, of course, both moral and political, but increasingly they too both have increasingly come to depend on, and are inextricably linked to, the endlessness, ubiquity, persistence and insistence of media discourse. The pursuit of political life, the management (or mismanagement) of markets, the conduct of diplomacy and the fighting of wars, as well as the construction of lifestyles and the capacity to get through the day, significant each in their own terms and perfectly capable in principle (once upon a time) of being conducted in exclusively unmediated or private contexts, are no longer free to be so.

If this is media-centrism, then so be it. It is time to grasp the nettle.

But nettles sting if they are not grasped firmly enough. The mediapolis is no exception. My attempt to grasp it has involved a number of different interrogations: into its status as a place where we will or will not find ourselves alongside the other in his or her dignity; into the consequences of the failures of representation above all in the demonization of the other; into its status as a discourse of multiple voices whose co-presence needs to be guaranteed and at the same time honoured; in its significance for the everyday lives of its audiences; in its claims for justice and in the justice of its claims; and in its significance for the emergence and sustenance of democratic, civil society, globally, nationally and locally.

There is nothing straightforward about this. This is, at least, blisteringly clear. The media are complex, contradictory and contested practices – but they are practices, not disembodied processes. And as such they are the product of human thought, judgement and action. And as such they are the principal means of connection (and disconnection), of symbolic inclusion (and exclusion), indeed of communication (and miscommunication) between human beings, without which, even in their distortion, social life is inconceivable. They are practices, too, pursued in contexts of significant technological and social change and instability. Perhaps this was always so. If we were to examine the history of communication and communication technology over the last hundred years, at least, we would certainly think so. But they are also practices pursued in the context of the exercise of power, both personal and institutional, in the symbolic as well as in the material realms. Indeed power is at the heart of it, since in the limits on appearance and the denial of hospitality, in the ideologies of misrepresentation and in the trashing of trust, real harm can be done: to individuals, to cultures and to nations – to us and our own and to others and theirs.

The mediapolis is a global and cosmopolitan phenomenon, though it is constructed in the local domains of the face-to-face work of production and consumption. It is a local phenomenon though it is distributed around the world, and across both national borders and domestic boundaries, without a sense of who is there to receive it, never mind, mostly, of whom it is who is doing the sending. The media represent, not uniquely but uniquely in their consequence, a perplexing mix of the human and the technological. Indeed it is technological change that continues to provide both the threats and opportunities that make the mediapolis such a rapidly changing phenomenon, and one whose moral status is both difficult to grasp and even harder to direct.

The current crisis, perhaps an eternal one, concerns the capacity of the global media to fulfil their responsibilities to a world which at the same time, in its political and economic dynamics, continues to undermine that capacity. The shifts in the marketplace that peer-to-peer technologies, for example, have created; the ease with which individuals can set up shop on the internet and reach an audience somewhere somehow for their views and opinions as well as their objects for sale; the mobile-phoning of still images and videos to broadcasters around the world in times of crisis or disaster; the refusal to read the daily press; the fracturing of audience cultures in the welter of lifestyle choices; the vulnerability of established markets both to new entrants and to the still increasing power of major corporations; the incapacity to control the flow of information: the commercially valuable (and arguably taxable) as well as the personally threatening and the politically seditious – though increasingly it appears to be the case that all of these flows leave their traces and therefore can be traced – each singly and together not only raise the levels of commercial, personal and political anxiety, but have significant consequences for how the world appears on its screens. And it is that appearance, that worldliness, as I have argued throughout this book, that constitutes the issue, the media's bottom line.

The concern in this final chapter is with the mediapolis as dynamic, changing and contradictory, but as something, in all of these aspects, that cannot be left entirely to its own devices. This is not a knee-jerk 'the market can't do it' kind of argument, but what I would consider is a vital undertaking in bringing the values of justice and responsibility into a domain of human activity that in their weakness or absence could do incalculable damage to the human condition. Many think that the media have already done this damage and that the trajectory of distortion, miscommunication, symbolic exploitation and polarization is too far gone. This may be right. But as I will shortly argue, if we can and do legitimately recognize and struggle against the damage being done by the human race to its physical environment, there is no reason why we should not also find and commit ourselves to struggling against the equivalent damage to our symbolic one. Indeed I would go so far as to suggest that the two are closely related, or at least relatable.

The locus and character of our regulatory concerns in the mediapolis, therefore, need to shift. In this rapidly changing media world, a world that still includes old media, and old but yet resistant values driving institutional processes of mediation, as well as the new, the concern with markets, competition, professional practice and content needs to be rethought. This is not only because of the decline of spectrum scarcity, or the incapacity of national governments to control international flows of information and communication, but because the media which now provide the infrastructure of the mediapolis are challenging what it means to be human, through their increasing salience as both information and communication resources, and as such as crucial components of our social life.

I am suggesting that an understanding of what it is to be human is, or certainly should be, the central question underlying, and in the final analysis regulating, the development of the mediated world in which more and more of us live, and by which almost all of us are affected. Indeed I am arguing that existing forms of media regulation, at best operationalizations of what can be called applied ethics (Christians 2000), at worst mindless enforcements of vested political or commercial interests, are not sufficient as guarantors of humanity or culture. Regulatory reform is still mostly a matter *for* governments and media industries and a matter *of* establishing professional and commercial guidelines for practice (variously enforced) without conscious attention to first principles of social action or media representation, and without addressing other ways of enabling not just a responsible and an accountable media, but a responsible and accountable media culture. A responsible and accountable media can be encouraged and regulated, however imperfectly and however vulnerably. A responsible and accountable media culture is another matter entirely, for it depends on a critical and literate citizenry (as well as a critical and literate, that is a reflexive, profession), a citizenry, above all, which is critical with respect to, and literate in the ways of, mass mediation and media representation.

We have seen how justice and responsibility can be considered as being in tension but that both are necessarily components of the morality of the mediapolis: justice leading to a concern with procedure and its regulation; responsibility leading to a concern with reflexivity and literacy. The two are not mutually exclusive. Regulation can encourage literacy and needs to be reflexive. Reflexivity and literacy need the supports of codes of practice and educational syllabi. The point is that regulation, by itself, either imposed or through various procedures of self-regulation, is not enough. It needs to be confined to specific levels of structural intervention. Meanwhile media literacy, both among producers and consumers, needs to be recognized as increasingly necessary, if not in the final analysis sufficient, for the present and future health and strength of the mediapolis.

And I also wish to suggest, unsurprisingly I hope at this stage of the proceedings, that at the core of such media literacy should be a moral agenda, always debated, never fixed, but permanently inscribed in public discourse and private practice, a moral discourse which recognizes our ultimate responsibility for the other person in a world of great conflict, tragedy, intolerance and indifference, and which critically engages with our media's incapacity (as well as its occasional capacity) to engage with the reality of that difference, responsibly and humanely. For it is in our understanding of the world, and our willingness and capability to act in it, that our humanity or inhumanity is defined.

Media as environment

Cees Hamelink has recently pointed out that the media are central to this increasingly urgent project of identifying what constitutes our humanity precisely because they are at the forefront in representing, through endless sequences of narratives and images, the 'historical reality of dehumanisation on a grand scale' (Hamelink 2000).

And the media are indeed quite central to our capacity to be and to act in the world, as Marshall McLuhan (McLuhan 1964) has once upon a time noted. It was he who most forcefully suggested that media, all media, are extensions of ourselves. They create and sustain an encompassing cultural environment which we all share. As we enter a digital age, one in which both the speed and range of communication seems to be have been so intensified; as we shift from, at best, an active engagement with our singular media to an increasingly interactive engagement with our converging media, media which give us the world, access to the world and information about the world, we are confronted with this McLuhanistic vision even more insistently.

Of course McLuhan profoundly misrepresented the totality and homogeneity of media as providing a kind of cultural blanket over all peoples of the world. He persistently disregarded the significance of geography and society, never mind institutional processes, as in turn mediating power and access to material and symbolic resources. Nevertheless, and despite its political innocence, this mediated cultural environment is as significant, I now want to argue, for the human condition as the natural environment is. Though it is rarely so remarked upon. Indeed both have holes in their ozone layers, chemical and moral in turn. Both are subject to the depredations and exploitations of the insensitive, the malicious and the self-interested. So although McLuhan's environmental perspective makes, perhaps, more sense now than it ever did, it leaves untouched the thorny questions of who and what we are, and of how what we are in turn affects the ways in which media emerge and develop. And it still fails to register mediation as both a social and a political process. In other words, the humanity and inhumanity at the heart of the dynamics of mediation are left unexamined; they are presumed to be unproblematic.

Like the natural environment, the media environment provides both the wherewithal, the resources, for the conduct of social life as well as the grounds of its very possibility.[1] In confronting media as extensions of the human, McLuhan argued that as technologies, merely as technologies, they constituted such infrastructural resources. Yet, of course, these resources, resources of instantaneity, of synchronous and asynchronous communication, of global reach and immediate connectivity, of digital compression and interactive communication, of infinite storage and endless searchability are, notwithstanding their technological base, always and only social. They only become resources in the hands and minds of human beings. They can be used, misused and refused. They can be distorted and enhanced. In other words, media resources are resources in and for practice, and it is in this practice that the issues of how they are to be deployed become so urgent.

Conventional regulatory discourses rarely examine why regulation should take place in the first place. Their presumptions about public interest, freedom of expression, rights to privacy, competition policy, intellectual property and the like presume an ordered or at least an orderable world, and indeed a world that would benefit from deliberative, and presumably accountable, regulation. They are not to be lightly dismissed. Yet at best regulatory procedures, focusing on producers but addressing consumers, are based on an acknowledgement and an acceptance of what I have already called applied or professional ethics: sets of morally informed but rarely interrogated prescriptions for, or proscriptions of, practice. Their justifications lie deeply buried in the regulatory cement, invisible to the naked eye of the practitioner, and equally opaque to their supposed beneficiaries. Indeed the main beneficiary of such regulatory impulses and practices is the putative citizen, in his or her public and private life, a citizen that predominantly is seen to need protection but is not necessarily being offered the resources to enable not just a personal defence against, but a critical and creative engagement with, precisely what it is that, in its worst manifestations, is seen to be so damaging.

The driving force of these arguments is that the otherwise determining bottom line of the global communication industry has to be tempered by the environmental status and civic role that the media have. The media are too important to be left to the media. This is not soggy liberalism, nor even radical socialism. It is, in a world of polarization, misunderstanding, and in the increasing exploitation of the image and the symbolic spaces of global representation, just plain common sense.

Home and away

In an earlier essay (Silverstone 1999) I argued that almost all our regulatory impulses, those that engage with the ownership of media industries on the one hand and those that concern the welfare of the family on the other, are between them concerned with the protection of home. What links them is a preoccupation with *content*: with the images, sounds, narratives and meanings which are transmitted and communicated daily, and over which regulators increasingly feel they have little control. What appears on the page or on the screen, what is represented, especially in its consistency or inconsistency, its decency or indecency, its intrusiveness, is deemed to be important precisely because it has been allowed to cross this principal threshold, seeping into private spaces and private lives. This was, of course, the impetus for the earliest impulses at content regulation, in the Hays Code, which was devised to regulate the young Hollywood cinema in the 1930s and which stayed in force until 1966. But these anxieties and the regulatory attempts to manage them have become more insistent as twentieth-century media migrated away from public to private screens, and from shared sitting rooms to solitary bedrooms.

Banal though it may seem, the media are seen to be important because of the power they are presumed to exercise over us, *at home*, a power that no amount of audience research can quite completely deny, and of course which most of us believe, one way or the other, naturally to be the case. Home, of course, needs to be understood in both literal and metaphorical senses. The defence of home is a defence of both the private spaces of intimate social relations and domestic security – the household; as well as of the larger symbolic spaces of neighbourhood and nation – the collective and the community. The two are complex in their interrelationship and do not always share common interests. Yet both are threatened by the media extension of cultural boundaries: both laterally, as it were, through the globalization of symbolic space, and vertically through the extension of accessible culture into the forbidden or the threatening. In both cases home has to be defended against material breaches of symbolic security.

The liberalization of mainstream media and telecommunications in the 1980s and 1990s by neo-liberal, and in the UK, Conservative, governments brought with it an unexpected and unwelcome reduction in the capacity to control the flow of media content into national space. Self-induced deregulation in one context and for one set of dominating economic reasons produced, as it was bound to, a moral panic in another context, that of culture. And in the UK, for example, something called the Broadcasting Standards Council was, as a consequence, created to protect both the vulnerable child at home and the vulnerable homeland as if it were a child. Debates on the future of public service broadcasting in the UK in the context of the renewal of the BBC's Charter have rehearsed the same dilemmas, for once again what was at stake was the moral integrity both of the home and the nation, in its citizen's capacity to exercise, both privately and publicly, meaningful choices (a precondition for a moral life) as well as a perceived need to protect that same citizen from the immorality of meaningless or threatening choices that unregulated commerce might be expected to bring in its train.[2]

In the meantime, while all of this activity is going on with respect to broadcasting and to a lesser extent the internet, the press, both in the UK and elsewhere, by and large remains outside the formal regulatory frame, at least as long as basic standards of decency, or the law of the land with regard to libel or sedition, continue to be adhered to. The public interest defence, the rights to the freedom of expression, the long history of market responsiveness, have enabled the press to secure a space for itself where self-regulation is regarded as sufficient. Self-regulation is a matter of professional practice, based on a presumption of responsibility. It is embodied in codes of practice, and enshrined, once again in the UK, in the institution of the Press Complaints Commission,[3] a body which is charged with maintaining 'the highest professional standards' for the press, principally through response to public complaints. It too produces a code, as does the Society of Editors, and most if not all newspapers or newspaper groups.

Indeed even competition policy is as much about, and has consequences for, such breaches of personal security and domestic integrity – of the rights of the person and the personal – as it is about cross-media owner-ship and the future of public service broadcasting and the public sphere.

And yet while regulators struggle to control and direct, to label and to license content (as well as competition), parents and families struggle over a personal and private culture, shaping and protecting the domestic spaces where public and private moralities are supposed to coincide. This is a struggle for control, a struggle which propagandists, advertisers, televi-sion schedulers and portal designers well understand. And it is a struggle which parents understand too, as they argue with their children over time spent on-line or their access to troublesome content. It is a struggle which at least in part defines, across lines of age and gender, the particular poli-tics of individual households.

Regulation is, then, a private as well as a public matter. It takes place in front rooms as well as in debating chambers, in the cut and thrust of discussions over viewing habits, as well as in international debates over V-Chips and trans-border media flows. In both these environments what is being fought over are the rights of, and control over, representation: of the availability of, and access to, the continuities and consistencies of both the immediacy, and the flow, of images and narratives. And in those rep-resentations what is at stake are the rights to define a relationship: between what is known and not known, between what is valued and not valued, between what one believes to be the truth and what one suspects as false-hood, and between what one lays claim to and what one can discard in one's relationship to the rest of the world. What is at stake, in these moments and mechanisms of regulation is, essentially, a moral order.

As we become increasingly dependent on the mediated word and image for our understanding of what takes place beyond our front door, as every-day life, in its taken-for-granted ordinariness, becomes inseparable from the mediations that guide us through it, and connect or disconnect us from the everyday lives of others, how the media position us, or enable us to position ourselves, becomes crucial.

As citizens we are expected to take responsibility for, and to act respon-sibly in relation to, ourselves, our neighbours and also the strangers amongst us. Such expectations have been, arguably, undermined by (among many other things) a century of electronic mediation, which has led to increasing privatization and individualization. The dominant trope in the analysis of twentieth-century public life has been the erosion of public life: the palpable decline in a culture of care, the paradoxical lack of, or breakdown within, public communication, and these weaknesses have been expressed in increasing alienation from the formal processes of politics and engagement in public life; perhaps not for all, but for many, especially in the wealthy and highly mediated democracies of industrial society. In the year 2000 in the US, more votes were cast for the candidates participating in the rock show *American Idol* than for the candidates for the US presidency (Galician 2004), a degree of public participation that has its later echoes around the world, not least in China where the winner of the show *Chaoji Nusheng* (the Chinese name for the equivalent show *Super Girl*) generated over 3 million votes in August 2005.[4]

But these societies, equally it goes without saying, are becoming increasingly connected to each other. What imperialism once enforced, globalization now enables, or indeed requires: a mutuality of increasingly highly stratified economic and financial structures and processes; a shared but still massively and unevenly discomforting physical environment; a political space that no longer knows, nor much cares about, national boundaries and territorial sovereignty; networks of information and com-munication that shrink social and cultural space and time to the size of a handset.

In this context, and taking the broadest sweep, problems of regulation become problems of governance, in which order and accountability are dreamed about on a global scale, and at the level of states and transna-tional non-governmental organizations. Foreign and domestic policy converges (Price 2004). Somehow even these dreams depend on a notion of citizenship, though a transcendent one, but they still require an engage ment with the human – and they challenge it too. In what ways, if at all, can or should this humanity be affected by our regulatory impulses and institutions? In what ways should this humanity (or its lack) inform and affect our attempts at regulation and governance?

Early commentators, both utopian and dystopian, on the emerging late nineteenth-century wireless and telegraphic space recognized the implications of what has subsequently come to be known as the double life of media and communication: recognizing that these media separate as well as connect, and I too have discussed this both in this work and elsewhere. This paradox inevitably calls the lie to any contemporary notion of the media's role in what is called the death of distance. It raises the question of isolation and not just privatization – and isolation of both the individual and of the group. It also raises the question of the illusion of connection: that in our mediated innocence, in our mediated naivety, that we are unable to recognize how imprisoned we are, how easily blinded we are, by the mediations that apparently link us together. And it is somewhat ironic to observe that the supposed revolution in media culture occasioned by the arrival of digital and on-line technologies should be seen to be so singular and radical, above all in their capacity to transcend the limits of electronic communication, limits perfectly well recognized (and feared) throughout the analogue twentieth century (de Sola Pool 1977; Marvin 1988).

As I have argued elsewhere (Silverstone 2005), there is often quite a fundamental confusion in much of the writing on the sociology and geography of new media. Time–space distanciation, or time–space compression, even ideas of the network society, suggest a profound and misleading elision between two kinds of distance: the spatial and the social. It is presumed in these discussions that the electronic mediation of physical or material connection provides at the same time social, cultural or psychological connection. The technologically enabled transformation of time and space which marked the entry into the modern world certainly provided new conditions and possibilities for communication, communication that provided connection despite physical separation. Yet the contradictions at the heart of such communication become even more profound the more we insist that electronic mediation brings no penalty when it comes to understanding and caring for the other. Indeed when we insist, on the contrary, that our world view is now global in its reach. That there is no escape. That nothing can be hidden, nothing can be, or is, ignored. But of course it can. There are all sorts of ways in which we can, and do, deny what we see, as I have argued in chapter 5.

My point is, and has been, that distance is not just a material, a geographical or even a social category, but it is, by virtue of all of these and as a product of their interrelation, a moral category. The overcoming of distance requires more than technology and indeed more than the immediacy of electronic communication. It requires what I have called proper distance. Proper distance is the critical notion that implies and involves a search for enough knowledge and understanding of the other person or the other culture to enable responsibility and care, as well as to enable the kind of action that, informed by that understanding, is in turn enabling. We need to be close but not too close, distant, but not too distant.

At the risk of merely repeating myself, let me review what the notion of proper distance is supposed to signify and try and relate it to the present discussion.

The media have always fulfilled the function of creating some sense of proper distance, or at least they have tried, or claimed to be able, to do so. In the reporting of world events, the production of news, the fictional representation of the past, the critical interrogation of the private lives of public figures, the exploration of the ordinariness of everyday life, what is involved, in one way or another, is a negotiation between the familiar and the strange, as the media try, though always imperfectly, to resolve the essential ambiguities and ambivalences of contemporary life.

Yet such mediations have tended to produce, as I have indicated, in practice, a kind of polarization in the determinations of such distance. The unfamiliar is either pushed to a point beyond strangeness, beyond humanity; or it is drawn so close as to become indistinguishable from ourselves. And, it should be said, there is also very little awareness that we are the objects of the others' gaze, that how *we* are seen and understood by those far removed from us also matters; we need to see and understand that too. Perhaps this has never been more the case than now. Indeed this is where my argument began in this particular book.

On the one hand we find ourselves being positioned by media representation as so removed from the lives and worlds of other people that they seem beyond the pale, beyond reach of care or compassion, and certainly beyond reach of any meaningful or productive action. Technology has a habit of creating such distance, and the bureaucracies that have been built around technologies have in the past, and with cataclysmic effects, reinforced this sense of separation and alienation, this *immorality of distance* (Bauman 1993). This is certainly and obviously the case in times of conflict, but it is rarely far away even in times of peace.

Per contra, the representation, just as frequent and just as familiar, of the other as being just like us, as recoupable without disturbance in our own world and values has, though perhaps more benignly, the same consequence. We refuse to recognize not only that others are not like us, but that they cannot be made to be like us. What they have we share. What they are we know. They are as they appear in our documentaries and in our advertisements. Such cultural neo-imperialism represents the other side of the immorality of distance, in its refusal to accept difference, in its resistance to recognizing and to valuing the stranger. Perhaps this could be called the *immorality of identity*.

In both cases we lose a sense of both the commonality and difference that should inform the ethics of how we live in the world. Either way we lose the capacity effectively to grasp both what we share and what we do not share as human beings. The irony of the electronically mediated century just passed, in which we have come to believe that the immediate and the visible is both necessary and sufficient to guarantee connection, is that this apparent closeness is only screen-deep.

Distance can, therefore, be proper (correct, distinctive and ethically appropriate) or it can be improper, as can (spurious) closeness. If improper distance can be, and is, created, *inter alia*, through the mediations that electronic technologies provide for us, then it follows that we can use the notion of *proper* distance as a tool to measure and to repair the failures in our communication with and about other people and other cultures and in our reporting of the world, in such a way as our capacity to act in it is enabled and preserved (Boltanski 1999). And it follows too that we can use the notion of proper distance as a way of interrogating those arguments, most recently in the analysis of the supposed miraculous capacity of the internet, that mistake connection for closeness, and closeness for commitment, and which confuse reciprocity for responsibility.

It is with the convergence between the public and the private, the personal and the social, that the notion of proper distance seeks to engage. And it is at this interface, perhaps increasingly confused and confusing, that social beings, citizens real or manqué, need to confront a moral agenda that is appropriate both to the conditions of the mediation of the world, and appropriate to the resulting mediated world, the world in which the other person appears to us – as through a glass darkly.

Towards media literacy

The issue is how this might be enabled. Media regulation is certainly one possibility. Regulation has always been a political and a technical activity. To suggest that it should also be a moral one has its dangers. Yet these dangers need to be confronted. What is missing so often in the regulatory discourse is the question: regulation for what, and for whom?

Media regulation, and by this I am referring principally to the intervention of governments, involves and is directed towards procedure. In my argument that links it to issues of justice, and to the enabling structures of the mediapolis. And that is where it should be. It is media justice which, ultimately, justifies the regulation of markets and competition to ensure that they are not overwhelmed by the powerful and that the voices of the weak, the less commercial and the marginal can be heard. It is media justice, in the requirement to enable hospitality, that underpins, and must continue to underpin, such interventions, not just in the name of competition or even freedom of speech, but in the knowledge that such intervention must result in the increased and meaningful presence of the other in the dominant spaces of national and global media systems.

Regulation in relation to the provision of public service in broadcasting is one obvious space where these issues do intrude and where it has a clear role to play. And while much attention might be given, in such regulatory debates, for example, to the ways in which such public services are funded and how they might in their fiscal and political extraction from the rigours of real competition themselves be distorting an otherwise perfect marketplace, such regulation, if it is actually oriented towards securing the widest possible range of voices to be heard, can indeed be said to be occupying its proper place and fulfilling its proper function. To suggest that this particular regulatory impulse, to protect a component of a national broadcasting system (or a global internet system) from the depredations of the market, is a consistently vulnerable one is hardly news, but it is inevitably part of my argument that it remains a significant one in many societies (even the US where debates over the funding and regulation of Public Service Broadcasting and National Public Radio, and indeed the internet, are eternal).

But regulation is like grammar. It addresses the rules of language, not how that language is spoken or what is said. Or it transgresses this fine line at its peril. Regulation's rules are rules of engagement, of process and of discrimination. They involve the law. They might and perhaps should, especially in the context of the mutuality of hospitality across nations, involve international law, in the form of treaties between, for example, broadcasters, both national and transnational, to ensure reciprocity of address, and the presence of the other in otherwise alien media space. But they should not, except indirectly in the ways that I have already indicated they ultimately do, focus on content. The production and consumption of media content must ultimately be a matter of individual responsibility, in the same way that natural speech is the responsibility of the individual who speaks. Regulation can, at best, provide the enabling infrastructures for that speech, and it can and should try to do so, and with principles of media justice firmly in mind; but, even so, the mediapolis cannot rely exclusively on regulation if it is to survive and prosper.

And in a world in which such political and legal intervention is becoming harder and harder to achieve, because of the globalization of media content, because of the ease of access to the internet both as producer and consumer, because of the extraordinary explosion of such production in cyberspace, and also because the communication of content is no longer a proprietary undertaking or a privilege only of the large corporation, but is something that anyone with a mobile phone or a network connection can do, then such attempts to control it, its flow, who has access to it, and what it actually is, become largely self-defeating. I say largely because of course states have an obligation to enforce the laws of libel and sedition just as individuals have the right to be protected against these (and other) threats; and indeed commercial rights holders also arguably have rights to enforce their copyright. So in each of these cases it is hard to see how national and international regulation is not appropriate and justified (though in each case it will be, and often is, contested). And there are those who argue that regulation is needed to make the media profession accountable and to enhance, if not guarantee, its trustworthiness (O'Neill 2002). I will return to this argument shortly.

But is such procedural regulation sufficient to guarantee justice in the mediapolis? Does it actually protect the media-weak from the media-powerful, the stranger from exclusion or expulsion by the putative host? Does it address the presence and absence, as well as the character, of the representation of minorities and the marginal in dominant media systems? Can it? And above all does it actually enable responsibility for what is undertaken in the media; does it not rather shield those who, as producers and consumers, as subjects and as audiences, engage on a daily basis with media as text, as discourse, as narrative, as news, and who need to understand the implications and consequences of that engagement?

Media regulation is a double-, if not a multiply, edged sword. It is clear that in a benevolent society that it can enhance the quality of the democratic process and enable effective and responsible commercial and professional practice. In less benevolent societies it can, and will, both effect and legitimate the opposite. In the unsteady progress towards something that might be called democracy, there is no guarantee that one of its principle supports, a free press and broadcasting system, will remain unconstrained. Neither post-Gorbachev Russia, nor post-Rafsanjani Iran, have managed to sustain what their predecessors were able to achieve, and the struggle continues across media in China, where the internet, despite every effort and in a context of quite significant state control of the press and broadcasting, still survives as a space for some kind of freedom of communication (Li 2005). And in the murky middle spaces of societies which are both at the same time, and that is of course most of them, depending on whose interests are being privileged, regulation will both restrict and enable. This is obvious enough.

There are two points to be made. The first is that media regulation must understand both its limits, and its possibilities. I have indicated what the limits are, both tangibly in the increasing practical difficulty of effecting direct control over the production and reception of media content and, less tangibly but just as significantly, in the risk of undermining individual and personal responsibility: an undermining which, paradoxically, is also the potential downside of codes of practice in the context of the regulation of the profession.

And the possibilities? Media regulation could and should address more vigorously and rigorously the wider and, I have suggested, the much deeper issue of our relationships to others, the relationships we have to those for whom we have no formal responsibility, to those who are distant in space or culture, the strangers amongst us, our neighbours abroad; but for whom our basic humanity requires that we should care. This is of course a tall order. However, it suggests a shift in regulatory attention as well as in its range, and one that, it might well be argued, is long overdue.

And this wider remit, indeed this widest of all remits, involves a step which necessarily in turn might be expected to require a move towards an international structure of regulation in which public and commercial providers of media content agree to a set of what might be seen as environmental standards of media practice. This would be the equivalent of a Kyoto for the media. And notwithstanding the weaknesses of that particular accord, it provides a possible blueprint for a way forward in dealing with the palpable pollution and erosion of the global media environment, an environment which ironically is entirely man-made, but at the same time invisible as such in these structural terms. I would go so far as to say that the securing of the future of the physical environment is going to be of limited value unless and until the mediated symbolic one is equally secured, however hard it will be to demonstrate the scale of the symbolic damage in quantitative terms. It is time for the global media environment to have its own movement if we are to be confident in humanity's capacity to secure the future of the planet.[5]

But without responsibility, without the individual's understanding of the ways in which the media work, in the everyday as well as in professional settings, and without the individual in each of those settings acknowledging the consequences of his or her participation in the process of mediation as a whole, then media regulation will fail and the achievement of a high level of media justice will be massively restricted.

And so the question is how to operationalize media responsibility.

I want to suggest that such operationalization needs to involve a shift away from regulation as narrowly conceived in the minds and practices of parliaments and councils, towards a more ethically oriented and reflexive profession, and towards a broadly based, educated and critical social and cultural practice which recognizes the particular characteristics of our mediated world. We used to expect that our populations should be literate in the predominant means of communication, the printed word, of their societies and their times. We still do. We recognize print literacy as a precondition for participation in society and engagement in the democratic process. Print literacy and democracy emerged hand in hand. I want to argue that the participative logic underpinning a project of mass literacy is as powerful today as ever it was. But we need to think about what it is and what it should be, now, in a global world, in an interactive world, in a world of mediated appearance. We need to think through what such literacy might be, and might mean, in our present intensely mediated century, in the mediapolis.

In one sense, as I have just indicated, we could say that we have been here before, at least in part. The mid- and late-nineteenth century saw, certainly in the UK but also in Western Europe and in the US, the rise of a political project, broadly speaking, to incorporate disparate and displaced populations into civic culture. The displacement was for the most part, internal: populations leaving the land and traditional cultures and finding themselves in cities and within urban and popular cultures. Industrialization was having profound social consequences, and the social consequences involved very significant and destabilizing shifts in the communicative infrastructures of everyday life. Such destabilization and the consequent danger of anomie amongst an increasingly concentrated population was clearly a source of anxiety amongst elites – both legitimate and paranoid anxiety. Nation-states were being consolidated and any source of political resistance was clearly a focus of concern. At the same time democracies were maturing and working-class movements were themselves encouraging the displaced and disadvantaged – the still excluded – to generate the necessary social and cultural capital to participate increasingly fully and meaningfully in the public affairs of the strengthening state. There were both campaigns for, and political commitments to enable, mass literacy. Workers' educational movements engaged the mature; increasingly universal primary and secondary education engaged the maturing (Altick 1957).

All participation is double edged. It is both enabling and constraining. The literacy of the book, the newspaper and the pamphlet brought with it both the means for incorporation into national culture and the means for the suppression of any alternative, but it also brought an increasingly informed, reflective and cultured citizenry. Vernacular literacy was a precondition of such participation and reflection. To pretend that this was not a regulatory project would be naive. At the same time, however, it was also a liberating one – and in essence and in intent, very often, a genuinely moral one, whatever we might think about Victorian ethics. The focus of that first regulatory impulse was clearly that of the nation-state, a state enabled initially by the Gutenberg revolution (Eisenstein 1979) and secured – at least for large slices of the twentieth century – by Marconi's and Baird's (Scannell 1989). The focus, now, arguably, is post-national, if by that can be meant the redrawing and puncturing of the boundaries around and between states in the face of globalizing culture (though this does not imply the imminent demise of the nation-state).

Whereas the nineteenth-century civic project required the literacy of the written text, a literacy that was both literal and critical, the twenty-first century civic project requires a literacy of mass-mediated, electronic texts – and this too needs to be both literal and critical. But there the similarity ends. For the twenty-first century brings with it a different cultural and political challenge, in which the different media, both analogue and digital, are differently implicated in the structures and dynamics of everyday life.

For most, the literacy of the book was a literacy of decipherment: to be able to read, to follow, to understand, to appreciate. It required considerable application and the acquisition of sophisticated skills. Media literacy in an age of broadcasting was thought to be much less demanding, and the ease of access to complex audio-visual texts was seductive. The mass media were seen as more powerful not just because they were mass, but because they dimmed critical skills, the skills of engagement and struggle with complexity (Rosenberg and White 1957). It was not thought that literacy, at least in the terms where it was appropriately applied to the written text, was necessary. Indeed the mass media were seen to be destroying and undermining that kind of literacy. It is possible, of course, to argue that the internet has created its own demands for a new kind of literacy – it is being called information literacy (Livingstone, Van Couvering and Thumim 2005) – text based but requiring new skills of organization and decipherment. Information literacy is more broadly based, for example in the requirement for skills in the searching for, and management of, information. This, it is suggested, is already transforming the structured illiteracy of the age of broadcasting. I would suggest that for the most part the literacy required for the internet is still seen to be essentially technical, and is rarely approached as requiring more sophisticated skills.

In both the new and the old media, therefore, very little attention has been given to media literacy as a critical activity. Very little attention has been given to media literacy as a civic activity. Very little critical attention has been given either to literacy or civics as an alternative to the blunderbuss of media regulation, or to the possibility of developing an ethical agenda which would inform such a project. Very little attention, therefore, has been given to what we could reasonably call (following Walter Ong's (Ong 1982) characterization of the cultural infrastructure of the first stage of the electronic revolution as secondary orality) *secondary literacy*. This would be literacy as based upon the literacy developed in the first phase of education in reading and writing, as it has been transformed through the prism of film, radio and television, into the literacy demanded by the new screen culture, hugely dependent on the written word, but also the continuing power of images and narratives, and significantly enhanced in its challenges by the sheer volume and complexity of mediated environment.

In a relatively recent paper Rüdiger Funiok (Funiok 2000) has addressed some of these particular questions of literacy through an interrogation of audience ethics, that is, the responsibility that users of the media can, and should, develop for themselves. He cites Cees Hamelink's (Hamelink 2000: 400) conclusion that 'Media consumption should be viewed, like professional media performance, as a social practice which implies moral choices and the assumption of accountability for these choices.' This is a complex demand, of course, and extends way beyond the still limited framework that I am pursuing here, though I have discussed it at length in chapter 5. Yet the notion of responsibility, again as I have been at pains to argue, is crucial: responsibility for oneself, and for others; in the context of the family, of course, but also in the context of neighbourhood and nation (imagined communities both) and, now, in the context of a global culture and a global imaginary, which the world's media are daily creating.

Media literacy in this context is a political project, just as media civics is a 'literacy' one. The former is a prerequisite for full participation in late modern society, involving as it does the critical skills of analysis and appreciation of the social dynamics and social centrality of media as framing the cultures of the everyday. Media literacy above all requires an understanding of the non-transparency of media and of the moral implications of that non-transparency. And it requires an understanding of mediation as a social and political process. Media civics, correlatively, depends on media literacy. Media civics, crucial to citizenship in the twenty-first century, requires the development of a morality of responsibility and participation grounded in a critical engagement with mediation as a central component of the management both of state and global politics and that of everyday life: those, in Habermasian terms, both of the system and the life-world.

There is very little surprise in these observations, at least from the point of view of the academic study of the media, and certainly in the context of the arguments of this book, but equally there is very little surprise in the observation that these fundamental critical principles have hitherto for the most part failed to inform both the deliberations of policy makers, and the judgements of citizens. At the same time it is important to recognize that media literacy, in various manifestations, has begun over recent years to make an appearance in public policy on the media (e.g., Ofcom 2004) and has come to be ensconced, at least in principle, in curricula and pedagogies, both in schools and universities. And of course it is also important to note that any initiative to promote media literacy is, ultimately, a matter of regulation or at least of public policy.

While it is not my intention to review or interrogate in detail the range of initiatives and discussions that are now, properly, beginning to emerge in this area, I do want to try and identify some of the key concerns and perhaps the key agendas. There are two points to be made at the outset.

The first is that literacy is intimately connected with, and presupposes, responsibility: at the very least responsibility for one's judgements and actions in the mediation of the world. The second is that literacy is not just a thing that audiences, readers and internet users have to have, but it needs to be considered as an emergent property of the mediapolis as a whole, and as such one can think of media-literate proprietors, or editors or journalists, and indeed illiterate ones too. Media literacy is also a property of the texts themselves, the news bulletins, the front pages, and the websites, insofar as they too might be expected to provide evidence of sufficient reflexivity in their own communications to offer the resources for readers to make the appropriate judgements on how they might be read, understood and criticized.

Media literacy is, or should be, a skill and capability of all those who participate in the mediapolis. It will take different forms depending on the level of power and involvement in the media environment and, of course, as that environment changes, the skills that are needed to participate fully in it will change as well.

In a recent and thorough review of the literature on adult media literacy, Sonia Livingstone and her colleagues (Livingstone, Van Couvering and Thumim 2005) indicate that media literacy can be seen as relevant to a number of different dimensions of social and cultural life: democracy, participation and citizenship; the growth of the knowledge economy and the resources for choice; and lifelong learning and personal fulfilment. My concern here is principally with the first of these, though I don't see necessarily a clear boundary between any of them. And in the context of the emergence of a discourse, academic as well as broadly political, around media literacy there are three distinctions to be made. Each, both implicitly and explicitly, has emerged in my account so far: the question of media literacy as a societal capacity or as individual competence; the question of the difference between media literacy and information literacy; and the crucial observation that media literacy should be seen as a product of the interrelationship between producers and consumers of media, and not necessarily as something that pertains only to the individual in isolation.

It is the latter, a view of media literacy as a dynamic of the mediapolis in which all who participate in it, as producers or consumers, or indeed as both (journalists are consumers of other people's media, just as readers, viewers and users of media are occasional producers of their own) must take responsibility for what they do and say within media space, that I want to take as the framework for what follows. I want to suggest, too, that media literacy is a matter for individual competence and that it will only be once it becomes so that it will emerge as a matter of societal capacity. And underlying all of this is the argument that, given the significance of the media in the world in which we live, literacy is not just a matter of cognitive or technical skills, but is a matter of morality and ethics.

Media literacy is justified as a social and political project because media, their production, distribution and consumption, are central to the conduct of the modern world. And its justification is buttressed by an understanding of that conduct as being in turn central to the ways in which the world is approached and comprehended, and in the necessity that those who live in that world with us are treated with respect, dignity and care.

There are a number of different levels at which such literacy needs to be recognized. From the top down, then.

There is a requirement for media literacy among proprietors and corporations; there is an equivalent requirement amongst editors and journalists; and there is a requirement that readers, audiences and users of media should also have the appropriate skills of critical engagement and understanding. In each case, of course, what counts as media literacy, or what might count as such, will be expressed in different ways.

It has been suggested (Lambert 2005) that public media corporations should have a responsibility to develop an ethics policy (interestingly enough, given my own arguments thus far, in the same way as other companies increasingly do whose activities have environmental consequences) and to declare, as part of their annual reporting, how they had fared against the standards they set themselves as ethical players in the media marketplace. There are a number of issues here, not least the viability of an essentially self-regulatory approach to media ethics at this level (as at others), which are of concern. Nevertheless if the notions of responsibility and accountability are to be incorporated into the development of media literacy as a property of the mediapolis then clearly those who exercise most power within it cannot be excluded, and at the very least the kind of institutional reflexivity that such a move might signal would be an important first step. Such a step indeed requires the kinds of judgement and reflexivity which underpin the idea of literacy at every level in the mediapolis: a critical understanding of media and mediation as a global practice with significant consequences for the way we all live in the world.

And what about journalists and their editors? Are they not by definition already media literate?

This is not the place for a developed analysis of professional ethics in journalism, even though such ethics have been sorely tested in recent times, both in the press and in broadcasting, and in many if not most of the developed as well as the developing nations. We can note however that in the West codes of practice exist, when they do, both at the mostly self-regulatory level of the profession (the Press Complaints Commission in the UK has already been referred to) and at the level of individual news-papers or broadcasting channels, and that the principle of self-regulation is avidly fought for, as much as anything else as a buffer against anything more stringently enforced by government. And we can also note the pressures that increasingly appear to be forcing journalists, particularly news journalists, to cut corners, to ignore codes and to undermine the trust that is the *sine qua non* of media representation: the fracturing marketplace, the multiplicity of competing and alternative channels and delivery systems, the pressures from governments, the decline in advertising.

The operating environment is tough and getting tougher. Is this a justification for the evident decline in standards? There are many who do not think so (e.g., Lloyd 2004). And there are many, too, who refuse to accept its inevitability (e.g., O'Neill 2002). Media literacy at the level of professional practice is not just a matter of technical skill: the composing of the perfect story, the unforgettable documentary, or the politically effective website. These skills are well developed and the media industry depends on their continuing development. I want to suggest that media literacy at this level, that is among journalists and their editors, once again, is a matter of informed and reflexive understanding of the nature of mediation as a practice and of the mediapolis as a social, cultural and political environment, in which their activities have significant moral consequences.

This should mean that journalists and editors need to present their readers and their audiences with the opportunities and resources for them to engage intelligently with their output. But it also means that, even in the linearity of the production process, they need to be equally clear in their communications with their subjects and informants in ensuring that they are as aware as possible of what is at stake in their participation in the news. Both subjects and audiences need to be treated with the respect accorded to them as fellow human beings, above all to be treated with dignity and without exploitation; in other words, with an acceptance, one way or another, of the obligation to provide them with, in whatever form is appropriate to the story being told, hospitality – with a right of access, and a right of voice.

Journalism is by definition, as I have already noted, a practice which both invites and then constrains hospitality: editing is a form of law. Newspapers and broadcasters need to find ways of enabling the presence of otherness, and otherness in its own terms, to appear on their pages and screens, even at times, and perhaps especially at times, of global polarization and when the political culture is so dominated by terror or its threat. At the very least, at the very least, we should be hearing from others around the world in our national media.[6] What are they saying about us? How can we engage intelligently with them? This too is a precondition for media literacy, indeed at every level. Is all this completely impractical? I do not think so. Is it going to be difficult? Absolutely. Is it important? I would say it was vital.

Media literacy at the level of the profession is a state of mind, or at least that is how it begins. It cannot depend on codes of practice, for codes of practice, however well intended and enforced, incline to overlook the issue of individual responsibility which journalists everywhere have to take for their judgements and their actions. This is not to suggest that journalists should be better than the rest of us as human beings (though why should they not be?), only that they should recognize that what they do continually and cumulatively has consequences for the rest of us as human beings. And if that is a burden, then so be it. What else should we expect of those whose responsibility it is to report the world, and in that reporting make it available to us as a political and social reality?

And finally to audiences, listeners, readers and users. It is here that the notion of media literacy has the widest and most established currency. For after all it is the consumer who needs to be literate: it is the child and the adult in the conduct of their everyday lives who needs to have the competence and skills to make effective and authoritative choices and judgements when confronted with the welter of information and narrative at his or her disposal and when confronted with the glossing simplicities of media representation. The territory for the attention of something called media literacy, however, is, like Topsy, just growing. And as the media environment itself explodes with newer opportunities not just to be intelligently (or ignorantly) selective in the relationship with what is being offered, but with opportunities for creative, never mind critical, engagement with a range of easy-to-use and easy-to-communicate resources (on-line, on-mobile), then what counts as media literacy and how it should be developed as a civic project becomes ever more urgent.

To be reminded, for the last time, why. It is because of the doubling of, and within, the mediapolis: that the mediapolis, to a significant degree, is the world and that it constructs the world. Media literacy emerges then not even in the relatively simple idea that we engage with its texts, seek to read them, parse them, criticize them and the rest, but that we both have to engage with the conditions of their production (Lewis and Jhally 1998) and more importantly we need to engage with the world that they bring to our front doors. Media literacy is not just about the message, nor even about the messenger, but it has to be about what lies behind both: the world of the stranger that would be invisible without them.

Media literacy, from this enhanced, but hopefully not too exaggerated, a perspective, is a matter for educational and broadly social and cultural policy. And it is a matter of pedagogy. The slogan? Let's say: 'Education, not regulation!'

More literally, one can point to syllabi in schools (K-12) in the United States that place issues of media, their role, their significance, their technique, their power, their influence, at the core of both social studies as well as language arts. The state of California has at least a declaration of such principles in their prospectus for Media Literacy (<http://medialit. med.sc.edu/california.htm> downloaded August 2005). It starts at Grade 4 in Language Arts with the evaluation of the role of media in focusing attention on events and in informing opinions on issues, and completes the curriculum at Grade 11/12 with the recognition of strategies used by the media to inform, persuade, entertain and transmit culture. And in social studies, beginning at Grade 9, it seeks to examine issues of historicity, evidence and point of view, the effects of the growth of media on the diffusion of popular culture, and the ways in which lobbying and media affect the process of law making and the conduct of American politics. American scholars working in this field (e.g., Kubey 2004), however, in pointing to the generically underdeveloped commitment to these issues across the United States, look to Europe and to the UK for evidence that programmes of media literacy are well established as part of the curriculum and cite the number of children doing media studies in high schools, as well the numbers taking university courses, as indicators that such a project is already well developed.

Indeed the UK has been doing media literacy (under any other and every other name) for at least a generation, within its school, further and higher educational systems. The sense that this is not what it was actually about; that the study of the media was at heart a civic, perhaps even a moral-ethical, project, may well not have emerged with sufficient clarity. My sense is that it did not emerge in this way much at all, and mostly because of the nervousness of the kind of pro-social agenda that went along with it, and a nervousness too of exaggerating the media's own significance.

Not any more.

Media literacy is, then, a complex of interventions grounded in a single moral expectation: that all those who participate in the mediapolis, who are involved in the processes of mediation, in one way or another, and in accordance with their status and their power, accept responsibility for their actions and their judgements in that participation. Since mediation continues in the minds and lives of those who are otherwise only at the receiving end of it, and since increasingly the consequences of that participation, or lack of it, feed back into the social realm and the democratic process, either directly in the increasing opportunities for interaction of one kind or another being offered by the new digital media, or indirectly in the willingness to vote, or to respond to the pain of the world in other ways, then such media literacy has a direct bearing on the nature of what we might call civil society and on the humanity of our relationships to each other.

Conclusion

Our regulatory impulses need to be both informed and moderated by these concerns. Citizenship requires responsibility and to exercise such responsibility well and thoroughly in turn requires the need to be able to see the world and to see through our media's often limited and inadequate representations of it. The mediapolis is both a reality and an ambition. As the former it presents itself as a space of global communication and non-communication, but a space in which, for many if not most of us, the world appears, and where those who wish to affect the world struggle to make their appearance. Of course it is fractured, polarized and dispersed as a communicative space, centrifugal rather than centripetal, and it may yet be stillborn. However, in its normative manifestation, the mediapolis is acknowledged as being a precondition for the future of humanity – members of which will need to learn to live with and understand each other rather more sensitively and responsibly. Without communication, this is unlikely to happen. And without the commensurate degree of media literacy, then communication itself becomes self-defeating.

I have proposed the notion of proper distance as a framing device for such a project. Our concern for the other has to burst the bounds both of the nation-state and of the narcissistic limits of attention only with the individual and the self. Its regulatory and responsive embrace should bring the other into its ambit. A sense of proper distance is a moral sense, one in which the relationship between proximity and distance is mediated by an effective measure of understanding, care and responsibility. We need to know about each other in a way that can only involve a constant critical engagement with our media's representation of the other. Such engagement is as important to our relationships to our neighbours as to the strangers, both amongst us and far away. The everyday, hitherto the site of a more or less unreflecting gaze, can, and should, be made more critically aware – for that is, after all, what our media can enable for us, if there is such a mind to do so. But this is not just about critique. It is about care. It is about hospitality. And at the heart of it lies, must lie, the dignity of the human being, what Jonathan Sacks (Sacks 2002) has called the dignity of difference. I am like you, but I am not you.

This difference is manifested in the contrapuntal, in the play of media voices, none of which should be silenced but of which each will be heard in its own space and time, in a context provided by the others. The contrapuntal is potentially a powerful metaphor in other dimensions of the mediapolis, in the connection and disconnection of technologies and technological uses, but it is as both an analytic and a moral principle of cultural formation and expression that it is valued here. And like the mediapolis it is both an empirical and a normative category. We can observe, and to degree hear, the to-ing and fro-ing of dominant and minority media, and we can and should value both, without idealizing the mutuality of their presence in a given society or their relationship to each other. There is, in reality, conflict, repression, discord. It would be good to try and reduce all of these. It would be good to pursue media justice more effectively.

Regulation is, therefore, not just a matter of production. And here as in other dimensions of media dynamics, production and consumption blur; and tangibly the boundaries between them, as digitalization takes hold, are becoming increasingly indistinct. Equally the full responsibility for a moral agenda informing media practices should lie not only with audiences and users, or indeed with producers, journalists or even, or especially, regulators. It is to be shared amongst all those who participate in the mediapolis. For it is the interests and understandings of audiences and users, the urgent requirements of citizenship, which should continue to constrain and increasingly determine the regulatory process. We are of course, responsible for ourselves. But, as Emmanuel Levinas insists, if we are to claim a full and proper humanity we must claim responsibility for the other.

And so to the Afghan blacksmith, with whom I began. What of him now? His voice and his judgements, audible momentarily, are now forgotten (though not by me). And what might we think of him as the world continues on its polarizing way and where terror, now, is home grown? Otherness is no longer a property of the other. Difference, intransigent, implacable, vilifying difference, is present amongst us as well as far away. What about, then, our own blacksmiths, our own Afghans, and our own terrorists? Are we to listen to them and give them the space to be heard? I believe we should. How else will we know what to do?

Notes

Chapter 1 Morality and Media

1 This formulation does not imply that the moral is ahistorical, though it is quite clear that morality is slow to change, and it is this resistance to the particular which underpins its significance as a constant at least within the major cultural traditions. This would certainly be true of what Jacques Derrida calls the Abrahamic (which includes of course Judaism, Christianity and, crucially, also Islam). (Derrida, Jacques, 2002, *On Cosmopolitanism and Forgiveness*, trans. M. Dooley and M. Hughes, London: Routledge.)

2 Of course some (but not all) kinds of tourism at least in industrial societies, and economic and other forms of migration more widely, are likely to be significant too.

3 I have used the term 'minor cosmopolitanism' (minor in the sense of key, not scale) to identify other dimensions of the globalization of identity, those that emerge, often perforce, in the diaspora or other less comfortable kinds of international mobilities. (Silverstone, Roger, 2001, Finding a Voice: Minorities, Media and the Global Commons, *Emergences: Journal for the Study of Media and Composite Cultures* 11 (1):13–28.)

4 The idea of media space as being a global commons has a wide reference – it addresses the internet principally as an open space free for all (as it indeed it was in its initial manifestations, albeit free for those who had the technology and skills to access it). It appears as a frame for discussion which is both legal (Lessig, Lawrence, 1999, *Code and Other Laws of Cyberspace*, New York: Basic Books) and political (Bettig, R. V., 1997, The Enclosure of Cyberspace, *Critical Studies in Mass Communications* 14:138–57; Silverstone, Roger, 2001, Finding a Voice: Minorities, Media and the Global Commons, *Emergences: Journal for the Study of Media and Composite Cultures* 11 (1):13–28.)

5 This is a point similarly made by Nick Stevenson, though his framing of the argument depends more on a perspective based on rights as opposed to obligations (see my argument below, in chapter 6):

> The diversity of political groupings and identities that make up civil society will increasingly see the mass media as the place where collective fates are decided. The struggle to see one's own life or shared culture represented fairly through the dominant institutions of the mass media is likely to intensify the more the same said media becomes determined by the global economy rather than public directives. This process is also likely to be heightened by the fact that the media in general are more caught up with the social definition of society than ever before. (Stevenson, Nick, 1999, *The Transformation of the Media: Globalization, Morality and Ethics*, London: Longman, p. 57.)

6

> I am not advocating an unconstrained relativism, for no arrangement, and no feature of an arrangement, is a moral option unless it provides for some version of peaceful coexistence (and thereby upholds basic human rights). We choose within limits, and I suspect that the real disagreement among philosophers is not whether such limits exist – no one seriously believes they don't – but how wide they are. (Walzer, Michael, 1997, *On Toleration*, New Haven and London: Yale University Press, pp. 6–7.)

7 Bryan S. Turner calls it cosmopolitan virtue. (Turner, Bryan S., 2002, Cosmopolitan Virtue, Globalization and Patriotism, *Theory, Culture & Society* 19 (1–2):45–63.)

8 Though there is of course a strong reactionary literature particularly addressed, in recent times, to television which expresses the fundamental concern with the undermining of culture by the media, see for example Postman, Neil, 1987, *Amusing Ourselves to Death*, London: Methuen, and Mander, Jerry, 1978, *Four Arguments for the Elimination of Television*, Brighton: Harvester Press. This is not without value, though for the most part it relies on a model of mechanical cause and effect which is not entirely sustainable; likewise there is little that looks beyond the critique to explore the possibilities for a different kind of media culture. There are also numerous websites that act as critics of, and commentators on, media representation, e.g., <www.mediachannel.org> and <www.mediawatch.org>.

Chapter 2 Mediapolis or the Space of Appearance

1 The act of listening is an implicit one in Arendt's philosophy of public space, but of course it is essential that it is granted its proper place. And in the context of what follows and my own arguments, listening and being heard is crucial. I discuss this more fully in chapter 6.

2

> It is the publicity of the public realm which can absorb and make shine through the centuries whatever men may want to save from the natural ruin of time. Through many ages before us – but not now any more – men entered the public realm because they wanted something of their own or something they had in common with others to be more permanent than their earthly lives. (Arendt 1998: 55)

3

> Judgement requires the moral-cognitive capacities for worldliness, that is, an interest in the world and in the human beings who constitute the world, and a firm grasp of where one's own boundaries lie and where those of other's begin . . . Whereas thinking requires autonomy, consistency, tenacity, independence, and steadfastness, judging requires worldliness, an interest in one's fellow human beings, and the capacity to appreciate the standpoint of others without projection, idealisation, and distortion. (Benhabib, Seyla, 2003, *The Reluctant Modernism of Hannah Arendt*, new edn. Lanham, Maryland: Rowman and Littlefield.)

4 The difficult and challenging philosophy of Emmanuel Levinas expresses an equivalent humanism to that of Arendt, and indeed it springs in significant degrees from the same cultural source, though in Levinas's case this is a religious rather than a secular Judaism and a critique of the same philosophical position – that of Martin Heidegger. As Colin Davis, in perhaps the most accessible introduction to Levinas's work, points out, the core of his thinking lies in a critique of the failure of western philosophy to address the Other. As such his philosophy has come to be seen as one of the major contributions to ethics in the twentieth century. See Davis, Colin, 1996, *Levinas: An Introduction*, Cambridge: Polity.

5 This is of course the Baudrillardian position, the paradoxically ontological core of the post-modern.

Chapter 3 The Rhetoric of Evil

1 Cf. Copjec:

> Kant's underlying question is historically posed. He does not ask himself how evil is possible, he asks, rather, how evil is possible given the act of freedom. He wants to understand how it happened that men who had recently won their freedom, who no longer needed to bow to external pressures, chose to calculate in terms of these pressures, that is chose to act immorally. That is to say, Kant sees evil as uniquely the product of a free humanity, and it is this which is new in his thought. (Copjec, Joan (ed), 1996, *Radical Evil*. London: Verso, x–xi.)

And cf. Bernstein and his discussion of the ineradicability of evil in the arguments of both Kant and Freud, in Bernstein, Richard, 2002, *Radical Evil: A Philosophical Investigation*, Cambridge: Polity, p. 159.

2

> 'Theodicy, in the narrow sense, allows the believer to maintain faith in God in face of the world's evils. Theodicy, in the broad sense, is any way of giving meaning that helps us face despair': Susan Neiman on Levinas's inclusion of a notion of theodicy in the wider non-religious context of attempting to reconcile us to suffering, without the framework of religion. (Neiman, Susan, 2002, *Evil in Modern Thought: An Alternative History of Philosophy*, Princeton and Oxford: Princeton University Press, p. 239.)

Levinas argued that theodicy was strictly impossible after Auschwitz.

3 Another way of putting this might be to say that it is possible to produce evil without conscious evil intent. The irony with which the lawyers representing the soldiers charged with the horror of Abu Ghraib were able to insist that their clients were only following orders would not be lost on many with even a modicum of historical sensibility.

4 The first time he had spoken there, that is during his first State of the Union speech on 29 January 2001, he had coined the now infamous phrase 'the axis of evil':

> States like these, and their terrorist allies, constitute an axis of evil, arming to threaten the peace of the world. By seeking weapons of mass destruction, these regimes pose a grave and growing danger. They could provide these arms to terrorists, giving them the means to match their hatred. They could attack our allies or attempt to blackmail the United States. In any of these cases, the price of indifference would be catastrophic (<http://www.white-house.gov/news/releases/2002/01/20020129-11.html>).

And for an account of the drafting of the axis of evil speech see Woodward, Bob, 2004, *Plan of Attack*, New York: Simon & Schuster, especially pp. 85–95.

5 The speech continues:

> I believe that communism is another sad, bizarre chapter in human history whose last pages even now are being written. I believe this because the source of our strength in the quest for human freedom is not material, but spiritual. And because it knows no limitation, it must terrify and ultimately triumph over those who would enslave their fellow man. For in the words of Isaiah: 'He giveth power to the faint; and to them that have no might He increased strength . . . But they that wait upon the Lord shall renew their

> strength; they shall mount up with wings as eagles; they shall run, and not be
> weary . . .'

He was obviously right about the end of communism.

My discussion begins, essentially, with the Reagan presidency. However there is a longer history, going back to the basic religiosity of the early years of the Federation; see Delbanco, Andrew, 1995, *The Death of Satan: How Americans Have Lost the Sense of Evil*, New York: Farrar, Straus and Giroux.

6 For a review of the media's response to 9/11 see Zelizer, Barbie, and Stuart Allan (eds), 2002, *Journalism After September 11*, London: Routledge.

7 Rogin sees the emergence of demonology in the US in terms of the flight from historically based social and political conflicts to a fake or imposed unanimity. From this perspective Reagan is one of a number of US 'imperial' presidents 'who personified America by absorbing the members of the body politic into their own mystic bodies and leading the regenerated American nation against its alien, demonic foes'. (Rogin, Michael Paul, 1987, *Ronald Reagan: The Movie*, Berkeley: University of California Press, p. xviii.)

8 'We are for the free enterprise system . . . We have fought our little Red brothers all along the line' (Reagan to the Los Angeles Rotary Club, 1948). As Rogin points out this evokes the native American Indians as well as referring to the Communists, bringing 'frontier individualism back into history again'. Ibid., p. 30.

9 One of the most astute commentators on the paradoxes in the relation between religion, state and society in the US was of course de Tocqueville in his *Democracy in America*.

10

>   ' To all my fellow Americans beyond this hall, I say, one thing we owe those
> who have sacrificed is the duty to purge ourselves of the dark forces which
> gave rise to this evil. They are forces that threaten our common peace, our
> freedom, our way of life . . . Let us let our children know that we will stand
> against the forces of fear. When there is talk of hatred, let us stand up and talk
> against it. When there is talk of violence, let us stand up and talk against it. In
> the face of death, let us honor life. As St Paul admonished us, let us not be
> overcome by evil, but overcome evil with good. (Speech delivered 23 April
> 1995, Oklahoma City: <www. Americanrhetoric.com/speeches/wjcoklahoma-
> bombing speech.htm>)

This speech was of course given before the name and nationality of the principal perpetrator of the bombing was established.

11 The words 'under God' were added to the Pledge of Allegiance during the Eisenhower presidency in 1954.

12 This can be found at <www.mcs.drexel.edu/~gcmastra/phots/news/lilface.jpg>. Such an identification of course involves a number of not entirely obvious cognitive steps: seeing a pattern in the smoke, interpreting it as a face, and believing that the face is the face of the devil.

13

> The clearest sign of a Christian, and, more specifically, evangelical, influence
> on Bush's ethics is his repeated invocation of conflict between good and evil.
> We have seen that Bush often talks of 'the evil ones', and even occasionally of
> those who are 'servants of evil.' He urges us to 'call evil by its name,' to 'fight
> evil', and tells us that out of evil will come good. This language comes straight
> out of apocalyptic Christianity. To understand the context in which Bush uses
> this language, we need to remember that tens of millions of Americans hold
> an apocalyptic view of the world. According to a poll taken by *Time*, 53 percent

of adult Americans 'expect the imminent return of Jesus Christ, accompanied by the fulfillment of biblical prophecies concerning the cataclysmic destruction of all that is wicked' (*Time*, Fall 1992, cited in Fuller, Robert (1995), *Naming the Antichrist: The History of an American Obsession*, New York: Oxford University Press.)

> One of the signs of the apocalypse that will precede the Second Coming of Christ is the rise of the Antichrist, the ultimate enemy of Christ, who heads Satan's forces in the battle that will culminate in the triumph of the forces of God, and the creation of the Kingdom of God on Earth. Projecting this prophecy onto the world in which they live, many American Christians see their own nation as carrying out a divine mission. The nation's enemies are therefore demonized. That is exactly what Bush does . . . David Frum, Bush's speech writer at the time of 'the axis of evil' speech, says of Bush's use of the term 'evil ones' for the people behind 9/11: 'In a country where almost two-thirds of the population believes in the devil, Bush was identifying Osama bin Laden and his gang as literally satanic.' (Singer, Peter, 2004, *The President of Good and Evil: Taking George W. Bush Seriously*, London: Granta, pp. 207–8.)

14 The work has yet to be done, to my knowledge, on Arnold Schwarzenegger's transformation from cyborg to Governor. I doubt that we will have long to wait.

15 Pierre Nora's seminal analysis of sites of memory as the articulations of a discourse that replaces history does not actually see how such sites also play a role in constructing the future. See Nora, Pierre, 1989. Between Memory and History: Les Lieux de Memoire, *Representations* 26 (Spring): 7–25.

16 Thus Rosenberg:

> The basic allegory of Pearl Harbor predated the attack itself. It fits preexistent traditions, updating the Custer and Alamo motifs that held such emotional power in national memory before World War II. Throughout the war, the rallying cry of 'Remember Pearl Harbor' served to remind Americans of the treacherous character of the enemy, to underscore the morality of the cause, to rally support for preparedness and for unrelenting military action if attacked, to warn against 'sleeping' and isolationism, against weakness and dissent. This infamy framework expressed the causes and justifications of the war in terms of national character rather than national interest. It rooted the story of the Pacific War not in geopolitics but in a highly personalised and religiously tinged language of retribution. (Rosenberg, Emily S., 2003, *A Date Which Will Live: Pearl Harbor in American History*, Durham: Duke University Press, pp. 32–3.)

17 Raimond Gaita cites Simone Weil in answer to this question:

> If you say to someone who has ears to hear: 'What you are doing to me is not just', you may touch and awaken at its source the spirit of attention and love. But it is not the same with words like 'I have the right . . .' or 'you have no right to . . .' They evoke a latent war and awaken the spirit of contention. To place the notion of rights at the centre of social conflicts is to inhibit any possible impulse of charity on both sides. (Gaita, Raimond, 2004, *Good and Evil: An Absolute Conception*. 2nd edn., London: Routledge, p. 6.)

18 I have identified these alternatives in the context of discussions of my notion of proper distance at various points in this book.

19 Tony Blair was also quite comfortable within the rhetoric of evil, see for example his televised speech to the Trades Union Congress on 12 September 2001: 'This mass

terrorism is the new evil in our world today. It is perpetrated by fanatics who are utterly indifferent to the sanctity of human life and we, the democracies of this world, are going to have to come together to fight it together and eradicate this evil completely from our world' (*The Guardian*, 12 September 2001). It is a sentiment that he has expressed a number of times. Nevertheless its salience in British culture is by no means equivalent to that in the US. There is another study to be done here.

Chapter 4 Contrapuntal Cultures

1 See, for example, the manifesto produced under the auspices of On Line/More Colour in the Media (OLMCM) to be found at <www.multicultural.net/manifesto/index.htm>.

2 There are real political issues here of course, centring on the claims of multiculturalism and assimilation as competing models for migrant and minority communities. I will argue in chapter 6 for the importance of an obligation of hospitality to the voices of the other, an obligation to listen, and a right to be heard. These obligations and rights are to apply to all media irrespective of their size or dominance.

3 I am aware that this begs huge questions as to the nature and significance of both writing and reading as practice. Such questions go beyond both my intentions in this book. This note is just to record that I am aware of them.

4

> In practical terms, 'contrapuntal reading' as I have called it means reading a text with an understanding of what is involved when an author shows, for instance, that a colonial sugar plantation is seen as important to the process of maintaining a particular style of life in England. (Said 1994: 78).

5

> The point is that contrapuntal reading must take into account [the processes of] imperialism and that of resistance to it, which can be done by extending our reading of the texts to include what was once forcibly excluded. (Said 1994: 79).

6 For a critique of hybridity see Harootunian, Harry, 2000, *History's Disquiet: Modernity, Cultural Practice and the Question of Everyday Life*, New York: Columbia University Press; Werbner, Pnina and Tariq Modood (eds), 1997, *Debating Cultural Hybridity: Multi-cultural Identities and the Politics of Anti-racism*, London: Zed Books. For Bakhtin, see Bakhtin, Mikhail, 1981, *The Dialogic Imagination: Four Essays*, Austin: University of Texas Press; and Bakhtin, Mikhail, 1984, *Rabelais and His World*, Bloomington: Indiana University Press.

7 The project, and network within which it was a component, was funded by the EU within the Fifth Framework Programme: grant number HPRN-CT-2000-00063. My colleague, and the front-line researcher, in this project was Dr Myria Georgiou.

8 The research was conducted between 2001 and 2003, that is before the EU's enlargement in 2004.

9 For a further discussion see: Georgiou, Myria, 2005, Mapping Diasporic Media Cultures: A Transnational Cultural Approach to Exclusion, in R. Silverstone (ed.), *Media, Technology and Everyday Life in Europe*, Basingstoke: Ashgate.

10 We did not undertake audience research so cannot produce data on the extent to which satellite television channels are actually consumed both on their own terms and in relation to other media by different minority groups.

11 Both Philip Schlesinger (1993. Wishful Thinking: Cultural Politics, Media and Collective Identities in Europe, *Journal of Communication* 43 (2):25–42) and Kevin

Robins (1994, The Politics of Silence: The Meaning of Community and the Uses of Media in the New Europe, *New Formations* 21.80–101) have articulated their doubts and their anxieties about the viability of a European culture; and in most respects in the ten years or so since they wrote little has changed. That is, little seems to have changed in mainstream culture. It is arguably the case, however, that trans-European cultures of a kind are forming precisely in the products of the activities of various diasporas multiply displaced across the member states of Europe.

12 Mirca Madianou (2004, Contested Communicative Spaces: Rethinking Identities, Boundaries and the Role of the Media among Turkish Speakers in Greece, *Journal of Ethnic and Migration Studies* 31 (3):521–42) describes the Turkish minority in Greece as a 'beached diaspora', a term which reflects the lack of meaningful homeland amongst a group of people who have 'always' lived in Greece.

13 The imagined communities of displaced minorities, while sustained significantly by the media which are produced for and consumed by them, are much more complex entities, and much less significantly bounded – that is the symbolic and the material boundaries of statehood can no longer apply – than their national predecessors, cf. Anderson, Benedict, 1983, *Imagined Communities: Reflections on the Origin and Spread of Nationalism*, London: Verso.

14 In this context the BBC provides or promises a range of digital resources which will both enhance and undermine its traditional role: its websites; a digital archive; an ultra-local service; video-on-demand and a range of downloadable educational material (see the Charter Proposal, <www.bbc.co.uk/thefuture>).

15 This relationship is, of course, claimed as key by C. Wright Mills, 1959, *The Sociological Imagination*, New York: Oxford University Press.

16 The point can be made that counterpoint is not always heard by the listener; the integrity of the fugue, for example, is constituted by the composition and not necessarily the sound. See Cook, Nicholas, 1990, *Music, Imagination and Culture*, Oxford: Oxford University Press, p. 35.

Chapter 5 The Mediapolis and Everyday Life

1 Klemperer, Victor, 2000, *The Klemperer Diaries 1933–45*, London: Weidenfeld and Nicholson. Saturday, 9 November, 1935, p. 133. Victor Klemperer, expelled from his tenure as Professor of Romance Languages at the Technical University of Dresden in 1935, miraculously survived both Nazi persecution and the British bombing of his city. His diary chronicles both his own daily existence, in its increasing deprivation and persecution, but also the rise and fall of Hitler's Germany from the point of view of his own everyday life experience.

2 The term audience comes from the discourse of broadcast media; the term user from the interactive world of, above all, the web. The convergence of technologies occasioned by the digital revolution is mirrored in the convergence between the different kinds of engagement that individuals have with their multiple media in their everyday lives.

3 Paradox is something, by and large, in this context, one may or may not recognize in the lives of others. In this sense I may be fairly charged with my own elitism in seeing paradox in the everyday as both something which those who live those everyday lives want to do away with, and at the same time as something analytically, in my own terms at least, I want to preserve and sustain.

4

> The absolutely other is the Other. He and I do not form a number. The collectivity in which I say 'you' or 'we' is not a plural of the 'I'. I, you – these are not individuals of a common concept. Neither possession nor the unity of number

nor the unity of concepts link me to the Stranger, the Stranger who disturbs the being at home with oneself. But stranger also means free one. Over him I have no *power*. He escapes my grasp by an essential dimension, even if I have him at my disposal. He is not wholly in my site . . . We are the same and the other. (Levinas, Emmanuel, 1969, *Totality and Infinity: An Essay on Exteriority*, Pittsburgh: Duquesne University Press, p. 39.)

5 Clearly there re-emerges the issue around the pronouns 'us' and 'we' here, which I identified in the first chapter in this book. Of course it is not possible, indeed it is invidious, to fold the diversity of possible responses into one singular category, and through a presumption which is quite obviously informed by a particular perspective (mine), and by class, ethnicity, gender and nationality. In a sense the pronoun 'we' can be considered, to some extent, a provocation: an invitation to the reader of this book to position him or herself in relation to it. However, it is also manifestly insufficient, for it is perfectly clear that there will be in the US (and the UK) individuals who would not at all see these images in the ways in which I am describing and challenging them.

6 The presence of play as a component of public or civic culture is of a piece with Hannah Arendt's own position on the space of appearance and public culture. See my discussion in chapter 2.

7 The notion of play in this sentence shifts its referent of course – towards play not as in a game but as performance (see Silverstone 1999).

8 Complicity turns to collusion, when, as increasingly is the case, media subjects seek, in their understanding of the process, to manipulate the setting in order to guarantee participation and visibility.

9 Collusion: 'secret agreement or understanding for purposes of trickery or fraud' (literally, and instructively, 'playing together') (*OED*).

10 Cohen cites and discusses Michael Ignatieff, *The Warrior's Honour: Ethnic War and the Modern Conscience*, London, 1998, especially, here, pp. 10 and 11.

11 Arendt's argument with respect to the domestication of public life is that genuine political activity, 'the drawn-out wearisome processes of persuasion, negotiation, and compromise' (Arendt, Hannah, 1973, *On Revolution*. London: Penguin Books, pp. 66–87), is itself compromised because compassion, an essentially private affair, 'abolishes the distance, the worldly space where political matters . . . are located . . . it is incapable of establishing lasting institutions' (idem, p. 8).

Chapter 6 Hospitality and Justice

1 Kant's understanding of hospitality depends on the acceptance of the visitor who comes, but then goes, and our obligation to him or her is limited by ephemerality. This is different, as I will go on to argue, to tolerance, even though tolerance may be considered more appropriate in a world in which the visitor does actually stay. My privileging the notion of hospitality over tolerance is not just a matter of analysis of the latter as constrained, provisional and ultimately political (see the following discussion) but also, and crucially, because in the post-modern contemporary 'cosmopolitan', nomadic, world, permanence (of residency or of identity, for example) can neither be assumed nor definitively accepted. I discuss the relationship between rights and obligations in the matter of hospitality later on in this chapter.

2

It is a question of knowing how to transform and improve the law, and of knowing if this improvement is possible within an historical space which takes place *between* the Law of an unconditional hospitality, offered *a priori* to every other, to all newcomers, *whoever they may be*, and the conditional laws of a right to hospitality, without which *the* unconditional Law of hospitality would be in danger of remaining a pious and irresponsible desire, without form and without potency, and of even being perverted at any moment. (Derrida, Jacques, 2002, *On Cosmopolitanism and Forgiveness*, trans. M. Dooley and M. Hughes, London: Routledge, pp. 22–3.)

3 It is clear what kinds of mediated content (hate-speech; paedophilia) would become unacceptable; each in their own way denies the rights of others, in mostly unambiguous and entirely threatening ways. I discuss this a little more below.

4 I am grateful to my colleague Terhi Rantanen for this thought.

5 For an opposite argument, that technologies can be considered moral, see Latour, 1992, in Feenberg, Andrew. 1999. *Questioning Technology*. London: Routledge, p. 85).

6 In practice, of course, this poses immense difficulties. On the one hand in the driving underground of the seditious that, because of their own intolerance, would not be welcome in the mainstream; and on the other in the response of those same voices to what they might see as their exclusion from the same mainstream. However, it is the refusal of hospitality rather than the exploitation (say through criticism of the host and his or her culture) that is the breaking point, for the latter, arguably, can be tolerated, whereas the former refuses the primary obligation and therefore justice.

7 For further discussions of these issues see, for example, Bowman, Shayne and Chris Willis, 2006, *We Media: How Audiences are Shaping the Future of News and Information*, The Media Center at the American Press Institute, 2003 [cited January 2006]. Available from <www.hypergene.net/wemedia>.

8 On the notion of virtue (including justice) as practice, see MacIntyre:

> By a 'practice' I am going to mean any coherent and complex form of socially established cooperative human activity through which goods internal to that form of activity are realized in the course of trying to achieve those standards of excellence which are appropriate to, and partially definitive of, that form of activity, with the result that human powers to achieve excellence, and human conceptions of the ends and goods involved, are systematically extended. (MacIntyre, Alasdair, 1985, *After Virtue*, 2nd edn, London: Duckworth, p. 187)

9 This is a question increasingly asked in media research, not least by John Thompson, indeed citing Jonas, in the last pages of *The Media and Modernity*. (Thompson, John B., 1995, *The Media and Modernity: A Social Theory of the Media*, Cambridge: Polity)

10

> The perspective of rights looks at these relationships from the position of those on the receiving end of treatment, whose first concern may be to claim their rights. The perspective of obligations looks at these relationships from an agent's perspective, where the first concern is to work out what to do, and more generally, how to live.(O'Neill, Onora, 1990, Practices of Toleration, in J. Lichtenberg, ed., *Democracy and the Mass Media*, Cambridge: Cambridge University Press, p. 160.)

11 This poses, of course, huge practical difficulties since not everything can be heard in the mediapolis, or in any other setting. My argument depends on the principle that everything spoken should be judged as *capable* of being heard, and that the regulatory infrastructures which emerge, in this facilitative dimension, that is the provision of news, information and claims for a particular understanding of the world, should maximize the chances of an equal access to an audience.

12 'Truthfulness implies a respect for the truth. This relates to both of the virtues that . . . are the two basic virtues of truth, which I shall call Accuracy and Sincerity: you do the best you can to acquire true beliefs, and what you say reveals what you believe. (Williams, Bernard, 2002, *Truth and Truthfulness*, Princeton: Princeton University Press, p. 11.)

Chapter 7   Regulation and Literacy

1 It is interesting to note that ethics has also been argued as being environmental; see for example Blackburn, Simon, 2001, *Ethics: A Very Short Introduction*, Oxford: Oxford University Press.

2 Here and in the following pages my account to some significant extent inevitably rests on examples drawn from the UK. Despite all the globalization talk, policy issues by and large are still a matter for states (the EU would be one overriding example) and as such remain quite distinct, grounded as they will be not just in the particularities of contemporary politics but in the distinct culture and history of the nations concerned. So while the generic issues seem to be the same across societies, the way in which they will be dealt with will vary hugely. The degree of press, broadcasting and media freedom, together with the regulatory impulse, especially after 9/11, to intervene even more draconically in otherwise private communication on the internet and through the telephone, as well as, in some countries, press and broadcasting, is a moving target, both historically and geographically. (The press in Russia and Iran are a case in point and the commandeering of the logs of mobile telephone calls in the US is one of a different but related kind.) To consider the differences between societies along the axis of regulation–literacy in a useful and systematic way is beyond the reach of this book. There is, furthermore, relatively little work that treats media regulation from a global perspective, but see Price, Monroe E., 2004, *Media and Sovereignty: The Global Information Revolution and its Challenge to State Power*, Cambridge: MIT Press; and Siochru, Sean O. and Bruce Girard, 2002, *Global Media Governance: A Beginner's Guide*, Lanham: Rowman and Littlefield.

3 This can be found at <http://www.pcc.org.uk/cop/cop.asp>.

4 I am indebted to Ziqi Guan for this information.

5 This may seem far-fetched and absurdly overambitious. I don't think it is, for all the reasons I have been offering in this book. Nor is it the case that, both embryonically and substantially, initiatives of this kind have not been envisaged already. The New World Information and Communication Order, launched under UN and UNESCO auspices in the 1970s, was perhaps the first initiative of this kind. The absence of an international project of global significance currently masks a range of smaller projects, some of which do extend beyond the national, and often based on the globalized reach of the internet, and it may be that these need to be mobilized more effectively at the highest strategic levels (for example see <www.reportingtheworld. org>).

6 *The Guardian* newspaper in the UK has a section, albeit much reduced since it was originally introduced, in which reports on global issues from the foreign press are published. This is rare but commendable. It is a start.

References

Altick, Richard D. 1957. *The English Common Reader: A Social History of the Mass Reading Public, 1800–1900*. Chicago: The University of Chicago Press.

Anderson, Benedict. 1983. *Imagined Communities: Reflections on the Origin and Spread of Nationalism*. London: Verso.

Anthias, Floya. 1998. Evaluating 'Diaspora': Beyond Ethnicity. *Sociology* 32 (3):557–80.

Arendt, Hannah. 1973. *On Revolution*. London: Penguin Books.

Arendt, Hannah. 1977. *Between Past and Future: Eight Exercises in Political Thought*. New York and Harmondsworth: Penguin.

Arendt, Hannah. 1978. *The Jew as Pariah: Jewish Identity and Politics in the Modern Age*, Ron H. Feldman (ed.), New York: Grove Press.

Arendt, Hannah. 1984. Thinking and Moral Considerations: A Lecture. *Social Research* 51 (1):7–37.

Arendt, Hannah. 1994. *Essays in Understanding 1930–1954*, Jerome Kern (ed.), New York: Harcourt Brace & Co.

Arendt, Hannah. 1994a. *The Origins of Totalitarianism*. San Diego: Harcourt Inc.

Arendt, Hannah. 1994b. *Eichmann in Jerusalem: A Report on the Banality of Evil*. New York and London: Penguin Books.

Arendt, Hannah. 1998. *The Human Condition*. 2nd edn. Chicago: University of Chicago Press.

Bakhtin, Mikhail. 1981. *The Dialogic Imagination: Four Essays*. Austin: University of Texas Press.

Bakhtin, Mikhail. 1984. *Rabelais and His World*. Bloomington: Indiana University Press.

Baudrillard, Jean. 1983. *Simulations*. New York: Semiotexte.

Baudrillard, Jean. 1993. *The Transparency of Evil: Essays on Extreme Phenomena*. J. Benedict (trans.). London: Verso.

Bauman, Zygmunt. 1993. *Postmodern Ethics*. Oxford: Blackwell.

Baym, Nancy K. 2000. *Tune In, Log On: Soaps, Fandom and Online Community*. London: Sage.

Beck, Ulrich. 2003. Cosmopolitan Europe: A Confederation of States, a Federal State or Something Altogether New? In *Desperately Seeking Europe*, S. Stern and E. Seligmann (eds). London: Archetype Publications.

Beck, Ulrich. 2006. *Cosmopolitan Vision*. Cambridge: Polity.

Benhabib, Seyla. 2003. *The Reluctant Modernism of Hannah Arendt*. New edn. Lanham, Maryland: Rowman and Littlefield.

Benjamin, Walter. 1970. *Illuminations*. London: Fontana.

Berlin, Isaiah. 1990. *The Crooked Timber of Humanity*. London: John Murray.

Berlin, Isaiah. 1997. *The Proper Study of Mankind: An Anthology of Essays*. London: Chatto and Windus.

Berlin, Isaiah. 2000. *Three Critics of the Enlightenment*. H. Hardy (ed.). London: Pimlico.

Bernstein, Richard. 2002. *Radical Evil: A Philosophical Investigation*. Cambridge: Polity.

Bettig, R. V. 1997. The Enclosure of Cyberspace. *Critical Studies in Mass Communications* 14:138–57.

Blackburn, Simon. 2001. *Ethics: A Very Short Introduction*. Oxford: Oxford University Press.

Boltanski, Luc. 1999. *Distant Suffering: Morality, Media and Politics*. Cambridge: Cambridge University Press.

Borradori, Giovanna. 2003. *Philosophy in a Time of Terror: Dialogues with Jürgen Habermas and Jacques Derrida*. Chicago: Chicago University Press.

Bowman, Shayne, and Chris Willis. 2006. *We Media: How Audiences are Shaping the Future of News and Information*. The Media Center at the American Press Institute, 2003 [cited January 2006]. Available from <www.hypergene.net/wemedia>.

Calhoun, Craig. 1998. Community without Propinquity Revisited: Communications, Technology and the Transformation of the Urban Public Sphere. *Sociological Review* 68 (3):373–97.

Canovan, Margaret. 1992. *Hannah Arendt: A Reinterpretation of Her Political Thought*. Cambridge: Cambridge University Press.

Castells, Manuel. 2000. *The Rise of the Network Society: The Information Age: Economy, Society and Culture, Volume I*. Oxford: Blackwell.

Chouliaraki, Lilie. 2006. *The Spectatorship of Suffering*. London: Sage.

Christians, Clifford. 2000. An Intellectual History of Media Ethics. In B. Pattyn (ed.), *Media Ethics: Opening Social Dialogue*. Leeuven: Peters.

Clark, Lynn Schofield. 2003. *From Angels to Aliens: Teenagers, the Media and the Supernatural*. Oxford and New York: Oxford University Press.

Cmiel, Kenneth. 1996. On Cynicism, Evil, and the Discovery of Communication in the 1940s. *Journal of Communication* 46 (3):88–107.

Cohen, Stanley. 2001. *States of Denial: Knowing About Atrocities and Suffering*. Cambridge: Polity.

Copjec, Joan, (ed.). 1996. *Radical Evil*. London: Verso.

Cook, Nicholas. 1990. *Music, Imagination and Culture*. Oxford: Oxford University Press.

Dahlgren, Peter. 1995. *Television and the Public Sphere: Citizenship, Democracy and the Media.* London: Sage.

Davis, Colin. 1996. *Levinas: An Introduction.* Cambridge: Polity.

Dayan, Daniel and Elihu Katz. 1992. *Media Events: The Live Broadcasting of History.* Cambridge, Mass.: Harvard University Press.

de Certeau, Michel. 1984. *The Practice of Everyday Life.* Berkeley: University of California Press.

Debord, Guy. 1977. *The Society of the Spectacle.* London: Practical Paradise Productions.

Delbanco, Andrew. 1995. *The Death of Satan: How Americans Have Lost the Sense of Evil.* New York: Farrar, Straus and Giroux.

de Sola Pool, Ithiel. 1977. *The Social Impact of the Telephone.* Cambridge: MIT Press.

Derrida, Jacques. 2002. *On Cosmopolitanism and Forgiveness.* Mark Dooley and Michael Hughes (trans.). London: Routledge.

Eisenstein, Elizabeth. 1979. *The Printing Press as an Agent of Social Change.* 2 vols. Cambridge: Cambridge University Press.

Feenberg, Andrew. 1999. *Questioning Technology.* London: Routledge.

Fineman, Howard. 2003. Bush and God. *Newsweek.* 10 March.

Frum, David and Richard Perle. 2003. *An End to Evil: How to Win the War on Terror.* New York: Random House.

Funiok, Rüdiger. 2000. Fundamental Questions of Audience Ethics. In B. Pattyn (ed.), *Media Ethics: Opening Social Dialogue.* Leuven: Peeters.

Gaita, Raimond. 2004. *Good and Evil: An Absolute Conception.* 2nd edn. London: Routledge.

Galician, Mary-Lou. 2004. Introduction: High Time for 'Dis-illusioning' Ourselves and Our Media. *Amercan Behavioural Scientist* 48 (2):143–51.

Ganguly, Keya. 2001. *States of Exception: Everyday Life and Postcolonial Identity.* Minneapolis: University of Minnesota Press.

Georgiou, Myria. 2005. Mapping Diasporic Media Cultures: A Transnational Cultural Approach to Exclusion. In R. Silverstone (ed.), *Media, Technology and Everyday Life in Europe.* Basingstoke: Ashgate.

Gunn, Joshua. 2004. The Rhetoric of Exorcism: George W. Bush and the Return of Political Demonology. *Western Journal of Communication* 68 (1):1–23.

Hamelink, Cees. 2000. Ethics for Media Users. In B. Pattyn (ed.), *Media Ethics: Opening Social Dialogue.* Leuven: Peeters.

Harootunian, Harry. 2000. *History's Disquiet: Modernity, Cultural Practice and the Question of Everyday Life.* New York: Columbia University Press.

Held, David. 2004. *Global Covenant: The Social Democratic Alternative to the Washington Consensus.* Cambridge: Polity.

Horkheimer, Max and Theodor Adorno. 1972. *Dialectic of Enlightenment.* New York: Seabury Press.

Husband, Charles. 2000. Media and the Public Sphere in Multi-ethnic Societies. In S. Cottle (ed.), *Ethnic Minorities and the Media*. Buckingham: Open University Press.

Jewett, Robert and Shelton Lawrence. 2003. *Captain America and the Crusade Against Evil: The Dilemma of Zealous Nationalism*. Grand Rapids, Michigan: William B. Erdmans Publishing Company.

Jonas, Hans. 1984. *The Imperative of Responsibility: In Search of an Ethics for the Technological Age*. Chicago: Chicago University Press.

Kant, Immanuel. 1983. *Perpetual Peace and Other Essays*. T. Humphrey (trans.). Indianapolis: Hackett.

Katz, James E. and Mark Aakhus (eds). 2002. *Perpetual Contact: Mobile Communication, Private Talk, Public Performance*. Cambridge: Cambridge University Press.

Klemperer, Victor. 2000. *The Klemperer Diaries 1933–45*. London: Weidenfeld and Nicholson.

Klusmeyer, Douglas and Astri Suhrke. 2002. Comprehending 'Evil': Challenges for Law and Policy. *Ethics and International Affairs* 16 (1):27–45.

Kristeva, Julia. 2001. *Hannah Arendt*. R. Guberman (trans.). New York: Columbia University Press.

Kubey, Robert. 2004. Media Literacy and the Teaching of Civics and Social Studies at the Dawn of the 21st Century. *American Behavioural Scientist* 48 (1):1–9.

Lambert, Richard. 2005. The Path Back to Trust, Truth and Integrity. *The Guardian*, 17 January.

Latour, Bruno. 1993. *We Have Never Been Modern*. C. Porter (trans.). Hemel Hempstead: Harvester Wheatsheaf.

Lessig, Lawrence. 1999. *Code and Other Laws of Cyberspace*. New York: Basic Books.

Levinas, Emmanuel. 1969. *Totality and Infinity: An Essay on Exteriority*. Pittsburgh: Duquesne University Press.

Lewis, Justin and Sut Jhally. 1998. The Struggle Over Media Literacy. *Journal of Communication* 48 (1):109–20.

Li, Xiguang. 2005. *Journalism in Transition: Critical Studies of the Chinese Press* (draft). Tsinghua University Beijing.

Livingstone, Sonia, Elizabeth Van Couvering and Nancy Thumim. 2005. *Adult Media Literacy: A Review of the Literature*. London: Ofcom: The Office of Communications.

Lloyd, John. 2004. *What the Media Are Doing to Our Politics*. London: Constable.

Lukes, Steven. 2003. *Liberals and Cannibals: The Implications of Diversity*. London: Verso.

MacIntyre, Alasdair. 1985. *After Virtue*. 2nd edn. London: Duckworth.

Madianou, Mirca. 2004. Contested Communicative Spaces: Rethinking Identities, Boundaries and the Role of the Media Among Turkish Speakers in Greece. *Journal of Ethnic and Migration Studies* 31 (3):521–42.

Mander, Jerry. 1978. *Four Arguments for the Elimination of Television*. Brighton: Harvester Press.

Marcus, George E. 1998. *Ethnography Through Thick and Thin*. Princeton: Princeton University Press.

Marvin, Carolyn. 1988. *When Old Technologies Were New: Thinking About Communications in the Late Nineteenth Century*. New York and Oxford: Oxford University Press.

Marvin, Carolyn and David W. Ingle. 1999. *Blood Sacrifice and the Nation: Totem Rituals and the American Flag*. Cambridge: Cambridge University Press.

Matar, Dina. 2005. News, Memory, Identity: The Palestinians in Britain and Social Uses of News. PhD. University of London.

McLuhan, Marshall. 1964. *Understanding Media*. London: Routledge and Kegan Paul.

Melchior-Bonnet, Sabine. 2001. *The Mirror: A History*. K. H. Jewett (trans.). New York: Routledge.

Mills, C. Wright. 1959. *The Sociological Imagination*. New York: Oxford University Press.

Moeller, Susan D. 1999. *Compassion Fatigue: How the Media Sell Disease, Famine, War and Death*. New York and London: Routledge.

Morrow, Lance. 2003. *Evil: An Investigation*. New York: Basic Books.

Neiman, Susan. 2002. *Evil in Modern Thought: An Alternative History of Philosophy*. Princeton and Oxford: Princeton University Press.

Nicholls, David. 1990. *American Experimental Music 1890–1940*. Cambridge: Cambridge University Press.

Nora, Pierre. 1989. Between Memory and History: Les Lieux de Memoire. *Representations* 26 (Spring):7–25.

Ofcom. 2004. Strategy and Priorities for the Promotion of Media Literacy: A Statement. London: Ofcom.

O'Leary, Stephen D. 1994. *Arguing the Apocalypse: A Theory of Millennial Rhetoric*. New York and Oxford: Oxford University Press.

O'Neill, Onora. 1990. Practices of Toleration. In J. Lichtenberg (ed.), *Democracy and the Mass Media*. Cambridge: Cambridge University Press.

O'Neill, Onora. 2000. *Bounds of Justice*. Cambridge: Cambridge University Press.

O'Neill, Onora. 2002. *A Question of Trust*. Cambridge: Cambridge University Press.

Ong, Walter. 1982. *Orality and Literacy: The Technologizing of the Word*. London: Methuen.

Peters, John Durham. 1999. *Speaking into the Air: A History of the Idea of Communication*. Chicago: Chicago University Press.

Postman, Neil. 1987. *Amusing Ourselves to Death*. London: Methuen.

Price, Monroe E. 2004. *Media and Sovereignty: The Global Information Revolution and its Challenge to State Power*. Cambridge: MIT Press.

Rawls, John. 1999. *A Theory of Justice* (revised edn). Oxford: Oxford University Press.

Robins, Kevin. 1994. The Politics of Silence: The Meaning of Community and the Uses of Media in the New Europe. *New Formations* 21:80–101.

Rogin, Michael Paul. 1987. *Ronald Reagan, The Movie*. Berkeley: University of California Press.

Rose, Nikolas. 1990. *Governing the Soul: The Shaping of the Private Self*. London: Routledge.

Rose, Nikolas. 1999. *Powers of Freedom: Reframing Political Thought*. Cambridge: Cambridge University Press.

Rosenberg, Bernard and David Manning White (eds.). 1957. *Mass Culture: The Popular Arts in America*. New York: The Free Press.

Rosenberg, Emily S. 2003. *A Date Which Will Live: Pearl Harbor in American History*. Durham: Duke University Press.

Rushing, Janice Hocker and Thomas S. Frentz. 1995. *Projecting the Shadow: The Cyborg Hero in American Film*. Chicago: Chicago University Press.

Sacks, Jonathan. 2002. *The Dignity of Difference: How to Avoid the Clash of Civilisations*. London: Continuum.

Said, Edward. 1994. *Culture and Imperialism*. London: Vintage.

Said, Edward. 2001. *Reflections on Exile and Other Literary and Cultural Essays*. London: Granta.

Said, Edward. 2003. *Freud and the Non-European*. London: Verso.

Scannell, Paddy. 1989. Public Service Broadcasting and Modern Public Life. *Media, Culture and Society* 11 (2):135–66.

Scannell, Paddy and David Cardiff. 1991. *A Social History of British Broadcasting, Volume 1, 1922–1939: Serving the Nation*. Oxford: Blackwell.

Schlesinger, Philip. 1993. Wishful Thinking: Cultural Politics, Media and Collective Identities in Europe. *Journal of Communication* 43 (2):25–42.

Silverstone, Roger. 1988. Television, Myth and Culture. In J. W. Carey (ed.), *Media, Myths and Narratives: Television and the Press*. Newbury Park: Sage.

Silverstone, Roger. 1999. *Why Study the Media?* London: Sage.

Silverstone, Roger. 2001. Finding a Voice: Minorities, Media and the Global Commons. *Emergences: Journal for the Study of Media and Composite Cultures* 11 (1):13–28.

Silverstone, Roger. 2003. Proper Distance: Towards an Ethics for Cyberspace. In G. Liestol, A. Morrison and T. Rasmussen (eds), *Digital Media Revisited*. Cambridge, Mass.: The MIT Press.

Silverstone, Roger. 2005. Mediation and Communication. In C. Calhoun, C. Rojek and B. Turner (eds), *The Sage Handbook of Sociology*. London: Sage.

Singer, Peter. 2004. *The President of Good and Evil: Taking George W. Bush Seriously*. London: Granta.

Siochru, Sean O' and Bruce Girard. 2002. *Global Media Governance: A Beginner's Guide*. Lanham: Rowman and Littlefield.

Sontag, Susan. 2004. What Have We Done? *The Guardian*, 24 May:2–5.

Stevenson, Nick. 1999. *The Transformation of the Media: Globalisation, Morality and Ethics*. London: Longman.

Thompson, John B. 1995. *The Media and Modernity: A Social Theory of the Media*. Cambridge: Polity.

Toulmin, Stephen. 1990. *Cosmopolis: The Hidden Agenda of Modernity*. Chicago: Chicago University Press.

Turner, Bryan S. 2002. Cosmopolitan Virtue, Globalization and Patriotism. *Theory, Culture & Society* 19 (1–2):45–63.

Villa, Dana R. 1999. *Politics, Philosophy, Terror: Essays on the Thought of Hannah Arendt*. Princeton: Princeton University Press.

Walzer, Michael. 1994. *Thick and Thin: Moral Argument at Home and Abroad*. Notre Dame: University of Notre Dame Press.

Walzer, Michael. 1997. *On Toleration*. New Haven and London: Yale University Press.

Werbner, Pnina and Tariq Modood (eds). 1997. *Debating Cultural Hybridity: Multi-cultural Identities and the Politics of Anti-racism*. London: Zed Books.

Williams, Bernard. 2002. *Truth and Truthfulness*. Princeton: Princeton University Press.

Williams, Raymond. 2003. *Television: Technology and Cultural Form*. Routledge Classics. London: Routledge.

Woodward, Bob. 2004. *Plan of Attack*. New York: Simon & Schuster.

Zelizer, Barbie and Stuart Allan (eds). 2002. *Journalism After September 11*. London: Routledge.

Index